THE BUILDINGS OF ENGLAND
BE 7
HERTFORDSHIRE
NIKOLAUS PEVSNER

10

69

The County of
HERTFORDSHIRE

Scale of Miles

0 1 2 3 4 5 6 7 8 9 10

BEDFORD-SHIRE

BUCKINGHAMSHIRE

Holwell
Ickle
Pirton
Hexton
Hitchi
Offley
Lilley
Ippoll
Temple Dinsley
Kings Walden
St Pauls Wal
Whitwe
Lawrence
Kimpt
Caddington Hall
Markyate
Ayot St Lawrer
Beechwood
Harpenden
Long Marston
Puttenham
Flamstead
Rothamstead
Wheathamp
Aldbury
Lt Gaddesden
Gt Gaddesden
Redbourn
Sandri
Tring
Wigginton
Nettleden
Childwickbury
Northchurch
Hemel Hempstead
Berkhamsted
Gorhambury
Boxmoor
Leverstock Green
ST ALBANS
Bovingdon
Tyttenhange
Frogmore
Kings Langley
Abbots Langley
Lon
Colne
Chipperfield
Buckshill
Garston
Flaunden
Langleybury
Shenley
Sarratt
Chandlers Cross
Radlet
Redheath
Aldenham
Chorleywood
WATFORD
Borehamwo
Croxley Green
Bushey
Elstree
Rickmansworth
Moor Park
Batchworth Heath
Oxhey
West Hyde
Eastbury
MIDD

The buildings of England

Hertfordshire

PEVSNER

720.942
P514b
v.7

Permabound

Hertfordshire

BY

NIKOLAUS PEVSNER

★

PENGUIN BOOKS
MELBOURNE · LONDON · BALTIMORE

FIRST PUBLISHED 1953

The author and publishers would be grateful
to any user of this book for having any errors
or omissions pointed out to them
in as much detail
as possible

MADE AND PRINTED IN GREAT BRITAIN
FOR PENGUIN BOOKS LTD
BY WILLIAM CLOWES AND SONS LTD
LONDON AND BECCLES

CONTENTS

*

*

*The map on pages 2–3 shows all those places,
whether towns, villages, or isolated buildings,
which are the subject of separate entries in the
text. The index on pages 310–313 gives references to the map square in which each
place mentioned will be found*

FOREWORD

Most of the facts which appear in the following pages were extracted and assembled by Miss G. Bondi. I want to place on record my gratitude to her for the care and circumspection with which she has worked on the published sources. In addition I had the privilege of my proofs being checked in great detail by Mr W. Branch Johnson and a team of members of the Hertfordshire Local History Council. I feel very much in their debt and should like to mention specially, in connexion with other comments and contributions, Mrs E. M. Hunt and Mr Gordon Moodey, of the East Herts Archaeological Society. Miss Robin Place wrote all the entries on prehistory and Roman antiquities, Mr Rupert Gunness generously helped on the eighteenth-century monuments, Mr C. H. Aslin, County Architect, provided information on the outstanding modern schools designed in his department, Miss M. F. Austin, former County Librarian, and Miss M. Swan, and Mr R. C. Sayell, of the St Albans Public Library and Watford Borough Library respectively, and also Mr Ian Nairn divers answers to out-of-the-way questions. The Reverend W. B. Farrer kindly lent me the photograph illustrated in plate 36a, and Mrs E. M. Hunt that of plate 7a (taken by the late Reverend J. W. Fall). To all of them I am most grateful.

I also wish to thank the many rectors and vicars of churches who gave me specific information, and the many owners of private houses, large and small, who allowed me access. Only one owner of an important country house refused entirely to let me see it. Many were most helpful. The least thing I can do for them is to say here most explicitly that the mention or even description of a house in these pages must not by any means be taken as an indication that it is open to the public.

As in previous volumes of this series by the courtesy of the Ministry of Housing and Local Government, who have a statutory duty to compile lists of buildings of architectural or historic

interest, I have had access to unpublished lists and much othe
information collected by the Chief Investigator of the Ministry
and his staff (here abridged MHLG). *I could also once more mak*
use of Mr H. S. Goodhart-Rendel manuscript notes on Vic
torian churches and Sir Thomas Kendrick's on Victorian glass
(referred to in this volume under CR *and* TK). *I have made fut*
use of the photograph collection of the National Building
Record and should like to express my sincere thanks to Mr
Cecil Farthing and Mrs M. Parry for all their help.

In spite of so much help received, I am, however, quite sure I
omitted to see and register large numbers of houses, especially
among the minor ones, partly because literature on these i
scanty, and partly because my own cross-country touring wa
not extensive enough to secure discovery of everything worth
recording. Interiors of houses especially will often be found in-
adequately treated. The reason here may be that privacy to
which I alluded before, or simply the fact that I had not seer
for myself. On the whole, however, I have made it a principle in
these volumes to examine everything personally before I decide
to include and try to describe it. Even so there remain no doub
plenty of errors and omissions.

INTRODUCTION

WITH about 630 square miles Hertfordshire is among the
six smallest counties of England. In population it is the
fourteenth from the top (1951); that means it is remarkably densely populated. This is due to its proximity to
London, a fact which one's eyes are hardly ever allowed to
forget. The landscape of Hertfordshire is naturally friendly,
green, gently rolling, with no large river, uneventful but
lovable. It possesses no grandeur, except perhaps occasionally on the height of the Chilterns, and it tends to be
dull towards the NE. It has long been under intense cultiva-
tion, and one cannot count on much solitude. London's
Green Line buses are likely to appear everywhere, and even
the familiar red buses cruise as far as Watford and St Albans.
At Barnet and Waltham Cross, London reaches solidly into
the county. Still separate, but likewise obviously part of
London, is the whole Bushey–Oxhey–Watford neighbourhood. The great number of large hospitals (especially mental hospitals) is also connected with nearness to the metropolis. Negatively the effect of this nearness is the absence of
any big city (Watford with 73,000 is the biggest town) and of
an old cathedral (St Albans was made a cathedral only in
1877).

In its industries Hertfordshire looks to London too.
Paper mills and printing works are as characteristic as market gardening and watercress growing, the latter two chiefly
in the E of the county.

More conspicuous than the rivers – the longest of which is
the Lea running E from somewhere near Luton past Wheathampstead, Hertford, and Ware and then turning S by
Broxbourne and Waltham and so into the Thames – are the
ancient roads. The Icknield Way is a pre-Roman track. It
comes from Ivinghoe and Luton and crosses the county
mainly between Hitchin, Baldock, and Royston. The chief

Roman roads are : (1) Watling Street, which enters Hertford
shire at Elstree. Passing through Radlett, St Stephen's, Veru
lam and Gorhambury Drive it leads across the fields to Bow
Bridge and Dunstable, and leaves the county at Markyate
(2) Akeman Street, of which only a small part is traceable
on its route from Aylesbury to Boxmoor, through Tring
and Berkhamsted. (3) Ermine Street which enters the
county at the hamlet of Ball Cross (in the parish of Ches
hunt) and follows the present road to Hamstead End
Thence it proceeds via Cold Hall, Elbow Lane, Hertford
Heath, Little Amwell, and Rush Green Farm to Ware
Vicarage, Braughing (where it crosses Stane Street), Bunt
ingford and Royston, where it leaves the county. (4) Stane
Street, which enters Hertfordshire at Bishops Stortford
passes through Little Hadham to Braughing, crosses Ermine
Street, and there leads through Hare Street, Clothall, and
Baldock. There are, in addition, traces of a road from
Verulam to Colchester, crossing Hertfordshire at Sand
ridge, Ayot, and Welwyn. Hertfordshire is also crossed by
two important canals, the New River built as early a
1609–13 as a conduit from Great Amwell to London, and the
Grand Junction (now Grand Union) Canal begun in 1792
and completed in 1805. It connects the Midlands with
London and runs through Hertfordshire from Tring by
Berkhamsted, Boxmoor, Watford, and Rickmansworth
The railway arrived in 1838. It is in several places conspicuous by fire brick viaducts.

Brick became the accepted building material in Hertford
shire only during the first half of the Tudor Age, although
the Romans had used brick extensively, and early medieva
builders had made ample use of Roman bricks (see St
Albans). But brick-making was not taken up for centuries in
Hertfordshire, as indeed in the whole of England. Details of
the reappearance of brick in the C15 and C16 will be given
later. Before then cottages were universally timber-framed
and for churches and large houses flint was extensively
used.* The most usual local stone is clunch; the best local
stone is the chalk from Totternhoe across the Bedfordshire

* Shenley church in 1424, etc., is of flint with brick dressings.

order, but oölitic limestone from Northamptonshire also appears. Geologically Hertfordshire is all young rocks, chiefly chalk on top of gault and London clay. The only more elevated land is the parts of the Chilterns which lie in the W of the county, NE of Tring. They are continued NE as a less conspicuous escarpment towards Royston.

The most important prehistoric evidence of Hertfordshire belongs to the area SE of the Chilterns and to as late a period as the Iron Age. Of the Stone and Bronze Ages there is no visible evidence except in museums, and what there is in these needs no special comment here. Cassivelaunus, the Belgic king who defied Caesar in 54 B.C., had his capital near Wheathampstead. His grandson moved it on to Verulamium. A third sizeable Iron Age settlement was at Welwyn, NW of the present road from Stevenage to Hatfield. Verulamium became one of the outstanding cities of Roman Britain, in fact the only *municipium* in the country. Much of the plan has been ascertained by excavations. The Museum possesses a most interesting collection. *In situ*, however, are only the theatre and one mosaic pavement. Roman stations were at Braughing, Reed, Thirfield, Clothall, and Wilbury Hill.

Saxon evidence is minor but not without interest. St Michael's at St Albans has its nave and chancel walls preserved, with window surrounds of Roman brick. Long-and-short work can be seen at Reed and Westmill.

Norman evidence is far more impressive. St Albans, one of the most powerful monasteries of Britain, is of course the prime monument. It was begun about 1078 and built very quickly. Much of the long nave, crossing, crossing tower, transepts, and chancel survives. Originally the E end was of seven stepped apses, two on the E side of each transept, two to the chancel aisles, and one to the chancel. Roman brick was extensively used where strength was required. The details are of the rawest and most severe. The church is specially remarkable for never having possessed a gallery like all the other major Norman churches of England, but only a triforium. Smaller English Norman parish churches have apses only rarely and as a rule only in the SE of

the country. Hertfordshire examples are at Wheathamp
stead (excavation results), Bengeo, Great Amwell, Grea
Wymondley, and Weston. Weston also has a Norman cross
ing tower and seems to have possessed a transept wit
apsidal chapels as well. Hemel Hempstead is an exception
ally complete later C12 town church. It has a square chance
with rib-vaults – the only example of Norman rib-vaultin
in the county * – transepts, a crossing tower, and a nav
with Norman clerestory and aisles. Saratt is a small Nor
man church on the very unusual Greek cross plan. Othe
Norman crossing towers exist or can be reconstructed a
Anstey and Pirton. Norman W towers are preserved a
Barley, Flamstead, Redbourn, and Stevenage; Norma
arcades, e.g. at Abbots Langley, Redbourn, and Walkern
Interesting overlaps of Norman and E.E. forms, provin;
how long into the C13 Norman detail was still used locall
can be seen at Kimpton and Kings Walden.

The paramount example of the E.E. style in Hertford
shire is, of course, the W parts of the nave and the retrochoi
of St Albans. The former were begun in 1195 and are thu
amongst the earliest examples of pure Gothic design in
Britain. Most of the work, however, belongs to c. 1215–35
It is exceptional for its date in having deep W porches and ;
triforium instead of a gallery. The retrochoir was begun in
1257. At Royston is an interesting fragment of a C13 parisl
church, much obscured by later alterations. Surprisingl
sumptuous chancel arches survive at Eastwick and Standon
In parish churches E.E. chancels are more frequent thar
E.E. naves; for the chancels were for the clergy, and ther
was no reason to enlarge them later, whereas naves grov
with congregations in the later Middle Ages. The finest E.E
chancel is at Anstey. Here the transepts are also of the C13
The same is true of Hatfield with odd W chapels attached t(
its transepts. A rare central plan survives at Flaunden – ;
Greek cross like Norman Sarratt. Examples of C13 crossing
towers are Northchurch and Wheathampstead.

* The E aisles of the Berkhamsted transepts are also rib-vaulted
They are, however, of the C13.

Those attracted by the fantasies of the Dec style of the
1st half of the C14 will be disappointed with what Hertfordshire has to offer. The Lady Chapel of St Albans, though of
1300–20, has nothing of the lavishness of Ely or Bristol,
and the restoration of part of the nave after 1323 is far from
original. The only places showing a more fanciful treatment
are the transepts of Wheathampstead. Chancel chapels with
Dec details are at Aldbury, Abbots Langley, and Benington.
Tracery on the whole is unimaginative. So-called Kentish
tracery, that is tracery with a motif of a quatrefoil with
spikes between the lobes, can be seen at Ayot St Lawrence
and St Paul's Walden. Designers need not have gone to
Kent for patterns. They appear as near Herts as, for example, Waltham Abbey.

As in so many parts of England, the later C14 and the C15
and early C16 were the high-watermark of prosperity in
wool or cloth towns and villages. Baldock and Ashwell
churches are two comparatively early examples of this (early
C14 and c. 1340–80). The majority of medieval work in
Herts churches is of the Perp style and chiefly the C15.
Important buildings are at Hitchin, Ware, and Watford.
Work in the village churches is not on the whole very inspired. Tracery is of no special merit. There are, however, a
number of stately W towers, the most beautiful, still of the
C14, at Ashwell. This and that at Baldock are crowned by a
recessed octagonal storey and then a thin spire. Extremely
thin recessed spikes are a peculiarity of the county. They
are known as Hertfordshire spikes.

Piers have a variety of sections. To return for a moment
to earlier centuries Norman arcades had circular piers, the
C13 usually octagonal ones (e.g. Ardeley, Flamstead, Great
Gaddesden, Much Hadham, Offley, Walkern). This latter
form was continued into the early C14 (Aldenham, Hitchin,
Wheathampstead, etc.). The W parts of St Albans of c. 1200
have a variation on this theme with four attached shafts in
the main axes. Quatrefoil sections of the piers are to be
found at Berkhamsted, Anstey, Gilston, and Sawbridgeworth. St Albans c. 1257 added to these four slimmer shafts
in the diagonals. Royston Priory did the same, but keeled

the diagonal shafts – not an unusual profile, also without the
keeling. Without capitals to the diagonal shafts the same
profile continues at Baldock and Ashwell, Albury and
Benington. Later at Ashwell the main shafts turn 3/8 in
section instead of semicircular, and at Clothall, also in the
C14, the diagonal shafts are also of 3/8 section. The most
usual C15 profile is four attached shafts and four hollows
in the diagonals (Cheshunt 1418–48, Barnet *c.* 1440–50,
Bishops Stortford, etc.). With 3/8 shafts instead of semicircular ones, the same section appears at Barkway, Furneaux Pelham, St Paul's Walden, and as late as 1532 at
Wyddial. More complex late medieval forms are at Tring
and Standon with double hollows in the diagonals, at Hatfield with treble shafts in the four main axes, and at Watton
and Ware. Perp piers have often capitals only to some shafts.
In Herts this characteristic habit is fully developed already
at Buckland (1348?).

With the exception of St Albans and Royston all the
churches so far mentioned were parochial. Herts was, in
fact, not rich in important monastic foundations. The power
of St Albans overshadowed all. To its liberty belonged
Abbots Langley, Aldenham, Barnet, Codicote, Elstree, Hexton, Northaw, Northchurch, Rickmansworth, Watford, and
divers other parishes, going across the border into Bucks.
The other monastic houses in the county of which remains
survive above ground were the Augustinian priories of Royston (founded C12) and Little Wymondley (founded C13),
the Benedictine nunneries at Sopwell and Markyate (both
cells of St Albans), the Carmelite house at Hitchin, the
house of the Bonshommes at Ashridge, the Dominican
friary at Kings Langley, and the Franciscan friary at
Ware.

There is no important medieval sculpture in Herts. The
shrines of St Albans Abbey are in a sadly fragmentary state.
Tomb-recesses and decorated tomb-chests are at Anstey
(*c.* 1300), Benington (*c.* 1330?, *c.* 1358?), Little Munden
(late C14), Aldenham (late C14), and Aldbury (1471). More
ambitious are the three chantry chapels of St Albans, dating
from 1447, *c.* 1460, and *c.* 1520. Of stone effigies the best of

he C13 are at Eastwick and Brent Pelham. A Purbeck marble effigy is at Walkern, a Purbeck slab with incised effigy at Sawbridgeworth, the former C13, the latter early C14. Alabaster effigies are rare, brasses extremely frequent. The earliest are of c. 1340 (Albury) and of 1356 (Berkhamsted); the best are the de la Mare brass at St Albans, c. 1396, of Flemish workmanship, and of English workmanship those at North Mimms c. 1360, Hemel Hempstead late C14, Furneaux Pelham early C15, Digswell † 1415, Watford † 1415, Sawbridgeworth c. 1433, Wheathampstead c. 1436, Watton-at-Stone mid C15, Standon † 1474, Broxbourne † 1474, a group of c. 1475–80 at Albury, Little Hadham, and Sandon, and Hinxworth † 1487(?).

For medieval wall painting St Albans is of national importance, especially the late C13 paintings of the Crucifixion on five nave piers, but also what survives in the chancel. Apart from St Albans only Flamstead with its C13 and C15 fragments, and smaller fragments at Bengeo (C13) and Widford have to be mentioned. Regarding medieval stained glass the figure of the Virgin at St Paul's Walden (early C14) and the Jesse tree at Barkway (late C15) are the best examples.

In church furnishings also outstanding works are lacking. There are plenty of preserved screens, but none of them first-rate. Of special historic interest is the one at Gilston, because it is clearly of before 1300 – a very early date. The stone pulpitum at St Albans is of the late C14, the stone reredos with its Victorian figures later C15. The best C15 timber screens are those of Hitchin. The coving of the rood loft is preserved at Redbourn and Kimpton. A great rarity is the Feretrar's Watching Loft at St Albans (c. 1500). Stallwork might be mentioned at Stevenage, misericords at Bishops Stortford, and a C15 font with carved figures at Ware. Decorated iron door-hinges survive at Little Hormead of a Norman date, at St Albans of the late C13. Also of the late C13 is the exquisite iron railing round the Gloucester Chantry at St Albans.*

* As in previous volumes of this series, church bells are not recorded.

That finishes the survey of medieval ecclesiastical architecture in the county. As for secular buildings, Berkhamsted
had the most important castle. It dates from the C12 and is
very poorly preserved. But its large circumference is still
impressive. At Bishops Stortford the mount of the Bishop
of London's castle survives, at Hertford also the mount and
some bits of masonry. Bennington has a small keep, now
part of a Neo-Norman domestic fantasy, Anstey big earth
fortifications and again a mount. Homestead moats, that is
moats originally surrounding manor houses, are a speciality
of Herts. The Royal Commission counts 141 of them. They
seem to date from the C13 to the C16. Hardly any of them
are mentioned in this volume.

With regard to manor houses the earliest at least partly
preserved examples are the Old Palace at Hatfield, Hinxworth Place, and the Rectory at Therfield. Hatfield, the
former country seat of the Bishops of Ely, is far more ambitious than the others can ever have been. It has a fine hall
with braced roof and is built of brick. Its date is *c.* 1480–90.
It marks the moment in the county when brick became
fashionable. Only slightly later is the brick gatehouse of
Hertford Castle and the brick frieze at Rickmansworth
Vicarage. Hinxworth and Therfield have characteristic
late C15 windows. In addition there exists another late
C15 hall at Cheshunt Great House. This was originally
much larger than it is now. It belonged to the courtyard
type also represented by Hadham Hall in its original
form and by The Lordship, Standon. The Lordship is
of brick, dated 1546. Its principal surviving feature is the
gatehouse.

Another big Early Tudor gatehouse of brick stands at Rye
House; and Hunsdon, which is now a much altered rectangular brick block, has yet another brick gatehouse close
by. The surviving house at Hunsdon was once one projecting wing of a symmetrical E- or half-H-shaped house. At
Knebworth fragments of the brick mansion of *c.* 1500 have
in the C19 been built into a new gatehouse. A characteristic
early C16 motif in Herts and altogether the brick districts
NE of London is the stepped gable (of Dutch and Flemish

derivation). It is to be found at Great Hormead, Furneaux Pelham, etc.*

The proof that brick had become equal in social status to stone is provided by its acceptance for church architecture. In Herts this is marked by the N aisle and N chancel chapel at Wyddial (1532) and the S porch at Meesden (c. 1530). The chancel chapels at Hunsdon and Stanstead Abbots (1577), and the tower top at Sarratt followed. They take us into the Elizabethan Age.

The wealth of Elizabethan and Jacobean houses in Herts is exceptional. It is no doubt to be explained by the nearness to London. They range in size from the Early Elizabethan hunting lodge of Queen Hoo to such palaces as the all but demolished Gorhambury (1568, etc.), the demolished Theobalds, and the gloriously surviving Hatfield of 1607-11. The Elizabethan style is complete in the Gorhambury porch with its classical columns and niches, and in the remaining range of Hadham Hall of c. 1575 with its classical pediments above many-mullioned and transomed windows. Of about the same age is Berkhamsted Place, built on the popular E-plan. The same plan occurs, for example, on a large scale at North Mimms, early C17, and on a small scale in the charming Water End Farm of c. 1610. Other examples of the style are Great Nast Hyde, Upp Hall, Delamere House Great Wymondley, Bride Hall Sandridge, and Letchworth Hall. The straightsided Elizabethan gables are still used in the early C17, but shaped gables consisting of concave and ogee curves are the more fashionable form (Astonbury, Barkway, St Monica's Priory Hoddesdon 1622). These are replaced from about 1630 onwards by a type of gable which is finished at the top by a pediment – a first concession to classical standards. Examples of this are at Rothamsted, at Hoddesdon in a house dated 1637 which also displays the novel scheme of orders of superimposed pilasters on the façade, and still in 1665 at Mackery End, otherwise a front belonging in its character to the time after the Restoration.

The dating of cottages is not easy. There are plenty of timber-framed structures in the villages which may in parts

* And as late as 1576 at Little Gaddesden Manor House.

go back to the C15 and in considerable parts to the C16. Bu
changes were slow, and a wholly new type of cottage wa
developed only after a change of legislation in 1775. Onl
then do the long low two-storeyed brick cottages with bric
modillion friezes appear. Anyway, the recording of cottage
in the pages of this volume is entirely inadequate, partly be
cause their strictly architectural interest is so small, partl
because there is little printed evidence beyond the Roya
Commission volume, and partly because I have not in
spected them systematically. The rule that narrowly space
uprights in a timber-framed house are an indication of earl
date holds only in a very general way. Chimney-stacks als
help in dating, their length, and their position diagonally o
otherwise.

A few specially fine barns may here be added, especiall
the timber-framed weatherboarded C15 barn at Croxley
Hall Farm, Croxley Green, and the splendid brick barn
140 ft. long, at Upp Hall, Braughing.

Of secular buildings other than houses, schools and alms
houses begin to appear in the C16. The Berkhamste
Grammar School of 1544 is the best remaining example. I
is built of brick and keeps still entirely within the Perp
tradition. Other contemporary schools are at Chipping
Barnet and Standon, and fragments at Buntingford and
Stevenage. Hale's School at Hertford is early C17, the Dew
hurst School at Cheshunt 1640. The earliest almshouses in
Herts date from 1580 (Watford), but the largest ones are
later than the Restoration.

The foundation of schools and almshouses took the place
after the Reformation, of the foundation of chantry chapel
in churches. Church architecture between the middle of the
C16 and the middle of the C17 was stagnant. The only com
plete church built during the century is St Peter at Bunting
ford (1614–26), a Greek cross in plan. The chapel at Oxhey
(1612) is still entirely Perp in character and details. The N
transept at Little Hadham has intersected tracery dating ap
parently from the late C16, the chancel chapel at Aspende
octagonal piers of 1622. However, these carry semicircula
arches decorated with strapwork, and the Morrison Chape

t Watford of 1595 and the Salisbury Chapel at Hatfield of
. 1610 replace Perp piers by Tuscan columns.*

The same development can be followed in much greater
detail in the monuments of *c.* 1550 to *c.* 1660. Again in
connexion with the Reformation they tended to grow more
and more self-confident and worldly. It is hard to choose out
of three dozen and more major examples what is to be regarded as outstanding or specially characteristic. The first
sign of dissatisfaction with the Perp motifs of decoration
appears in a tomb-chest of alabaster at Wheathampstead,
which is dated 1558. Strapwork, the new abstract art of
ornament which the Elizabethan style took over from the
Netherlands, appears in full maturity at Aldbury in 1570,
but the majority of the more ambitious monuments belong
to the C17. Some are good enough to be in Westminster
Abbey, first and foremost that of the Earl of Salisbury at
Hatfield, by *Colt*, a large free-standing composition with
kneeling allegorical figures at the angles and the effigy of the
Earl above and as a cadaver below. At least as good *Nicholas
Stone's* moving figure of Sir Richard Cyrle † 1617, in a
shroud. This is also at Hatfield. Works like these would
hold their own in any county. Many others are cruder in
style and showier in decoration. The chief types are one
with kneeling figures facing each other across a prayer-desk,
usual mostly for epitaphs on a smaller scale but occurring
also in standing wall-monuments, and another with a recumbent effigy (or two, one being placed behind and a little
above the other) or a semi-reclining effigy, under an arch,
shallow or deeper and coffered, between columns carrying
an entablature with an achievement. Particularly good
are the examples at Bayford (1612) and Hunsdon (1617).
Others at Braughing (1625), Broxbourne (1609), Hatfield
(1612), Hertingfordbury (1622, *c.* 1650), Hunsdon (1612),

* Elizabethan and Jacobean CHURCH FURNISHINGS are of no
great interest. It is sufficient here to mention the Early Renaissance
decoration (the earliest in the county) of the screen of *c.* 1540 at Digswell, the early C17 screen at Wyddial, and the screen and family pews
at Hunsdon of about the same date. The style remained unaltered for a
long time. The pulpit of 1658 at Bishops Stortford is still wholly in the
Elizabethan tradition.

Sawbridgeworth (1625), Standon (1587, 1606), Watfor
(1599, 1628), and Wheathampstead (c. 1630–5). An odd cas
of Gothic survival is the canopy of the Ravenscroft Monu
ment at High Barnet of 1630. Rarer types are those with bust
(an early example at Braughing, 1597, wider popularit
during the reign of Charles I: Hadley, by *Nicholas Stone*
1616, then Berkhamsted 1627 or 1634, Aspenden 1634 o
1623, Meesden 1626, Buckland 1634, Sawbridgeworth 1637
Willian 1656), those with seated and those with standin
figures. The most famous seated effigy is Sir Francis Bacon
at St Michael's St Albans, 1626 (an earlier example 1605 a
Radwell); the only standing figure is Bridget Gore † 165ς
She is in her shroud, a type made popular by the Donn
Monument in St Paul's Cathedral.

The Restoration brought a noticeable change in the styl
of monuments. It is clearly indicated in the beautiful epitap
of Judith Strode at Knebworth (1662) with its purely Italian
nobly handled bust and extremely restrained detail. On
type specially favoured shortly after the Restoration has n
effigy, though often two mournful putti, and Italian detail i
a grand Baroque manner (several examples at Little Gad
desden, also Cheshunt). Busts remain in fashion. (Ardele
1673, Barnet 1680, 1689, Wyddial 1687, etc.) Semi-reclinin
figures occur even more frequently than before and thei
style now becomes more spectacular. Roman costume ap
pears, and the proudly carried wigs of an extremely self
assured age. One of the earlier displays of this self-impor
tance of the prosperous nobleman at the time of William o
Orange is the Viscount Hewyt Memorial at Sawbridgeworth
(1689). He is portrayed standing in front of us in an attitude
as if he were Louis XIV himself. A standing statue also M
Lytton † 1710 at Knebworth (by *Thomas Green*?). The
Lytton Chapel at Knebworth contains the most sumptuou
series of monuments in the county. The large monument
to Sir William Lytton † 1705 and Sir George Strode † 170
by *Edward Stanton* have stately semi-reclining figures wear
ing wigs and big reredos backgrounds. Two semi-reclinin
effigies (arranged à la Guglielmo della Porta's tomb of Pop
Paul III) at Tring (by *Nost*, 1707). As the c18 progressed

e composition of monuments became more varied.
he sources are Italy and France; the style moves from a
mewhat ponderous Baroque to a remarkably elegant
ococo. Herts is rich in many types and examples by many
ands. Reclining figures with assistant allegories at Offley
599, at Abbots Langley (by *Cheere*) 1732; two standing
gures with a tree in the background at Offley (by *Nollekens*)
777; allegories singly or in pairs, seated or in other atti-
ides, without effigies at North Mimms 1716, Offley (by
aylor) 1752, Abbots Langley (by *Scheemakers*) 1756,
hrocking (by *Nollekens*) 1770, Flamstead (by *Flaxman*)
782. Of other sculptors *Rysbrack* is represented by four
five works, none amongst his most important, *Roubiliac*
y one extremely charming but minor piece (Hertingford-
ury 1727), *Bacon* by two (Sawbridgeworth; Watton 1793).
he *Stantons* appear at Flamstead (1690) and Barkway,
cheemakers made the Freeman Monument at Braughing to
thenian Stuart's design (1772). Lesser sculptors of monu-
ients are *T. Bull* (Redbourn), *B. Palmer* (Graveley), *John*
ichards (Buckland), and *W. Woodman* (Cheshunt). The last
eorgian decades have produced less interesting monu-
ients (two more *Flaxmans*, at Great Gaddesden 1782 and
acombe 1815, one *Thorwaldsen* at Wheathampstead, an ex-
ellent *Westmacott* at Little Gaddesden 1823, more *Westam-*
tt at Kings Langley, *Chenu* 1796 and 1820 at Barkway,
endrick at Barkway and Great Hormead). Not all the best
ionuments are signed. There are, for exmple, in various
laces, a number of delicate epitaphs of *c.* 1760–80 in white,
ink, and biscuit-coloured marbles with portrait medallions,
herubs' heads, etc., whose authors are unknown.

In houses the classical style which Inigo Jones opposed to
ie current Jacobean made an early appearance in Herts;
ut the first examples are of a characteristically impure,
iough by no means transitional, kind. They do not employ
acobean motifs any longer, but use the Italian idiom awk-
ardly and with a broad accent. The result is academically
bjectionable, but original and robust. Balls Park of *c.* 1640
s one of the earliest examples of this peculiar Carolean
tyle which has recently been connected with the name of

the London architect *Peter Mills*. Tyttenhanger of *c.* 1655–
60 belongs to the same group, though its brick quoins,
window pediments, hipped roof, and squat cupola are in
keeping with the correct style of Pratt at Coleshill, etc.
The staircase at Tyttenhanger is one of the earliest in the
country to have a railing of openwork foliage panels. Of
the late C17 and the early C18 there are quite a number
of pleasant, simple, comfortably proportioned brick houses
(Brent Pelham Hall, Golden Parsonage 1705, Redheath
1712, Chipperfield Manor House 1716, Temple Dinsley in
its original form 1717, and so on to Much Hadham Hall,
Cumberland House Redbourn, and many others in villages),
but nothing on a grand scale. Grandeur appears only with
Leoni's Moor Park, a stone mansion with splendid giant
Corinthian portico and a hall with paintings by *Amigoni*.
The chief country houses after 1750 are Brocket Hall by
Paine (*c.* 1755–75), curiously solid and unadorned outside,
Gaddesden Place by *Wyatt* (1768–73), Gorhambury by
Taylor (1777), and Woodhall Park by *Leverton* (1777), the
latter three Palladian of characteristically different idioms.
In 1782 at Pishiobury *Wyatt* appears mildly medievalizing
in a thoroughly Neo-Gothic style Panshanger was built
about twenty years later by the younger *Repton. Soane* did
some of his most original Neo-Greek work at Marden Hill,
and one should regard Hyde Hall near Sawbridgeworth of
1806 and the enlargements at Bayfordbury of 1809 in
relation to his style. A specially handsome small Neo-Greek
villa is Tewin Water of *c.* 1815.

There are plenty of pleasant Georgian town houses in
such towns as St Albans, Hitchin, Hemel Hempstead, Ware,
Hertford, etc.

Secular buildings other than houses are *James Adam's*
Shire Hall at Hertford (1768–9), the Corn Exchange at
Bishops Stortford of 1828, and the Town Hall at St Albans
by *George Smith*, who did much work in the county (1829).
The most extensive almshouses are those of Bishop Ward at
Buntingford 1684, and the Duchess of Marlborough's at St
Albans 1736. The Old Hall Academy was built as a Roman
Catholic College in 1795–9 and enlarged in 1805, a building

much more extensive and unified in composition than school
buildings other than Catholic were in the c18. However, in
1809 Haileybury College appeared with its long Neo-Greek
açade and quadrangle by *Wilkins*.

The only church building of a comparably representational character is *Nicholas Revett's* at Ayot St Lawrence
1778–9, on an unusual plan and with a severe Greek Doric
portico. Church work before 1800 otherwise is negligible
(St Paul's Walden Chancel 1727, Offley Chancel *c*.1750, Totteridge 1790). Several village churches have their box pews
and three-decker pulpits (Stanstead Abbots) preserved. The
most remarkable font is that at Essendon, of Wedgwood
black-basalt earthenware. Excellent early c18 ironwork is
at Hatfield churchyard (from St Paul's Cathedral) and in
Hatfield church (from Amiens) and Knebworth church.

Early c19 churches are of no special architectural merit,
some classical, some of that starved Gothic which charac-
terizes the period of the so-called Commissioners' Churches.
A number are Neo-Norman, and London Colney of 1825 by
J. Smith must be one of the earliest examples of a Norman
Revival in Britain.

Several of the leading Victorian church architects are
represented in Herts: *Pugin* with the ambitious chapel at
Old Hall Green 1845, *Butterfield* with Holy Saviour Hitchin
1865 and the successful re-modelling and enlarging of the
High Barnet Parish Church 1876, *Bentley* with the outstandingly fine Holy Rood Watford 1883, etc., and so on.
Pritchett's High Wych of 1861 deserves to be specially mentioned as an eminently typical example of High Victorian
design at its most revolting, *Seddon's* Ayot St Peter of 1875
is a work by an early adherent of the Morris reform. Other
churches by *Blomfield* (Stevenage), *Jekyll* (Lilley), *Norman
Shaw* (Boxmoor), *Carpenter & Ingelow* (Long Marston),
and so on to *Lutyens's* remarkably original and forceful but
unfinished St Martin's Knebworth 1914.*

* The best Victorian Stained Glass is that of *William Morris* at Furneaux Pelham 1866, 1873, Kings Walden 1867, Rickmansworth 1891,
and Hatfield 1894, of *Kempe* in his early years at High Cross 1876 and
Bishops Stortford 1877, and of *Selwyn Image* at High Cross 1893.

Lutyens married into the Lytton family at Knebworth and so got several jobs at Knebworth. Homewood of 1900 is one of his most original early houses, Temple Dinsley of *c* 1908 one of his biggest enlargement jobs. The Early Georgian house sinks into insignificance under the weight of *Lutyens's* Neo-Georgian wings. The chief Late Victorian houses are Goldings by *Devey* (1870), Denham, Totteridge by *Norman Shaw* (1877), New Place, Welwyn by *Philip Webb* (1880), and the American *H. H. Richardson's* Lululand at Bushey for Herkomer the painter (*c.* 1885). Of this only the massive entrance is preserved. *Devey* also built Blakesware, *Waterhouse* Easneye (1868). Of the next generation, *Lutyens's* generation, *Voysey* is represented by some of his best work, The Orchard at Chorleywood (1900) and other houses at Chorleywood, Bushey, and Eastbury, *Walton* by The Leys Elstree (1901), and *Macartney* by Firthwood House Eastbury (*c.* 1900). *Leonard Stokes's* All Saints Convent at London Colney (1899) is institutional architecture of the same generation at its best, a very free Neo-Tudor.

For architectural development in the C20 few counties are as interesting as Herts. Here the first independent garden city was built: Letchworth; and the second: Welwyn.* Here of the seven planned satellite towns of London three are situated: Stevenage, Hemel Hempstead, and Hatfield New Town.‡ Letchworth was designed by *Parker & Unwin*, the pioneers of town planning of their generation, Welwyn by *Louis de Soissons*. The Stevenage plans are by Ash Gordon, those for Hemel Hempstead by *G. A. Jellicoe*, those for Hatfield by *Lionel Brett*. The principle behind their creation is a logical development of that underlying Ebenezer Howard's book on *Garden Cities of the Future* and Parker & Unwin's designs for Letchworth. The satellite town as well as the garden city is meant to be an independent town with its own factories and all urban amenities. The creation of more such cities than Letchworth and Welwyn

* More on the principle of the garden city will be found under Letchworth, p. 153.

‡ And Harlow in Essex is only just across the border.

became urgent when *Sir Patrick Abercrombie's* and *Mr J. H Forshaw's* plans for the County of London and for Greater London had shown up conclusively the necessity of 'decanting' some of London's growing population. The necessity seems alas to be for one whole town of 50,000 inhabitants to be completed every year, or else the desired relief for London will not take place. As it is six new towns were begun near London: Harlow and Basildon in Essex, Crawley in Sussex and the three mentioned above in Hertfordshire. They were started on paper with much enthusiasm. The idea had been to progress beyond Letchworth and Welwyn by giving them a more urban character. But as nowhere building has started in the natural way from the centre, what can so far be seen is nearly as suburban and loosely laid out as the garden cities. The only difference is the consistent use of terraces of houses and the occasional interjection of blocks of flats (Stevenage). The only completed shopping centre at the time of writing was at Hemel Hempstead. However, things may look very different in a few years time, if, as much be hoped, the rate of growth can be geared up. So far building of houses seems to be slower than in many less convincingly planned housing estates in Herts built, for example, by the London County Council. If in the end the New Towns come to be anything like their present plans, then they will be the first towns in England since Bath of which their inhabitants and the country can be unreservedly proud.

In addition the *Herts County Architect's Department* is remarkably active in taking over, converting, adjusting, and thereby saving, good Georgian and Victorian houses and in erecting new buildings which are intelligently designed and built. The outstanding case is that of the county's schools programme. The case has rightly received wide publicity at home and abroad, but must here in conclusion be summarized, especially because it will not be possible to mention all the exemplary new schools built since 1946. They now (Summer, 1952) total over fifty. The programme was based from the beginning on extensive, very ingeniously conducted research, as to how materials can be ordered beforehand

and stocked by the manufacturers, how delays in sanc
tioning can be avoided, and how local contractors ca▪
be made use of. The answer to these questions is a system
of galvanized steel frame units bolted together on the site
with pre-cast vibrated concrete units for walls and roofs
This very complete system of prefabrication allows ex
tremely rapid assembly, and as only the basic units (on
module originally of 8 ft 3 in. now of 3 ft 4 in.) are stan
dardized, also extreme freedom in grouping. At first th
system was used only for single-storey primary schools
but it has now been extended to two- or three-storey build
ings, so as to allow the construction of secondary schools
Recent developments have also taken place in the use o
concrete and timber frames to overcome the steel shortag▪
and also in the use of plastic and other cladding materials
These experiments have been designed on the new 3 ft 4 in
planning module. However, in spite of all this research and
technical ingenuity, these schools would be merely an
achievement of engineering and organization if the com
position and finishes were not the work of a team of ex
ceptionally sensitive and modern-minded designers. From
the balancing of block against block down to the colours o
the walls, the curtain patterns, and the door handles, every
thing is carefully considered and elegantly done. It is a
delightful experience to walk around and through some o
these schools. In the following pages only a dozen selected
examples are mentioned.*

So this account of the history of architecture can end on a
note of cheer and optimism, which is more than one can say
of modern developments in many parts of Britain.

A few lines must be added on the printed sources on
which the information contained in the following pages i
based. The chief sources are the *Victoria County History* (
vols, 1908–14) and the Hertfordshire Volume of the *Roya*
Commission on Historical Monuments. This, however, being
the earliest volume published by the Commission (1910) i

* See Boreham Wood, Cheshunt, East Barnet, Essendon, Heme
Hempstead, Hertford, Hitchin, Oxhey, St Albans, Stevenage, Ware
Welwyn Garden City.

ot as detailed as its successors. In addition such guidebooks the *Little Guide* (by H. W. Tomkins) and *Kelly's Direcry* were used. Of more specialized literature the histories Herts by Chauncy, Clutterbuck, and Cussans are of lue, of periodicals *Country Life* and the *Transactions of the ast Herts Arch. Soc.* and of the *St Albans and Herts Arch. Arch. Soc.* On the whole, however, not much strictly chitectural research has been done in Herts monuments, d the present volume will no doubt reflect that shortage.

HERTFORDSHIRE

*

ABBOTS LANGLEY

ST LAWRENCE. A church of exceptional architectural interest, thanks to its Norman nave arcades and Dec s chancel chapel. The church is not large. It has a low w tower with diagonal buttresses on the lower stage only. That stage is of the C13, as indicated by its small lancet windows. Its top is a plain brick parapet. The nave is short, of two bays, the chancel lower than the nave. Its windows have Early Perp tracery. The aisle windows are later Perp. So is the clerestory, although remains are noticeable of an earlier clerestory (c. 1300) with pointed trefoil-headed windows. The s chancel chapel has a sumptuous exterior with a chequer pattern of flint and stone mixed with brick, while the rest of the church is flint with stone dressings. The tracery of the windows in the chapel is typical Early Dec. Remains of the w window show that the s aisle was renewed later. A s, and also a N, aisle had, however, existed long before. On entering the church one sees at once that the nave arcades belong to the C12. The N arcade has one circular pier with scalloped capital and w and E responds of the same design. The roundheaded arches are decorated with zigzag placed at right angles to the wall surface and an outer billet. The s arcade has the same arches and responds, but the pier was renewed in the early C13 with a shallow stiff-leaf capital, at about the same time at which the tower was built and received its arch to the nave with an elaborate moulding and large and more expressive stiff-leaf capitals. The w window of the s aisle proves part of that wall also to be a Norman survival. The nave arcades were continued in the late Middle Ages (four-centred arch on the s side). The Dec s chancel chapel opens to the chancel by a two-bay arcade with

sharply pointed two-centred arches of double-chamfere
moulding. The nave roof is handsome C15 work of kin
post type with the closely set rafters showing and th
spaces between them plastered.

FURNISHINGS. FONT. Octagonal, Perp, with shiel
inside quatrefoils (in two panels coarsely carved angels i
stead). – PAINTING. SS Lawrence and Thomas, high
on E wall of S chancel chapel. Much of what is seen now
Professor Tristram's 'restoration'. The style is clear
that of the chapel itself, that is first third of the C14.
COFFER. German, C16, with reliefs alluding to origin
sin and redemption, no doubt from the Protestant Nort
as the dialect of the inscriptions also proves. – STAIN
GLASS. S chapel E window, 1909, with a lush display
white foliage between the small scenes. By *Powell's*
Whitefriars. – MONUMENTS. Unimportant brass of 16
in the N aisle. – In the S chapel Anne Combe † 1640, t
usual epitaph with kneeling figure, and Dame Anne Ra
mond † 1714, an epitaph of unusual design, with the pri
cipal figure in timeless costume seated frontally, dignifi
and urbane. The representation of the three gran
children in their cradles on the plinth is, however, still
the naïve C16–C17 tradition. – The two principal mon
ments are placed against the aisle W walls: the first Lo
Raymond † 1732, by *Cheere*, semi-reclining figure wi
wig, with a seated allegory on the l. holding a portra
medallion, and putti on the r., the whole against a broa
pyramid; lively diagonal composition. – The secor
Lord Raymond † 1756 with black sarcophagus again
black obelisk in the centre and seated allegories of ho
and plenty to the l. and r. By *Scheemakers*.

THE VICARAGE, big and square, Georgian, behind th
church, the gabled and cemented MANOR HOUS
neglected at the time of writing, to the SW. To the NE th
Georgian LANGLEY HOUSE (Breakspear R.C. Colleg
so called because Nicholas Breakspear, later Hadrian I
the only Pope of English nationality, was born at Abbo
Langley), *c.* 1770, the usual five-bay, two-and-a-hal
storey structure, stuccoed *c.* 1830 and enlarged.

ther buildings around: the large, ugly, yellow and red
brick LEAVESDEN MENTAL HOSPITAL (1868–70), by
Giles & Biven. Between it and the village one of the
pairs of MODEL COTTAGES has been erected in 1856
which *Henry Roberts* designed at Prince Albert's request
for the Society for Improving the Conditions of the
Labouring Classes. The first of them could be seen at the
Great Exhibition of 1851. The cottages are characterized
by open recessed staircases and some Neo-Jacobean trim.
They were meant to be model units for larger and higher
blocks of flats.

ANGLEYBURY *see* p. 152.

ALBURY

r MARY. As in so many churches in this neighbourhood
the chancel is the earliest surviving part: C13 with
original N and S lancet windows. The nave and aisles are
mid C14, as shown by the aisle windows with very unusual, rather ugly, heavily flowing tracery. The arcades
have piers with big round shafts and thin shafts in the
diagonals. The arches are two-centred and double-chamfered in the S, more complex in the N. The chancel arch is
of the same style, the very tall tower arch evidently a hundred years later. The tower has diagonal buttresses, a low
stair-turret, and a spike. – PULPIT. C18 with inlaid shield.
– SCREEN. Tall, C15. – PLATE. Chalice, 1626. – MONU-
MENTS. Tomb-chest with five quatrefoils with shields.
On it the defaced effigies of a Knight and a Lady of *c.*
1400. – Brass to a Knight in armour and his Lady,
elegant somewhat mannered figures of under 1½ ft length,
c. 1475 (nave floor). – Brass to Thomas Leventhorp
† 1588 and wife and children; husband and wife turned
towards each other (S aisle). – Brass to John Scrogs † 1592
with wife and child; one plate with tapering sides.

ALDBURY

n exceptionally charming village green. To the E the woods
p the hillside towards Ashridge. The church recedes

from the sw end of the green, and several excellent co
tages lie NE and w of the church (especially Nos 11–13) an
N of the green along Stocks Road. In the distance on th
brow appears the MONUMENT (a Greek Doric colum
with an urn) to the third Duke of Bridgewater, erected i
1832 to commemorate his pioneer work for English canal

ST JOHN THE BAPTIST. Tall, slender w tower with sli
diagonal buttresses. In contrast to its vertical elevatic
the long, relatively low nave and yet lower chancel, an im
pressive opposition of vertical and horizontal. The chan
cel is embattled. Its masonry is the oldest part of th
church, as proved by a small C13 lancet window in the
wall and a low-side lancet in the s wall. The nave arcade
are early C14 with octagonal piers carrying moulde
capitals typical of that date and double-hollow-chamfere
arches. One pier on the s side is broader than the other
perhaps for a screen. The staircase in the s aisle does no
however, correspond to it. It led to the parvis above th
porch. The E bays have renewed piers. The N chanc
chapel must also be early C14. The tower arch is a littl
later. – In the N aisle wall is a figure CORBEL, very coarse
yet probably later than the C13, which is the date sug
gested by the Royal Commission. – LECTERN. C16,
timber. – PLATE. Cup of 1514; secular.
   The most remarkable part of the church is the PENDLE
CHAPEL. It is divided from the aisle and the chancel b
an excellent stone SCREEN with original Perp tracery an
a castellated top. In it is the MONUMENT to Sir Rober
Whittingham † 1471 and his wife, two recumbent ston
figures on a tomb-chest with weepers alternating wit
shields. The monument and the screen came from Ash
bridge in 1575–6. Against the E wall the later epitap
to Sir Richard Anderson † 1699 and his wife, with tw
elegant busts. – MONUMENTS in other parts of th
church; Sir Ralph Verney † 1546 with wife and childre
large brasses on stone tomb-chest decorated with shields
Also from Ashbridge. – Tiny brass to John Davies (
respond, N arcade), late C15. – Epitaph to Thoma

Hyde † 1570 and his son † 1580 (N chancel chapel) with
exquisite strapwork decoration but no figures.

ALDENHAM

ᵗ JOHN THE BAPTIST. The church stretches out im- 12
pressively S of the Green, long and well-proportioned,
with a W tower, nave, and aisles of four bays, and chancel
and chancel chapels. Exterior and interior look at first a
unity, but they represent quite a long and complex building history. The exterior is all flint with stone dressings,
the window shapes will be mentioned later. The W tower
has diagonal buttresses, a NE stair-turret higher than the
tower battlements, and a thin, long (renewed) timber
spire. The oldest remaining fragment is a Norman window at the W end of the S aisle, perhaps not in its original
position. The lower parts of the W tower (*see* windows) are
C13. C13 also is the chancel, with deeply splayed lancet
windows, completely renewed sedilia, and a trefoil-
headed piscina recess.* The S chancel chapel has windows
with typical tracery of *c.* 1300, with trefoils and pointed
trefoils. It is separated from the chancel by short octagonal
piers with broadly moulded capitals and double-chamfered arches. The nave and S aisle were rebuilt about 1340
(*see* the octagonal piers with capitals decorated by fleurons
and the double-chamfered arches and also the tracery of
the two-light windows). To the Perp style belong the N
arcade and wide N aisle (the capitals of the piers are finer
and have faces as well as fleurons as decoration), the N
windows, the N chancel chapel, the tower arch towards
the nave, the upper parts of the tower, and the clerestory
with small two-light windows. The brick N porch is C19.
The roofs are good C15 work, especially in the nave and N
aisle. Both are of very flat pitch.

FURNISHINGS. FONT. Square, C13, undecorated, on
five supports. – SCREEN. Between S aisle and S chancel
chapel, C15, much renewed. – COFFER. 10 ft long, oak

* The E window was inserted by *Sir Charles Barry* during the restoration of 1840.

trunk scooped out; the sides are 3 ft thick. With iro
bands and many hinges. Dated c14 by Roe. – STAINE
GLASS. By *Kempe*, 1891–1900; the earliest the Cruc
fixion in the N chancel chapel. – PLATE. Cup, 1565; Cup
1635; several c19 pieces. – MONUMENTS. An unusu
wealth of BRASSES, not of high aesthetic quality, but in
teresting as illustrating the changes of costume: in th
chancel man, woman, and eight children, c16; mar
woman, and eleven children, c16; Lucas Goodyere, 154
draped in a shroud; in the S chancel chapel a series fro
the early c16 to the early c17 (man and wife, *c.* 152c
man head missing, *c.* 1520; man and two wives, *c.* 1525
lady, *c.* 1535; Joan Warner † 1538; E. Brisko † 16c
and wife). – Of stone monuments the most importar
is that to two ladies of the Crowmer family in the
chancel chapel. Two identical tomb-chests with quatre
foil decoration. Recumbent effigies on them in late c1
costume. Canopies above with cusped four-centred arche
and embattled top cornices. The two monuments forr
one composition. – John Coghill † 1714, ascribed by Mr
Esdaile to *R. Crutcher*, two effigies on tomb-chest; he re
clines and seems to talk to her; she is behind him in
half-sitting position. Contemporary costumes. – Rober
Hucks and his wife † 1771, good unsigned epitaph i
various marbles, with double profile medallion. – Vice
Admiral Sir John Chambers White † 1845, Gothic epi
taph, very Dec in style, made by *Poole* of Westminster.
In the churchyard big urn on pedestal to Lt-Gen. R
Burne † 1825. On the pedestal the places in Europe
Asia, and America are enumerated where he fought
amongst them Buenos Ayres and The Suburbs of Buenc
Ayres.

EDGE GROVE, N of the church. Late c18, with four-colum
Ionic porch, much altered in Edwardian days.

WALL HALL, N of Edge Grove. Castellated, turreted, and
cemented house of *c.* 1800 (then given the fancy nam
Aldenham Abbey) and *c.* 1830. Big Gothic conservatory
some artificial ruins, an Ionic covered garden seat and a
ice house in the grounds.

PATCHETTS GREEN, S of Aldenham, a pair of exceed-ingly picturesque farmhouses with weatherboarded out-buildings.

DELROW, SE of Patchetts Green, gabled cemented house with a few preserved Jacobean-looking fireplaces. One rainwater-head bears the date 1666.

BATLERS GREEN, 1 m. E of Aldenham, an excellent C16–C18 house. The street front is of eight bays, early C18. Behind, an L-shaped Tudor house with a plastered and pargetted gabled E front and contemporary timber and brickwork. In one room ceiling with moulded beams.

ALDENHAM HOUSE, 2 m. SE. A fine brick house of c. 1700, much enlarged c. 1870 and later, for instance by an in-congruous tower. *Sir Arthur Blomfield* is supposed to have been the architect of 1870. The earlier house has a W front of seven bays with two storeys, hipped roof, dor-mer windows, a carved pediment, and a pedimented porch on detached unfluted Ionic columns, and a S front with central polygonal bay window and crowning vases. The Venetian window to the l. of the W front is Early Georgian. What valuable features the interior possesses are all boarded up at the time of writing.

ANSTEY

GEORGE. An architecturally interesting and externally very impressive church. Internally the aesthetic effect is spoilt by the very features which make the building archaeologically remarkable. The crossing tower seems Norman in its lower stages: four narrow roundheaded arches inside with shafts with extremely primitive volute or spiral capitals on the W side of W and E arches. The arches have roll-mouldings thickening at narrow, regular intervals into a kind of Norman shaft-rings, a motif used in the mid C12 decoration of the Slype at St Albans Abbey. The shafts also have such rings, but here they seem the proper shaft-rings of the Early Gothic style which were introduced in France about 1150 in a com-pletely different context and do not appear in England

before Canterbury in 1175. So this 'Norman' work
probably as late as *c.* 1200, a time-lag worth rememb-
ing. The chancel and both transepts were rebuilt late
the C13. The S transept front seen from the S is a fi
sight, with C13 lancet windows and a round stair-turr
Behind it appears the crossing tower with diagonal b
tresses right up to the top, C14 bell-openings and a He
spike. The chancel has on its S and N sides typical late c
windows with two lights with pointed trefoil heads a
quatrefoils above (no bar tracery yet). Inside the chan
is a fine display of C13 detail. The E end has two bla
lancets to the sides of the C19 E window, the N doorwa
label on very unusual stops, and the S side an equally u
usual piscina and sedilia arrangement combined with t
windows and a doorway. It is all so odd that one wond-
whether it has not been, in some way, tampered with.
the S transept S wall an exquisite though, alas, mutila
tomb-recess with a canopy and pinnacles. The cano
of the same type as those of *c.* 1300 in Westmins
Abbey (blank trefoil in the top). It rests on naturalis
leaf stops. The pinnacles have blank tracery and a
naturalistic leaves. Under the cusped arch of the canop
woman's head with a wimple. The effigy in the recess (
below) does not seem to belong. The date of the cano
is probably the earliest years of the C14. Only a little, i
all, later the nave arcades (four bays) with big quatre
piers with moulded capitals and two-centred alm
straight arches. The C15 clerestory windows are quat
foil-shaped. The aisle windows are Late Perp, as is th
porch with two-light windows and blank panelling. T
inner and outer doorways of the porch have blank quat
foils in the spandrels. – FONT. Very crude Norman w
four mermen holding their split tails with both th
hands; the design makes a symmetrical pattern along t
four sides of the bowl. – CHANCEL STALLS. Plain C15
C16 with MISERICORDS (large leaves, a shell, a head w
tongue out, two profile heads). – STAINED GLASS. S ai
window by *Heaton, Butler, & Baines*, 1907. – PLA
Set of C18.

'CHGATE. C15 or earlier. Tripartite; but one third
altered into a lock-up.

ARBURY BANK *see* ASHWELL

ARDELEY

LAWRENCE. Unbuttressed W tower with spike. The W
window C14. Embattled aisles, clerestory, and chancel.
The aisle and clerestory windows mostly Perp. The N
porch tall with two-light windows, also C15. Only in the
chancel do two lancet windows show an earlier stage of
the church. The windows are matched by the fine piscina
and the N recess, both with short shafts and dog-tooth
ornament. The nave N arcade consists of three bays with
octagonal piers, and these must also be C13 (simple
moulded capitals, double-chamfered arches). The S arcade
is a little later: C14, as is presumably the chancel arch.
The nave and aisle ROOFS of the C15 have bosses, angel
brackets, and some tracery in the brackets. – The ROOD
LOFT with painted rood and rood canopy (but no screen)
was given in 1928. It was designed by *F. C. Eden*. –
FONT. Octagonal with big faces in the four diagonals. The
date is difficult to determine; probably C14. – PLATE.
Chalice, Paten and Almsdish of the late C17. – MONU-
MENTS. Brasses to Philip Metcalffe, Vicar of Ardeley,
† 1515, to Thomas Shotbolt with wife and children
† 1599, and to W. Wyndham Malet, Vicar of Ardeley,
† 1885 (profile, turned towards the altar). – Mary Mark-
ham † 1673, epitaph with lively demi-figure in niche with
telling gestures. On a ledge in front her baby. Fine
quality. – Cartouche to Henry Chauncy † 1703; also very
good.

RDELEY BURY. A Late Tudor house of brick of which
little remains except some walls. The rest mostly the work
of a fanciful architect of 1820 who converted the manor
house into an enchanted castle. He added a circular flint
tower, two polygonal brick turrets, divers pinnacles, and
so on, made the windows Gothic, erected a baronial hall

with a big fireplace, a minstrel's gallery and a plaster⁣
timber roof, and inserted Gothic vaulting in other room⁣
Long avenue, lake, and Tudor boathouse.

THE GREEN was made in 1917 by the Lord of the Man⁣
A brick well in the middle, white thatched cottages, V⁣
lage Hall, and terraces of cottages around, designed ⁣
F. C. Eden (a Blaise Castle Revived, though without t⁣
capriciousness of the original).

At Cromer, 1 m. NW, CROMER FARM, a specially attracti⁣
farmhouse with overhangs, exposed uprights, and gable⁣

ARKLEY

ST PETER. Rough brick church of 1840 with aisleless na⁣
and transepts. Lancet windows. The chancel was adde⁣
in 1898 (by *Traylen*; GR). – STAINED GLASS. E windo⁣
1903 by *Kempe*. – MONUMENT. Very simple epitaph ⁣
Enosh Durant † 1848, at whose expense the church w⁣
built; the epitaph is signed by the *Westminster Marb⁣
Company*, not by an individual sculptor, a sign of t⁣
coming Victorian times.

WINDMILL. NW of the church. Built probably early in t⁣
C19. Repaired in 1930.*

ASHLYNS *see* BERKHAMSTED

ASHRIDGE *see* LITTLE GADDESDEN

ASHWELL

13 ST MARY. The glory of the church is its W tower, in fou⁣
stages with tall angle buttresses. It is 176 ft high, crowne⁣
by an octagonal lantern with a leaded spike, the same pa⁣
tern as at Baldock.‡ The tower is clunch-built and mo⁣
ambitious than any other of a Herts parish church, and ⁣
has never been explained why just Ashwell should ha⁣
gone to such an enormous expense. It was begun in t⁣

* Information kindly provided by Mr Rex Wailes.
‡ The leading was last renewed in 1948.

first half of the C14.* The church itself is of the same
date, the chancel was apparently completed in 1368, and
the whole building in 1381. The body of the church is of
clunch and flint, relatively low and not embattled except
for the chancel. Most of the windows are usual C15 Perp,
but the clerestory windows and the tower w window prove
that the Dec style was still alive when the building went
up. The s porch is two-storeyed, higher than the aisle,
with a fine outer doorway and two-light windows (the
vault is C19). The N porch of one storey has three-light
windows. Both porches are of the second half of the C15.
The interior bears out the building history surmised for
the exterior. The arcades of the nave look indeed a little
earlier than 1350. They change their details from E to W
(piers with big attached shafts and thin ones without
capitals in the diagonals, then piers with the big shafts
slightly thinner, then with the big shafts of semi-octagonal
section). The aisle roofs are good, solid C14 work. The
chancel arch corresponds to the earlier parts of the nave,
the tower arch to the later. To link up nave and tower a
blank piece of wall was left standing and decorated with a
blind two-light Perp arch as high as the whole nave. The
clerestory windows stand above the spandrels, not the
apexes of the arcade. The chancel is aisleless with large
windows, and as these have no stained glass it appears
very light. The whole church is indeed spacious and
broad, rather than tall. The walls are whitewashed, the
stone parts light. The effect is decidedly puritanical, especially as the church has surprisingly little of furnishings. –

* This is proved by the extremely interesting graffiti inside the N
wall of the tower. They say in Latin: 'MCterX Penta miseranda ferox
»lenta . . .(? pestis) superest plebs pessima testis' and 'In fine ije
»cundae) ventus validus. . . . . Maurus in orbe tonat MCCCXI,
50, wretched, wild, distracted. The dregs of the mob alone survive
tell the tale. At the end of the second (outbreak) was a mighty
nd. St Maurus thunders in all the world.' The date of this excep-
»nal gale was 1361. Higher up] on the tower wall (N) there is a fur-
»er inscription, in much smaller script: primula pestis in MterCCC
it l.minus uno. Also on the N wall a remarkably detailed and accurate
:atching of the s side of Old St Paul's cathedral.

PULPIT. 1627. The usual blank arches in the panels ar
made up of diamond-cut pieces. – LADY CHAPE
SCREEN. Very elementary C15 tracery. – STAINE
GLASS. Small C15 fragments in clerestory windows.
PLATE. Paten, 1632; Chalice, 1688. – No monuments (
importance. – LYCHGATE. Attributed to the C15.

[4] The village has perhaps more architecturally worthwhil
houses than any other in the county, and they are beside
thanks to an uncommonly discriminating and public
spirited landowner, in a very good state of preservatior
But the village is so big that the houses cannot be taken i
visually as a whole. They are nearly all of the timber
framed or the gabled brick type. The C18 has not adde
much (chiefly two houses near the E end of the Hig
Street, one of five bays with a hooded doorway, the othe
of seven bays). In the centre of the High Street, especiall
excellent, the long ST JOHN'S GUILD HALL with it
narrowly spaced timber uprights and the neighbourin
cottages with bold rustic fancy pargetting of 1681. Re
mains of C15 houses have been analysed recently i
Country Life. Towards the W end of the High Street th
CHANTRY HOUSE with a two-light C18 window, an
opposite WESTBURY FARM, plastered with symmetric;
gables. S of the church the TOWN HOUSE (Museum)
two-bay gabled C16 house with overhang and narrowl
spaced timbers. (In the Museum a C15 silver Reliquar
originally of the Guild of St John.) – W of the church th
humble two-bay brick house which was founded by th
London Merchant Taylors as a school in 1681. To the
of the grounds of Ashwell Bury DUCKLAKE FARM,
house with bold, good ornamental Tudor wall painting
in one room.

ASHWELL BURY. A sizeable Early Victorian house re
modelled, chiefly inside, by *Lutyens* in 1922–3. The sky
lit staircase is particularly notable. The lowest steps fr
the well right across, before the staircase narrows to th
width of the second and third flights. In a very Lutyensia
way, the architect left one window in an inconspicuou
position unaltered so as to show what he started from.

SHWELL END, BLUEGATES FARM (N of Ashwell Bury).
Two more C16 farm-houses, a little further out.

RBURY BANK, ¾ m. sw, between Claybush and Newn-
ham Hills. Iron Age hill-fort in the shape of an elongated
horseshoe, sw–ne across a hilltop. The size is 300 by 220
yd. The bank is highest at the sw, where the ground is
steepest.

ASPENDEN

T MARY. Cemented and much restored (1873, by *Sir A.
Blomfield*). Unbuttressed w tower with spike. The interior mostly Perp and much C19. In the chancel lancets,
proving its C13 date. The s porch is quite lavish with a
decorated doorway and two-light window. It was built *c.*
1525 and paid for by the widow of Sir Robert Clifford.
Inside, the s aisle arcade (octagonal piers, moulded
capitals, two-centred arches) must belong to the mid C14.
The s chancel chapel is the most interesting part of the
church. It was remodelled in 1622. It opens to the chancel
in two bays with the usual octagonal piers, but the arches
are now made semicircular, and strapwork decoration
is applied. – C15 Roofs in nave, s chapel, and s aisle. –
Perp RECESSES in the N chancel wall (ogee canopy and
crenellation) and the s chapel. The latter houses the tomb
of Sir Robert Clifford † 1508. Tomb-chest with shields on
three lozenges. Depressed panelled arch. Against the back
wall brasses of the Clifford family. Quatrefoil frieze above
the arch and top cresting. – *Morris & Co.* windows of
1913 in the s porch. – MONUMENTS (cf. above): Man and
woman, 1500, 18 in. figures (nave, N wall). – Ralph and
William Freman † 1634 and 1623, big epitaph with
broken segmental pediment and beneath it, not in niches,
two frontal busts. The two brothers hold each other's
hands. – John Boldero † 1789, with urn above inscription; white, grey, and pink marble.

ASTON

ST MARY. The chancel shows signs of its erection in the
C13 (one lancet window, Double Piscina). The rest, as far

as visible, is c15 (w tower with diagonal buttresses wit
five set-offs) or c19 (s porch, nave s windows, whole
aisle). – PULPIT. c17, very simply panelled. – SCREEN
Simple, but handsome, c. 1500. – PLATE. Chalice and tw
Patens, 1571; Chalice, 1612. – BRASS. John Kent † 159
and wife (nave, E end).

ASTON HOUSE. Brick house of c. 1700, remodelled in th
c19. The old work well visible on the E side. The stable
are more interesting in design than the house: also
1700, brick chequer with rubbed dressings. Blank arcade
on the ground floor, alternating circular and oval window
on the upper floor. Lantern turret.

ASTONBURY HOUSE. Three-storeyed Jacobean brick man
sion with remains of a first building period of c. 1540
Symmetrical s front (with big trees close to the E end)
Two broad gabled projections contain two original stair
cases; two chimney stacks in the angles between the pro
jections and the centre of the house which is occupied b
the hall. On the N side a porch (rebuilt) leads into the Hal
The gables here are shaped with ogee above conve
curves. The principal windows are mullioned and tran
somed. Handsome open well timber staircase (E) with ta
obelisks on the newel posts and banisters whose uppe
half is the mirror image of the lower part.

FROGMORE HALL. Red brick Neo-Gothic mansion wit
big square tower (chequered parapet, two large Per
windows). Whom by?

AUBREYS, THE, see REDBOURN

AVENUE FARM see IPPOLLITTS

AYOT ST LAWRENCE

OLD ST LAWRENCE. The old church in the village is i
ruins. Tradition has it that Sir Lionel Lyte began to pu
it down when he had decided to build (as one would the
have called it if to-day's jargon had already existed) a
ultra-modern church in the grounds of his house. Th

Bishop heard of this when demolition had gone some way, and prevented further destruction. The damage was not repaired, and so the picturesque ruin which we see to-day resulted, a sight which would no doubt have pleased Sir Lionel and his friends. What survives of the building shows that the church had a NW tower, nave, chancel, N aisle, and N chancel chapel. The windows in the N wall of the N chapel tell of Dec tracery (one has a combined star and quatrefoil motif in the head, known as Kentish tracery). The W arch of the same chapel with early C13 stiff-leaf capitals was originally that of the nave arcade. – A decayed C15 tomb-chest under the tower with recumbent effigies of a Knight and Lady.

he house, AYOT HOUSE, looks an early C18 building, with its segmentheaded windows and the characteristic vertical strips and window trim of rubbed bricks. The main front is of three storeys and five bays with the middle bay slightly projected. Additions were made *c.* 1850 and in 1933. STABLES with cupola and a portico or verandah of tall thin polygonal timber posts. The old manor house close by is of Tudor construction, with a front renewed in the late C17.

EW ST LAWRENCE was designed by *Nicholas Revett* and 14b built in 1778–9 partly to replace the old church, partly to serve as an eye-catcher from the house. Hence its 'gloriette'-like far-spreading front. The church itself, no larger than, and rather similar to, an early C19 cemetery chapel, has a Grecian front, a thing unheard of at that time. The Grecian Revival had only just begun with *Revett's* and his colleague *James Stuart's* voyage to Athens and their publication of the *Antiquities of Athens* (vol. 1, 1762). To let one of them do a church or chapel with a real Greek temple roof proved a client to be eminently progressive (or ambitious, or perhaps just wanting to be fashionable). The portico with its columns only fluted at the top and foot is copied from the Temple of Apollo at Delos. But the whole composition with side colonnades and little outer aedicules is not at all Grecian. It is a purely Palladian composition, that is the type of composition

which was customary for English country house
right through the C18. To have churches really copyin
Greek temples another fifty years had to go. The groun
plan of *Revett's* church is remarkably original. A rec
tangular centre with coffered ceiling and a short w ar
with a screen of two columns and a coffered tunnel-vaul
Transepts of the same length and height, also tunne
vaulted. The E end is a coffered apse, again of the sam
height and width, with two curved recesses. The sma
organ is original. – In the outer aedicules stand the urns t
Sir Lionel Lyte and his wife.

BRIDE HALL, 1 m. s. Jacobean manor house of brick, bui
on the E-plan with central two-storeyed porch. The
projecting wing has a straight gable. On the r. wing th
has been replaced by a hipped roof. The windows are re
newed. Staircases, door frames, and in the Hall a fireplac
and moulded ceiling-beams remain. Weatherboarde
barns to the r. and l. The area between them and in fron
of the house handsomely turfed by the present owner.

AYOT ST PETER

ST PETER. 1875, by *Seddon*. Red brick with blue bric
decoration and stone dressings. Asymmetrically place
thin tower with broaches connecting the square with a
octagonal upper stage on which rests a spire. Clock wit
fancifully designed face in a shade of blue. Nave an
apsed chancel plus a polygonally projecting s orga
chamber. Corresponding to this on the N side a large ros
window on the ground floor flanked by lancets. It is a
very capricious and deliberately original. The interior i
an exceptionally complete example of church furnishin
about 1880 by an architect in sympathy with the the
recent Arts and Crafts tendencies: chancel arch, an earl
work of the *Martin Brothers*, who had their pottery a
Southall from 1873 to 1915, thin iron chancel screer
elaborate tiling of the chancel, font with mosaic-work o
the circular bowl. – STAINED GLASS in the W window
(1880) designed by *Seddon* and incompetently executed

in the apse windows (1879) by an unknown glass artist. –
PLATE. Chalice and Paten of *c.* 1640–50.

the small cemetery, ½ m. W, a mortuary chapel, once the
E end of a previous church of 1863 by *Pearson*. Pearson's
church replaced one of 1732 which was octagonal and had
a campanile.

YOT PLACE. Excellent though modernized farmhouse of
1615, partly timber-framing and plaster (N wing), partly
timber-framing and brick (E wing). The hall is in the E
wing and has a 'minstrels' gallery'.

YOTBURY. A fine well-kept house, the centre block of
which is of 1672. Additions of 1913.

BALDOCK

Γ MARY. A roomy church, architecturally in several points
the sister of Ashwell, a few miles away. Big broad W tower
of the early C14 with Dec windows, and on the embattled
parapet a small octagonal lantern crowned by a Herts
spike. The body of the church also embattled, mostly of
flint. But the lower part of the chancel is of stone. Here
traces can be found of C13 windows and a Double Piscina
with a C13 shaft. The S porch is two-storeyed with a turret
in the NW angle and an outer doorway of the early C14.
The other windows are Perp. The interior is in its appear- 18b
ance almost completely early C14: tower arch, arcades of
six bays, chancel arcades of two bays, Sedilia and Piscina
in the S chapel with nodding ogee arches. The piers are
quatrefoil with additional thin shafts (without capitals) in
the diagonals (just as at Ashwell), typical moulded capitals
(on the S side slightly more finely detailed than on the N),
and double-chamfered arches. Good contemporary head
corbels for the outer labels. C15 clerestory roofs (on head
corbels). The aisles are wide and on the low side. The
church is generally broad and roomy: a wealthy town
church. – FONT. Octagonal, on nine shafts; C13. –
SCREENS. A complete C15 set across aisles and chancel
arch, the rood screen, of course, more ornate than the
others, but all three relatively elementary in their tracery.

– STAINED GLASS. W window 1849, looks as if it might b
by *Wailes*; E window similar; N aisle Simpson Window
1881, a typical early *Kempe*. – PLATE. Chalice and Pater
1629. – MONUMENTS. C13 Purbeck marble coffin-li
with cross (N chapel). – Brasses to a nun, *c.* 1400, sma
(nave, W end); to a man and woman, *c.* 1400, smallish (
chapel); to a man and woman, later C15, larger figure
(N chapel); to a man and woman, shrouded, *c.* 1520, *c.* 3
long (N chapel). – Monument to Georgiana Caldecot
† 1846, by *Baily*. She lies on a couch mourned by a knee
ing young woman, while an angel in the background of th
relief carries her soul up to heaven. – Many minor epi
taphs (e.g. by *Gaffin*).

PERAMBULATION

To judge from the houses of Baldock its wealth was of th
C18 rather than the C16–C17. One remembers Georgia
but no Tudor or Jacobean houses, red brick but no half
timber. What one chiefly remembers, however, is the in
teresting way in which the four main streets meet at th
centre. They arrive from the four main directions read
to form the usual cross, a visually unsatisfactory thing fo
a town centre, because the unimpeded views across do no
allow the eye to come to a halt in the middle of the town
At Baldock instead islands are inserted at the N end of th
High Street and the W end of White Horse Street so that
from wherever one approaches the cross, the eye is alway
stopped by a wall of houses or at least a house projecting
into the facing street. The most ingenious arrangement i
at No. 1 HIGH STREET (Late Georgian) with a canted
corner towards White Horse Street. The High Street i
much wider than the other streets, especially after th
island is passed. Part of the island (opposite No. 1) is th
FIRE STATION BUILDINGS of 1897 (by *Talbot, Brown
& Fisher* of Wellingborough), uneventful red brick with
a tower at the corner. In the High Street the best house
are near the N end. On the E side No. 9, the most ambi
tious house of Baldock, now unfortunately half hidden
by trees. Early Georgian with segmental pediment to

the door and an order of giant Corinthian pilasters of
rubbed brick, with finely carved stone capitals and entablature. No. 11 is early C18, No. 21 late C18. No. 21 lies
back, has seven bays of which the middle three project
slightly and carry a pediment into which cuts the arched
central window. Plain porch and pretty cast-iron gate-
posts. – Opposite is an equally stately group: Nos 12–14a
(Early Georgian) with plainer details. Otherwise on the w
side only Nos 32–42, WYNNE'S ALMSHOUSES of 1621,
one-storeyed, brick, with a raised gateway in the low
brick wall separating the front area from the street and
Victorian bargeboarding to porches and dormers. On the
E side Nos 21–23 is SIMPSON'S BREWERY, Late Georgian. It consists of a five-bay, three-storeyed, chequer
brick dwelling house and the brewery proper with a seven-
bay façade plus lower detached side buildings. The centre
is refaced in yellow brick. Behind it the manufacturing
parts with one range with giant blank arches, all of
chequered brick.

Much less of note in the other streets. HITCHIN STREET is
quite short and has on the S side some plastered gabled
cottages, especially No. 27 with overhang on canted bays.
No. 31, very narrow, is dated 1632. No. 33 lies back. It is
early C18 brick and has seven bays. Opposite is No. 16,
mid C18 with quoins and a pedimented doorcase with
fluted pilasters. At the w end No. 37, three-storeyed, red
brick with white brick quoins, a doorcase with fluted
pilasters and a plaque with the date 1755. – In CHURCH
STREET Nos 4–16, a Late Georgian terrace of two-
storeyed brick cottages, No. 3 a large C16 plastered half-
timber house with its r. half handsomely refronted in the
early C18 (typical doorcase with frieze rising in the
middle). At the far end No. 50 (BULL'S HEAD) with
close vertical timbers. – Finally in WHITE HORSE
STREET, which has the width of a High Street, No. 13
with a later Georgian three-bay, three-storey brick front
and a doorcase with fluted Ionic pilasters, No. 22 on the
other side, also later Georgian, but two-storeyed with
giant angle pilasters and parapet. Back on the other side

No. 31 of five bays and two storeys with doorcase with
fluted pilasters and pediment, and No. 35 with two C17
brick gables and the rest of the front remodelled in the
late C18.

BALLS PARK

Balls Park is one of the most puzzling houses of Hertfordshire. At first sight it appears to be Early Georgian, and it
is only when details are examined that plenty of motifs
are noticed which are far too individual, even perverse,
even uncouth, to be possible in the Augustan Age. The
dates as recorded in fact point to a date about 1640, and
that again seems extremely unlikely considering the total
absence of those semi-Jacobean, semi-Dutch elements
(pedimented curved gables) which occur in such houses
as Swakeleys (Middlesex; 1629–38). Yet the dating is
fairly reliable. The house is illustrated in Chauncy, that is
in 1700, in exactly its present form, except for the pediments and one or two other features. Chauncy also says
that the house was built by Sir John Harrison who was a
rich supporter of King Charles, deprived of his estates in
1647 and only reinstated after the Restoration. He died in
1669, and it seems unlikely that he could have spent
money on a new house at any time later than c. 1640.*
Does the house then go with such a date? What contra-
dicts it is its unbroken block shape, 7 by 7 windows. One
expects a more lively, restless general relief of the façades.
But Tyttenhanger c. 1654 is no less plain and even. Moreover a close study of the main entrance on the N side with
the window above reveals some inconsistencies and mannerisms characteristic of the first coming of the classical
idiom. Tuscan pilasters with waist bands are placed l. and
r. of the doorway so that they half hide slightly higher
Ionic pilasters. The Tuscan pilasters are of stone, the
Ionic pilasters of brick. The doorway is arched and on its
apex stands a flat panel with a stunted pilaster in it. On
the capitals of the Tuscan pilasters are two big corbels
incongruously placed. They support a balcony (with an

46b

* John Evelyn noted the house as newly built in 1643.

C18 railing). The arched door to the balcony has a frame
with typical angular ears (cf. Tyttenhanger) and volutes
scrolling out at the foot. The composition was originally
continued in a semicircular pediment flanked by unicorns.
The two storeys of the house are divided by a broad band
of shaped bricks. The angles have brick quoins and two
orders of brick pilasters. Of the three plus three windows
to the l. and r. of the doorway the middle ones have
equally odd stresses (short pilasters on the ground floor,
arched heads on pilasters on the upper floor). All these
details point to exactly such a date as tradition tells. They
place the house near the beginning of a series of about six
others which Professor Geoffery Webb grouped together
some twenty years ago and called his 'six houses in
search of an architect.' That architect has partly been
found by Howard Colvin to be *Peter Mills* who practised
in the City of London. Balls Park is not ascertained by
him or Professor Webb, yet undoubtedly is in the same
style. On the other hand, the pediments, the S porch, and
some other alterations tally with Salmon's statement in
1728 that the house was 'greatly augmented and improved' by Sir John Harrison's sons who were in possession from 1705 to 1725.

Inside is a big central hall originally in all probability
an open courtyard. The whole E side on the upper floor is
filled by a long gallery. Several rooms have noble plaster 47
ceilings with that very division into large panels, octagonal, circular, semicircular, and so on, which the mid
C17 liked.

A new N wing with a large Dining Room and main staircase was added in 1924–5 by *Sir Robert Lorimer*, and, for
the purposes of the Training College which now is in-
stalled at Balls Park, a GYMNASIUM standing on its own.
It is very handsome work of the H. C. C. Architect's Department (*C. H. Aslin* and *J. T. Pinion*).

BARKWAY

ST MARY MAGDALENE. A big, broad, spreading-out
church with a w tower (diagonal buttresses; tower arch

Perp), rebuilt in 1861 with pinnacles (not a Herts pattern
The s porch is also C19. The chancel is the oldest par
C13, as proved by the lancet windows (E window tracer
C19, chancel arch Perp). The N and S aisle arcades ar
characteristically Late Perp with piers consisting of semi
octagonal shafts and hollows in the diagonals. Charac
teristically Late Perp windows with very depressed
almost straight-sided, two-centred arches at the top
and elementary 'panel' tracery. – FONT. Octagonal, Perp
with fleurons on the coving. – STAINED GLASS. Remain
of a Jesse window (E end S aisle): In the centre light fou
kings above each other, surrounded by leaf scrolls; othe
figures in the side lights; late C15. – PLATE. Chalice
Paten, and Flagon, 1714; small Chalice, 1807. – MONU
MENTS. Brass to Robert Poynard † 1561 with wives an
children (S aisle wall). – Standing wall monument to S
John Jennings, Rear-Admiral, a Governor of Greenwic
Hospital, Ranger of Greenwich Park, M.P., etc., † 174
(against the tower W wall). For the great London man th
most successful London sculptor was engaged: *J. M
Rysbrack*. The monument is signed. Tall broad base wit
inscription and very classical, typical *Rysbrack* detail. O
it bust on plinth with two fine putti l. and r. – Severa
earlier epitaphs, e.g. Judith Chester † 1702, signed *Stan
ton*; Mary Chester † 1703, Stantonish; Thomas Smoul
† 1707, signed according to Mrs Esdaile by *R. Harts
horne* (Stanton workshop). – James Andrew † 1796 an
Thomas Talbot Gorsuch † 1820, both epitaphs by *P
Chenu* and done as *pendants*. They are also placed side b
side. The earlier with a seated figure of Hope, the latte
with Father Time. The change of style in the details is in
structive. – John Baron Selsey † 1816, epitaph with
draped urn and bits of willow branches behind; b
Kendrick.

MANOR HOUSE, S of the church. Brick, L-shaped, firs
half C17, with mullioned and mullioned-and-transome
windows and shaped gables.

NEWSELLS PARK, 1 m. N. The big house was accidentall
burned during the Second World War. Newsells Bur

lies immediately to its w, in the grounds, a small brick
house of the late C17.

OKENACH, 1 m. NE. Formerly known as Cockenhatch. A
composite history. The core is of 1716. Hence the segmentheaded windows. Additions of 1833, and more ambitious additions in 1925.

BARLEY

T MARGARET. 1872, by *Butterfield*, except for the w
tower and the s aisle. The w tower is of the C12 with a
typical Norman tower arch, a ground-floor window with
deep splay and also roundheaded upper windows. The
top stage Early Perp. The s doorway with the aisle is of
the C14. The s arcade may be a little earlier than this
doorway: octagonal piers, plainly moulded capitals. One
typical C14 window. The Butterfield interior is not impressive. The master's hand is only noticeable in the
tower top, not a Herts spike but a Butterfield spike. –
SCREEN. C15. Parts of the tracery re-used against the N
wall of the chancel. – PULPIT. Good 'Jacobean' work,
with bookrest, fine back, and fine tester with pendants.
The actual date is 1626. – STAINED GLASS. Crucifixion
N aisle E window and Head of God N aisle w window, C14
to C15. Some demi-figures of 1536. – PLATE. Steeple
Cup, 1612; small Paten, 1618. The inscription in an
exquisite script. – BRASS. Andrew Willet † 1621, praying,
not quite frontal.

OWN HOUSE. Early Tudor with outer stair to the upper
floor which is one room with original timber roof. It was,
amongst other purposes, 'used and employed for the
keeping of maides' marriages'.

IG HOUSE. Shaftenhoe End. E and N fronts early C18.
Doorways with hoods on carved brackets. But on the s
side porch with overhang on figure brackets and the inscribed date 1624, and longer wing with big outer
chimney and diagonal chimney stacks.

retty overhanging cottages by the entrance to the village
from the N.

BARNET see CHIPPING BARNET, EAST BARNET, NEW BARNET

BATCHWORTH HEATH
1¾ m. SE of Rickmansworth

BATCHWORTH HEATH HOUSE is a nice three-bay Georgian red brick house.

The S ENTRANCE GATES TO MOOR PARK, see Moor Par[k]

BATLERS GREEN see ALDENHAM

BAYFORD

ST MARY. 1870, by *Woodyer*. Stone, in the E.E. style,.wit[h]
brick quoins and a flèche. The S vestry roof is the nav[e]
and chancel roof carried lower down without a break (
happy effect). – FONT. Perp, octagonal with simple tracer[y]
and quatrefoil motifs. – MONUMENTS. George Knighto[n]
† 1612, excellent recumbent marble effigy in armour. Le[t]
into the back wall the brasses of two men in armour, [c.]
1550 and *c.* 1590.

BAYFORDBURY. The long white façade of twenty-five bay[s]
stepped up gently towards the centre, makes an exceedingly fine effect of Regency elegance, set behind an ornamental lake. In fact the house belongs to two period[s]
1759–62 and 1809–12. Of the first are the seven-ba[y]
centre and the pedimented outer wings with their cupola[s]
of the second the connecting links containing one larg[e]
room each towards the garden, and the porticoes. Th[e]
garden portico is of unfluted Ionic columns, that toward[s]
the entrance of heavy Greek Doric columns, and attache[d]
Greek Doric columns are also used on the same side fo[r]
the new intermediate parts. An iron balcony on thin iro[n]
shafts runs all along the garden façade which is also extended still further by an orangery wing on the r. and [a]
screen-wall of the same design on the l. Inside, the En[]
trance Hall has still its stucco ceiling and fireplace in th[e]

Rococo taste of 1760, and the stucco work of the room to
the l. of the Entrance Hall is of the same date. The rest, as
far as it has datable decoration at all is in the style of 1810,
notably the staircase with its curved sweep up to the
upper floor gallery, its iron balustrade and circular dome,
and the two ingeniously contrived corridors with an excessively elongated groined vault and small saucer domes
decidedly Soanian in character. The fireplace in the
present Library was originally in the Egyptian taste which
was the latest fashion in 1810 (thanks to Napoleon's
Egyptian campaign and Denon's publication of 1803).
The two side figures of mottled marble are preserved.
he grounds are of famous beauty. A group of cedars on the
E side of the lawn was planted in 1765. Close to the kitchen
garden are the stables, plain and utilitarian but dignified
(1812).

BEECHES see BRENT PELHAM

BEECHWOOD
1½ m. SW of Flamstead

'he house stands close to the site of a suppressed nunnery. 50a
But no remains exist now older than the Elizabethan
period, and what there is, is quite minor. The beauty of
the house is its NE façade of 1702. It is of red and purple
brick chequer with stone quoins and lively stone surrounds of the windows. The central doorway of the nine-
bay, two-storeyed front has a broken segmental pediment
on fluted Corinthian pilasters. – Central three-bay pediment, hipped roof, and dormer windows. The central
courtyard of the house was converted into a Hall with skylight in 1859. To the SE front a wing was added in 1819
with the Library. *Soane* had something to do with the
house (according to information kindly provided by Miss
Dorothy Stroud), and the blue marble fireplace of the
Library may indeed well be his. – Splendid fireplace, door
frames, and ceiling of *c.* 1740 in the drawing room to the N
of the Entrance Hall.

BENGEO

ST LEONARD. The rare example of a virtually intact Nor
man village church; nave and chancel with apse. Thi
again is a rarity, at least in Herts (but cf. Great Amwell)
The apse has small roundheaded windows in the dee
inner splays, the nave has one such window on the N side
On the s side the windows have been enlarged and altere
in the C14 and C15. The brick s porch dates from the C18
the timber bell-cote from the C19. The s and N doorway
are original, and the chancel arch has an order of colon
nettes with one scroll capital and the other with the face o
a man. The chancel and apse are surprisingly roomy. –
DOOR. Probably C14. – COMMUNION RAILS. C18.
PAINTING. On the nave E wall a C13 Deposition from th
Cross and indications of quatrefoil patterns. In the chan
cel painted ashlaring and a later, superimposed red
lozenge pattern. – TILES. Some of the C14 below the
Communion Table (cf. Much Hadham). – PLATE
Chalice and Paten, 1626. – MONUMENTS. John Ryde
mural tablet of 1665, by *William Stanton*. – Humphre
Hall, 1742, by *Thos. Adey*, profile medallion held b
two putti with rather vacant faces. The background th
usual obelisk. – Daniel Minet † 1790, a modest tablet b
Nollekens.

BENGEO HALL. E front of 1745 with two canted bay win
dows, and a late C18 doorway to which a staircase witl
handsome mid C18 iron railings leads up. The third floo
of the front hides three earlier gables.

BENINGTON

ST PETER. Essentially a late C13 to early C14 church, al
though the w tower with angle buttresses and a Hert
spike belong to the C15, as do the clerestory with big two
light windows and the chancel s windows. The Sedilia i
the chancel are the earliest pieces in the church, much re
stored, but certainly made some time before 1300: stiff
leaf, and crocket capitals and cusped pointed arches. Th

Piscina is a little later; it has an ogee arch. Its style goes with that of the nave N windows. The N chancel chapel was added yet later, say about 1320–30. It is the most important part of the church. The windows have modest flowing tracery, the arcade to the chancel quatrefoil piers with thin shafts in the diagonals and simple moulded capitals (cf. Ashwell and Baldock). The labels rest on excellent corbels (head of a woman wearing a wimple, man piercing his body with a sword, etc.). The arches are of finely moulded sections. Under one of the two arches stands a MONUMENT with two more than lifesize effigies, a cross-legged Knight and a Lady wearing a wimple. The figures are defaced. On the sides of the tomb-chest mourners in arcades with triangular heads. The arch above is surrounded by a big crocketed ogee canopy flanked by thin buttresses on which some tracery is exactly identical with that of the windows. The style seems to exclude a date later than c. 1330; yet the heraldry is supposed to point to 1358. To the E of this chantry a smaller opening with a four-centred arch was pierced through early in the C15 for the placing of another MONUMENT with two effigies. The heraldry here indicates the date 1432. Ogee niches on the tomb-chest. The arch is panelled inside and has in the centre of the panelling the figure of an angel holding the little souls of the deceased in a cloth. Between the two openings BRASS of a priest, upper half only, C15. – FONT. Octagonal, with projecting, coarsely moulded shafts in the diagonals (cf. Walkern). – BENCHES. Simple C15. – PLATE. Chalice and Paten, 1639.

The VILLAGE GREEN is almost perfect, with individual scattered cottages, showing their timber-framing, or plastered and with overhangs and gables (BELL INN). Benington possesses besides several bigger houses of interest.

THE LORDSHIP, a Georgian house converted into a Neo-Norman fantasy to match the scanty remains of the KEEP of Benington Castle. This was a structure of flint with stone dressings 44 by 41 ft in size with thick walls

and flat pilaster strips. The wall fragments stand to the
height of 9 ft and are ivy-clad and adorned with Neo-
Norman doorways, etc. A Neo-Norman gatehouse was
also added between house and keep. This was designed
we are told, by a landscape gardener, *Pulham* of Broxbourne, not by an architect, a fact eminently characteristic of the age of the Picturesque.

OLD RECTORY. 1637. Brick front with three gables and a
two-storeyed porch with Tuscan pilasters and a simple
pediment. The windows all altered. Originally they were
no doubt mullioned and had hood-moulds (*see* the windows in the gables).

BERKHAMPSTEAD, GREAT, *see* BERKHAMSTED

BERKHAMSTED

In contrast to the neighbouring Hemel Hempstead the
church at Berkhamsted lies right along the High Street
more or less in line with the houses on the N side. This gives
the church a decidedly urban character.

ST PETER. The result of much adding and enlarging. At
least five periods can be distinguished (apart from *Butterfield's* restoration in 1871): chancel *c.* 1200 (lancet windows with nook shafts); crossing piers and N transept
walls of the same date; nave with both arcades of seven
bays (not at all in line with the chancel) late C13 (begun
from the E with quatrefoil piers on the s, an alternation of
circular and quatrefoil piers on the N side, and continued
to the w with circular piers only; simple moulded capitals
double-chamfered arches); N transept E aisle with rib-
vaults *c.* 1300; s chancel chapel early C14 (ogee reticulation in the window tracery; ogee-headed Piscina; two
tomb-recesses, the E one with a renewed arch), outer
aisle mid C14 (with a wooden post separating it from the
inner aisle); s aisle, w part of outer aisle (originally a
porch), and clerestory C15; upper parts of the crossing
tower 1535–6. The crossing tower dominates the external
appearance of the large flint-built church. It is big and

powerful with a NE stair-turret rising higher than its
battlements. The body of the building spreads broadly
along the street and faces on the other side across the
churchyard the old Grammar School. – SCREEN. In W
tower arch; C15, much renewed. – STAINED GLASS.
Some C14 glass in chancel N widows. – S aisle window
with three Saints, by *Kempe* 1880. – PLATE. Chalice,
1629; Almsdish, 1637; Paten, 1706. – BRASSES. Richard
Torrington (?) † 1356 and wife (N aisle). – Demi-figure
of Priest, *c.* 1400 (chancel). – Woman, *c.* 1360 (N aisle). –
Richard Westbroke † 1485 (N aisle). – Thomas Humfre,
c. 1470, shrouded, with wife and children, and figure of
St Michael; re-used on the reverse for John Waterhouse † 1559 and wife (N transept aisle). – John Raven
† 1395 (St John's Chapel). – Katherine Incent † 1520,
shrouded (St John's Chapel). – MONUMENTS. Knight
and Lady, late C14, defaced stone figures on tomb-chest
with ogee-headed niches and shields. – James and John
Murray † 1627 and 1634, epitaph with busts of the two
brothers in a circle. They died young and are here seen
holding hands. One of them reads in a book. Good
quality (chancel). – Thomas Baldwin, 1642, by *Nicholas
Stone*, large tablet without figures (s aisle near w end). –
Elizabeth Cradock † 1704, standing wall monument of
shallow relief; no figures; by *F. Hardy* (s transept). –
Mary Isabella Smith † 1834, with large kneeling figure,
apparently unsigned.

CASTLE. Large but only very fragmentarily preserved. The
situation is unimpressive. The remains consist of an
outer and an inner moat surrounding an area of *c.* 450 by
300 ft. In the NE corner is the motte or mount, *c.* 45 ft
high, on which originally stood a shell-keep. The bailey
was surrounded by a wall with some semicircular projections. Living quarters were on the W side and in the NE
corner. From here two bridges crossed the narrow ditch
between bailey and mount and a staircase led up to the
keep. All that remains of stonework are stretches of flint
walling nowhere more than 15 or 20 ft high. The castle
was probably first erected with earth walling and stockades

late in the C11 (William's half-brother, Robert of Mor
tain) and rebuilt in stone during the ten years whe
Thomas Becket held it in his quality of Chancellor. Docu
ments refer to building work between *c.* 1160 and *c.* 118c
In 1216 the castle was besieged by King Louis of France
Later it became an appendage of the Dukes of Cornwal

The Castle lies on the N bank of the river Bulbourne (an
the N side of the railway), the HIGH STREET runs paralle
with the river some distance to the S. Its centre is th
church and the houses surrounding it. To the SW of th
church COURT HOUSE, C16, timber-framed, very re
newed, with a projecting upper storey. To the N of th
church across the churchyard the GRAMMAR SCHOOL
Its nucleus is the building erected *c.* 1544 from the en
dowment of John Incent, Dean of St Paul's. It consists o
a long brick-built room with kingpost roof and six three
light windows with four-centred heads. Gabled addition
to E and W as houses for schoolmaster and usher, and
large more recent additions behind to the N. – E of th
church in CASTLE STREET nice quiet terraces of houses
Nos 1–4 brick and timber-framing, Nos 5–9 early C1ͅ
purple and red brick.* Finally, S of the church, that is i
the HIGH STREET proper, the best house of Berkham
sted, INCENT'S HOUSE, half-timbered with overhangin
upper floor, carefully restored. This is followed to the E
still facing the church, by Nos 117–121, three quie
houses of *c.* 1800.

The HIGH STREET is best visited from its W end. It begin
in an informal villagey way with only a few individua
houses worth noting. BOXWELL HOUSE (S), broac
three-bay design of *c.* 1700, cemented front with quoin
and quoins to the middle bay. A pediment over this
Doorcase with Ionic columns. – Then SAYER ALMS
HOUSES (S), 1684, one storeyed row of six brick house
with big segmental pediment in the centre. – Opposit
several nice Early Victorian villas with trellis porches
etc. – No. 189 (S), early C18, blue and red brick chequer. –

---

* Beyond the Grammar School in Castle Street a pretty, irregula
group of timber-framed cottages, Nos 49–57.

No. 222, 1737, former Bourne Charity School, brick. – By the War Memorial the street narrows on the N side forming a very effective angle, where the BELL INN with plastered gabled side appears behind some trees planted with discrimination. – Opposite the KING'S ARMS, three-bay red brick, with three oriels on the first floor; the second floor is an addition. – Then the SWAN INN, C17, with two symmetrical plastered gables, and close to it Nos 135–137, early C18 with quoins and dressings painted black in the early C19 way. – Past the church the RED HOUSE HOTEL, the most ambitious C18 house in the town: seven bays with a fine porch with Ionic columns and pediment; big Venetian window above. – Then Nos 103–109, an urban terrace of early C19 yellow brick houses with pretty iron balconies. – After that the architectural interest lessens.

On the other side the High Street is continued in GOS-SOM'S END, first with solid rows of early C19 cottages, then with individual houses. Gossom's Lodge (with Gothick windows) and Gossom's Cottage, both of three-bay width; Nos 77–80, a half-timbered group; and Edge-worth House, three-bay, cemented C18 house, with tall pilasters, lying isolated under old trees.

BAPTIST CHURCH, High Street, 1864. Yellow and red brick, with an ugly, asymmetrically placed turret. Typical of its date.

FRIENDS MEETING HOUSE, High Street, 1818. Simple pedimented brick structure with arched door and two arched windows.

THOMAS CORAM (FOUNDLING HOSPITAL) SCHOOL, 1933–5, by *J. H. Sheppard & Partners*. The statue of Coram by *W. Calder Marshall*. A large axial composition of pale brick buildings connected by colonnades. The detail restrainedly Neo-Classical.

BERKHAMSTED PLACE. Gabled, symmetrical Elizabethan house with central hall and central entrance. The wings project in two steps. All this is only the remains of a courtyard house of *c.* 1580, altered in 1610–11, and again in 1662 after a fire had destroyed two-thirds of the house.

Original C16 work on the NW side, stone and flint chequ
pattern. At the NE end an original oriel window. Inside
large original fireplace with late C17 alterations and a goo
plaster ceiling on the first floor.

ASHLYNS, 1 m. s. *c.* 1800 with bow-fronted centre with iro
verandah. 'The whole building, gracefully set on the to
of a slope, has a light and easy air' (MHLG).

HARESFOOT, 2 m. s. Late Georgian five-bay two-store
house with stuccoed frontages.

GRIMS DYKE. Traces of this Saxon boundary line can b
followed near Berkhamsted. They are on the opposite sic
of the Bulbourne valley in the parishes of Northchurc
and Wigginton. Grims Dyke is a ditch of *c.* 35 ft acro
and a bank of which two stretches survive, one 800, th
other 500 yds long. Its purpose was probably rather pro
tection against cattle raids than against strictly militar
aggression.

BISHOPS STORTFORD

Visually Bishops Stortford has little to compare with, sa
Hitchin or Hertford, let alone St Albans. It does not giv
one the impression of the wealthy late medieval or Georgia
town which one might expect. The town consists chiefly c
the crossing of four main streets with the market square an
the Corn Exchange in the centre and the church along th
side of one of the four.

ST MICHAEL. A big, low, embattled Perp town churc
with a W tower and tall spire, prominent for a long di
tance around, not owing to the early C15 which built
(set-back buttresses, low stair turret) but to the year 181
when a tall, slim upper stage of light brick was adde
with buttresses at the angles and pinnacles above and
lead spire. The contrast between the business-like sturc
ness below and the fragility above is that between Goth
and Gothick. The whole church is otherwise of the C1
(except for the C19 N chancel chapel and tall S vestr
with typical Late Perp windows, with depressed se
mental or depressed pointed arches (the latter with almo

straight sides), with a N porch two bays deep and a S porch. The chancel clerestory and chancel E window belong to the C19. The original E window of three lights is now in the S wall. The interior is big and airy. Tall [19] tower arch on thin responds, six-bay arcade with thin piers (four main shafts and four hollows in the diagonals) and two-centred arches, two-light clerestory windows, lower chancel. The roofs of nave, chancel, and aisles are original. In the nave the arched braces are traceried, and they rest on stone corbels with the figures of the Apostles. In the aisles instead of these there are grotesques and also such genre figures as a gardener with pruning knife, a cook with ladle, a woodman with bill-hook, etc. – FONT. C12, square, of Purbeck marble, with shallow blank arches; on five supports. – ALTAR AND SURROUND. 1885, by *Sir A. Blomfield*. – PULPIT. Locally made for £5 in 1658, an extremely late date for so purely Elizabethan a piece. The angles have termini pilasters decorated with raised ovals and diamonds. This and the decoration of the main panels with arches in feigned perspective probably comes straight from some pattern book. – SCREEN. C15; big, with two tall four-light sections on each side of the entrance. – CHANCEL STALLS. C15, with poppy-heads at the ends of the front stalls and MISERICORDS for the [31a] back seats. They represent *inter alia* heads of human figures and animals, very well carved, an angel, a swan, an owl, a dragon. – DOORS. Original, both in N and S porches. – STAINED GLASS. Chancel S window, by *Powell*, 1853 (TK), still in the painting tradition of the C18; not yet medievalizing. – W window, by *Kempe*, 1877, a very characteristic example of his early manner. – PLATE. Paten, 1563; Chalice, 1597; Chalice, 1683; two Flagons, 1721; Almsdish, 1741. – No monuments of any importance.

ALL SAINTS, Stanstead Road, Hockerill. 1937, by *S. E. Dykes Bower*. In a position overlooking the whole town. Big square tower with hipped roof and three excessively elongated lancet windows. The two entrances into the aisles with curiously lobed arches. Interior with tall

circular piers, a long aisleless chancel and a rose E wi
dow with C20 flowing tracery.

CONGREGATIONAL CHURCH, Water Lane, 1860. Said
be by *W. F. Poulton*. Stock-brick on an elongated centr
plan with two façade towers. The trim is Italianate.

WAYTEMORE CASTLE, Bridge Street, on the other side
the river from the town, that is in a position just like Ber
hamsted Castle. Of the rectangular shell-keep only fou
dations remain. It was on a narrow mount, 40 ft high. T
the S was the bailey (now pleasure grounds).

CORN EXCHANGE. The secular centre of the town, bu
1828 in a self-confident Neo-Greek style. Ground flo
with Tuscan piers in the accentuated places, upper floc
with a giant Ionic portico to the N, a portico *in antis*
the W. Architect: *G. Perry* of Bishop Stortford.

BISHOPS STORTFORD COLLEGE. The original buildin
in the Gothic style 1867 by *J. Clarke*, boarding houses
1914, etc. The Memorial Hall by *Clough William El*
(1921–2) in a 'Colonial' Georgian much more elega
than most of the Neo-Georgian work of the period.

HOCKERILL TRAINING COLLEGE. Red brick wi
diaper pattern and stone trim. By *J. Clarke*, 1852. Lat
additions.

PERAMBULATION

The corner of High Street and North Street is the GEORG
HOTEL. With its two-storeyed gabled and pargetted o
part and its three-storeyed completely urban Early Vi
torian E part it marks the span of the building history
the town. HIGH STREET has the church on one side, o
the other houses mostly of no special merit. But No.
(C17, gabled with second floor overhang) and especial
No. 30 (broad, with three irregular gables; the overhan
rest on canted ground floor bays; central entrance arc
half bows to connect it with the projecting bays, a pret
C18 adaptation of the C17) are worth a look. The Hig
Street is continued in the wider, more suburban WIN
HILL. The houses here are more loosely placed an
mostly early C19. An eminently picturesque group is N

15B, C17 cottages with malthouse and granary. –
NORTH STREET has a good assortment of houses on the
w side, ranging from the HALF MOON INN (No. 31) to
the tall early C19 CHEQUERS HOTEL with its two three-
storeyed bay windows, and to Nos 7 and 9, both Victorian business Gothic of stock brick with stone and red
brick trim, No. 7 Northern (c. 1868), No. 9 Tuscan in
design.* Facing the N end of North Street THE
CHANTRY, an irregular group of mainly C18 buildings
and a glaring example of how a shop and a bit of showy
sham-half-timbering can ruin an important vista. To the
r., down NORTHGATE END, again bigger suburban
houses, the best BROOKE HOUSE, white brick, three
storeys, with Roman Doric doorcase and lower wings.
The approximate date can be guessed from some cottages
opposite called Waterloo Place.

rallel with North Street runs WATER LANE with large
detached houses whose gardens look towards the river
(e.g. the house facing Barrett Lane). Water Lane runs
into BRIDGE STREET. Here first a group of C17 plastered
houses (Nos 2–6), and then the BLACK LION, a C16 57a
building with exposed timbers, overhang and gables, very
picturesque, although rather over-restored. Opposite No.
11, early C17, with nice interiors. Across the bridge and
past the Castle DANE STREET turns s. Here and in DELL
LANE pargetted houses mixed up with industrial building.
From the Castle HOCKERILL STREET runs up the hill.
No. 29 is nice Late Georgian, Nos 37–41 a specially handsome group of the C17. At the top, facing Hockerill
Street, is the COCK INN, early C17. Turning N a good
way out in PARSONAGE LANE CHURCH MANOR, C18
brick frontages and fine early C18 gables with a cupola,
blank oval and circular windows in the front and a large
blank Venetian window on the side. Farther out on the
DUNMOW ROAD the NAG'S HEAD, 1936, by E. B.
Musman, once famous as one of the few architecturally
modern pubs, now rather dated with its exact symmetry.

* The change of taste was contagious. The shop front opposite at
o. 14 was also remodelled in Tuscan Trecento.

The Public Bar and the Saloon Bar are in their shapes ar
positions absolutely one the echo of the other. No di
tinctions of character, no use made of the capabilities
the corner position.

s of the centre the main streets are more thorough
modernized. Only farther out a few things of interest. *
the beginning of SOUTHMILL ROAD as the MHLG h
rightly emphasized, some excellent examples of late C:
and early C19 malthouses, etc. (N earlier than s). At tl
beginning of SOUTH ROAD the house where Cec
Rhodes was born, typical, dignified, semi-detached, ear
C19 house with heavy Tuscan porch-pillars.

Two FARMHOUSES in the neighbourhood may be single
out as specially handsome: WICKHAM HALL, 1¼ 1
NW, and STORTFORD PARK, 1½ m. W.

BLAKESWARE see WIDFORD

BOREHAM WOOD

ALL SAINTS, 1910, by *Francis & Minty* (GR). Arty-craf
and not good of the kind.

Some nice houses along the road W of the town, bo
Georgian residences and a farm (NICOLL FARM) wi
outbuildings.

64 COWLEY HILL COUNTY PRIMARY SCHOOL, see Intr
duction, p. 28.

BOVINGDON

ST LAWRENCE. 1845, by *Talbot Bury*, to whose memo
(he died in 1877) a stained-glass window was put up in tl
church (N aisle). *Bury's* building is flint, clearly in tl
Herts style, no longer with the freedom (and ignorance)
the earlier C19. Only the aisle windows have a trace
design not historically documented. – STAINED GLASS.
window by *Lavers*, 1856 (TK). – MONUMENT. Toml
chest with stone effigy of an unknown Knight in armo
of c. 1400 (pointed bascinet).

RENTSTREET FARM, ½ m. SE. Brick and timber-framin

The ground floor probably C16, the upper floor C17; *see* the closer spacing of the uprights below.

BOXMOOR

ᴄ JOHN, 1874, by *Norman Shaw*. Surprisingly uninteresting compared with Shaw's later churches. Nave, aisles, chancel, and chancel aisles, turret on the nave away from the w end. Simple, small, mostly two-light windows in the style of *c.* 1300. Inside, quatrefoil piers.

ᴏɴɢʀᴇɢᴀᴛɪᴏɴᴀʟ CHAPEL, Box Lane. Built in 1690, but the outside now of an appearance as if re-done early in the C19.

ᴇꜱᴛʙʀᴏᴏᴋ HAY. Large, stuccoed early C19 façades with curved and shallow rectangular bay windows. A rustic entrance lodge at the N gates.

BRAMFIELD

ᴛ ANDREW. So much restored in 1840 that it appears an Early Victorian building. The w tower is hardly taller than the nave roof and has a spire. The tower arch is characteristically thin and bodyless. – PLATE. Chalice, 1562; Paten, 1617; Breadholder, 1757. – MONUMENTS. Two epitaphs to George Viscount Grandison † 1699 and the Rev. Edward Bourchier † 1775, of identical design.
ᴜEEN HOO *see* p. 188.

BRAUGHING

compact village with the church in the centre. The main llage street E of the church. The churchyard is surrounded ⸱ houses to the W, S, and E. To the W behind them a ᷓeam, which can only be crossed by footbridges and fords, ᴅd on the other bank another street higher up parallel to ᷓe main street.

ᴛ MARY. With the exception of the chancel (N lancets) entirely early C15.* W tower tall, of three stages, with set-back buttresses and a recessed spire rather than a spike.

* In 1416 John Kyllan of London left £5 for the work on the church.

w door with ornamented spandrels and niches to the
and r. Two-storeyed s porch with ornamented spandr
to the doorways, large two-light side windows, a tw
light upper s window with niches. Battlements and ang
pinnacles (that is, everywhere a show of a little mo
money spent than by most of the neighbouring churche
Embattled clerestory with three-light windows, rood l
turret at the SE end of the nave. Late Perp N and S ai
windows. Tall W tower arch, arcades of four bays w
piers of four main shafts and four hollows in the diagona
the latter without capitals. The arches are re-used from
earlier arcade. Fine nave roof with the sub-principals ca
ried on angels and the E bays panelled and decorated wi
bosses. – BENCHES. A few C15, buttressed. – STAIN
GLASS. E window of 1916–17, just going C20 in style, th
is with the leading getting heavier and more severe. (I
whom?) – PLATE. Chalice, Paten, and Flagon, 1718.
MONUMENTS. Brass to man and woman, c. 1480, mu
rubbed off, 18 in. figures (s aisle). – Brass to Barba
Hauchett † 1561. – Tablet to Sir John Brograve † 159
without figure. – Epitaph to Augustin Steward † 159
frontal bust, very stiff. – Large standing wall monume
to John Brograve † 1625 and his younger brother, tw
stiffly reclining figures, their heads propped up on the
elbows, in a reredos framing with big columns and ar
between them; in the spandrels the figure of an ang
blowing soap bubbles (Vanity) and Father Time. – Lar
monument to Ralph Freman, D.D., of Hamels, † 17
and his wife as well as two other Freemans and the
wives. The portraits are in three medallions, each wi
two profiles, the main one on the severe sarcophag
which forms the centre of the composition. Two putti l
a little awkwardly on their bellies on the volutes of t
curved top, Michelangelo's Medici allegories in revers
the other medallions are on the sides outside the mon
ment proper. The monument was designed by *Jam*
Stuart (Athenian Stuart) and carved by the young
Scheemakers.

w of the church a handsome cottage with pargetted upp

door, s of the church one with exposed timbers and brick nogging. In a kind of square E of the church a late C17 three-bay brick house and a C17 overhang house with two gables. THE BURY, NW of the church, the older manor house, also C17, with gables, quite extensive.

AMELS *see* p. 104.

BRENT PELHAM

MARY. Essentially mid C14, save the C15 W tower (with diagonal buttresses and Herts spike). The restoration of 1861 added the S porch and renewed the S, N, and chancel E windows. In the chancel the N and S windows are original. But the most interesting tracery is that of the preserved S DOOR: early C14. The interior is wide, tall, and bare. Tall tower arch with big shafts with capitals and thin diagonal shafts without. – SCREEN. Some of the tracery of the C15 rood screen used in the tower screen. – PLATE. Chalice, 1628. – MONUMENTS. C13 black marble slab with foliated cross, angel above it holding a soul in a cloth and around him the symbols of the four Evangelists; a very remarkable work. – Brass to the two wives of F. Rowley † 1625 and 1627, two seemingly identical women with ruffs and hats.

RENT PELHAM HALL. E of the church, a fine, broad, late C17 brick front of nine bays with slightly projecting pedimented three-bay centre and two-bay outer wings. Modillion frieze, hipped roof. Some of the chimney-stacks behind this front prove that the structure is earlier. A date-stone marked 1608 indeed remains.

HE BURY, ¼ m. N of the church. Farmhouse dated 1677 yet still with overhang and diagonally set 'Tudor' chimney-stacks.

EECHES, 1 m. ESE of the church. Early C17 house with big outer chimneys with fine octagonal shafts and moulded capitals. In two of the chimneys are two-light mullioned brick windows. The main front altered in the C18.

BRICKENDON BURY
1¼ m. ssw of Hertford

Connected with Hertford by Morgan's Walk, an avenue ¾
long. The house seems to be Georgian, with giant pilast
on the entrance front, but redone in 1885–6, when
Italianate tower was added, and again in 1898, when
other fronts were made pretty with half-timbering a
ornamental plasterwork.

BRICKHOUSE *see* GREAT HORMHEAD

BRIDE HALL *see* AYOT ST LAWRENCE

BRIDGEWATER MONUMENT *see* ALDBURY

BRIGGENS *see* STANSTEAD ABBOTTS

BROCKET HALL

A big square red brick mansion by *James Paine*, in a lar
park. The main vista from the house is the river Lea co
verted into an undulating lake with a bridge by *Paine*
the s end. The landscaping of the grounds is the work
Mr Wood of Essex. As for the house, which was beg
about 1755 and completed externally in 1775 and i
ternally about 1780, the most surprising thing about it
its utilitarian exterior as compared with its generous si
and its magnificent interiors. It is a square block with
stone facings, no stone window trim, no portico. To r
lieve uniformity, no more is done than to give the salo
unusually large arched windows (the basement belo
them was only created when a formal garden was laid o
in front of this façade), to add canted bay windows on t
saloon (w) side and the E side, to give the main entran
(s side) attached columns and a pediment, and to enlar
some windows to the Venetian triple-window patter
That is not much; it leaves the three-storeyed house a b
structure inspiring more respect than affection. But insi
splendid things were done. The plain Entrance Hall
connected with the central staircase, which starts with o

arm and continues in two at right angles. On the first
floor level a gallery runs round three sides of the staircase
with fluted columns (the lower part spiral-fluted) and
little circular and oval saucer domes. The centre above the
staircase itself has a large glazed oval dome. The iron railing is of a delightfully lively honeysuckle pattern. Of the
other rooms a few (the Billiard Room and the Study, the
latter an asymmetrically shaped room cleverly balanced
by the insertion of two columns to divide it into a main
part and, as it were, an alcove) have Palladian mid C18
decoration, the others are frankly in the more fashionable
taste of *Robert Adam*, with exquisite daintily detailed
plaster ceilings. Most of the stucco work is white, but in
the Saloon, a room of remarkable size, the coved ceiling is
gilt, with paintings, on a scale very different from the
dainty, playful, a little finicky scale of the Adam circle.
These paintings were indeed designed and begun by *John
Hamilton Mortimer*, an artist of genius who was capable
occasionally of real Sturm und Drang savageries, and
completed by *Wheatley* after Mortimer's early death in
1779. The Saloon is undoubtedly the climax of the house;
and that is as it should be.

BROOM HALL see WATTON-AT-STONE

BROOKMANS see GOBIONS

BROXBOURNE

⸗ AUGUSTINE. A large church, entirely of the C15–C16. 2
Tall w tower with angle buttresses and a sw stair-turret
higher than the tower. Decorated w door and four-light
w window. Nave and two aisles, chancel, and two chancel
chapels. The whole church is embattled, except for the N
chancel chapel or Saye Chapel which has a parapet with
an inscription recording its erection in 1522. The chapel
is stone-faced, as is also the s chapel, whereas the rest of
the church is flint. The s chapel was built before the N
chapel, in 1476, by *Robert Stowell* who later built St Margaret's church by the side of Westminster Abbey. All

the windows of Broxbourne church are Perp. Of p[...]
medieval only the s porch doorway, semicircular wi[...]
complex classical surround. It may be c. 1650. There is [...]
chancel arch, so that the arcades run through from w to [...]
Tall thin piers of four shafts and four hollows in t[...]
diagonals. The same design appears in the taller tow[...]
arch. The roof of the nave is original, so is the handsor[...]
panelled ceiling of the chancel, adorned with bosses. [...]
FONT. Octagonal, Norman, with shallow blank arcadin[...]
two arches per panel. – STAINED GLASS. In the N chan[...]
chapel, by *Willement*, 1857 (TK), with medallions contai[...]
ing scenes in strong colours. – PLATE. Chalice and Pate[...]
1606; Paten, 1633; Chalice and Paten, 1824. – MON[...]
MENTS. Between chancel and s chancel chapel Sir Jo[...]
Say † 1474 and wife, tomb-chest with shields in bla[...]
arcades. On the lid good brass effigies of Knight and Lad[...]
the figures c. 3½ ft long. – Between chancel and N chan[...]
chapel tomb-chest with canopy to Sir William Say a[...]
family: early C16. Plain chest; the supports of the cano[...]
polygonal, the canopy with depressed arches, quatref[...]
frieze and cresting. The effigies were of brass and let in[...]
the E wall. They have disappeared. Brasses in the chan[...]
to a priest, late C15; to another priest, early C16; in t[...]
nave to a knight carrying a mace (Sir John Borrell?), ear[...]
C16. – Standing wall monument to Sir Henry Cock † 16[...]
with wife and children. Stiff effigies, she recumbent, [...]
semi-reclining behind and above her. The children [...]
usual kneeling against the front of the base. Coffered arc[...]
on solid side supports. Achievements and obelisks on to[...]
Not of high quality. – Sir William Monson and wi[...]
† 1734, two busts above a long inscription tablet. – G. [...]
Williams † 1736 and wife; big epitaph.

MONSON ALMSHOUSES, High Street, 1728. Red brick, [...]
four bays and two storeys, with widely spaced window[...]
Simple doorcase; above it a recess like a blank windo[...]
with a cartouche and inscription.

The church is quite a distance from the High Street, to b[...]
reached from it by an avenue. The High Street is part [...]
that long ribbon of houses, C17–C20, timber-framed an[...]

plastered or of Georgian brick outer-suburban-London-
types which stretches N all the way from the Middlesex
border to Hoddesdon. The nicest houses on the
Broxbourne stretch are by the bridge across the New
River.

BUCKLAND

ANDREW. Nave, chancel, and s transept C14. An inscription in some stained glass is recorded giving the date
1348 for the construction of the church. W tower c. 1400,
s aisle and s porch later C15. The W tower has diagonal
buttresses. The nave and chancel have windows typical of
the mid C14, the s aisle and s porch (depressed arch,
two-light windows) belong to the late C15 or even early
C16. The s aisle arcade has odd and very pretty piers consisting of shafts with capitals only for the inner order of
the arches themselves. Towards the nave and aisle there
are no capitals. Demi-figure of an angel on the W impost.
Head-stops on the labels of the nave windows. – STAINED
GLASS. C15 canopies in N windows. – MONUMENTS.
Brasses to Alice Boteler † 1451; to William Langley,
Rector of Buckland, † 1478; and to John Gyll † 1499
with children (chancel). – Susan Clarke † 1634, epitaph
with bust and small Mannerist figures on the l. and r. –
John Clare † 1772, big epitaph with bust above an asym-
metrical Rococo cartouche with inscription. By *John
Richards* of Bishopsgate.

the village street BUCKLAND HOUSE, a fine Early
Georgian house of chequered brick: seven bays, with
projecting centre and a doorcase with attached fluted
Ionic columns. A Venetian window above; the side parts
filled in with Gothick timber panels.

BUCKSHILL
2¼ m. sw of Kings Langley

BUCKSHILL BOTTOM. Two fine farmhouses. One of them,
of brick and timber-framing with projecting porch, is
in its unrestored state a perfect example of rural C17

building in West Herts. The setting also helps, in a d
with no other houses in the neighbourhood.

GREAT WESTWOOD FARM. Good house of *c.* 1740. Bric
five bays by three, and hipped roof. Nothing ornament·
More attractive farmhouses on the road to Chandler
Cross.

BUNTINGFORD

The little town possesses an enjoyable High Street, or
architecturally very remarkable church, and the statelie
Almshouses in the county.

14a ST PETER. Built in 1614–26 as a chapel-of-ease to Laysto
Brick, on the Greek cross plan to which in 1899 a por·
and apse were added. The windows were also altere·
Kept in the church is a C17 BRASS PLATE showing tl
interior of the church.

60a WARD'S HOSPITAL. Immediately N of the church, tw
storeyed, ashlar-faced along three sides of a courtya·
open to the street. The wings are two bays wide and fi·
bays deep, the centre bay is crowned by a pediment ar
the doorcase by a scrolly open pediment. The windo·
are low, of two lights with stone mullions. The hospit·
was endowed by Bishop Seth Ward in 1684. Seth War·
the mathematician and astronomer, Bishop of Exeter ar
(1667) of Salisbury, friend of Christopher Wren ar
Chancellor of the Order of the Garter had, as the i·
scription in the centre of the hospital says, been 'born
yis town Wthin the parish of Aspden & education in
free-school of Buntingford'.

LAYSTON COURT, near the S end of the High Street, th
is a little farther N than the hospital and on the other si·
of the street, is the former Buntingford Grammar Scho·
It dates from the early C17 and consisted originally of o·
room with open timber roof. The roof is now sub-divid·
into two storeys and several rooms. At right angles to
towards the street is the late C17 schoolmaster's house.

The HIGH STREET is long and straight, part of the Rom·
Ermine Street. The houses, especially those of the C1·
look remarkably wealthy. They stand right at the S en·

No. 19, for example, is only three bays wide, yet has giant angle pilasters. No. 21 is detached and lies back, five bays, two storeys, with an Ionic doorcase. Opposite a small early C18 five-bay house with lively keystones and a door surround with alternating rustication. A similar doorcase was inserted at No. 41 (opposite), a C17 house with overhanging upper storey. The overhang rests on late C17 brackets. More overhang (e.g. No. 22) and more red brick houses follow. No. 46 is early C19, Nos 65 and 71 are Georgian. Opposite TUDOR HOUSE, with overhang and some fancy pargetting, then No. 66 also C17 overhang, and finally Nos 84–86, the most ambitious C18 house: five bays plus addition on the l., probably originally seven bays. Doorcase with scrolly carved brackets which may have carried a hood.

REENWAYS ESTATE, on the road to Baldock. *c.* 70 houses by *P. Mauger & Partners*.

ARE STREET *see* p. 104.

AYSTON *see* p. 153.

BUSHEY

ushey, including Bushey Heath, extends along the A41 ad to Watford for over two miles in a NW direction. At the W end it merges into Watford. There is a nucleus of the llage still by the church; the rest is hard to define: outer ondon suburban, Watford suburban, and in addition veral large schools in their grounds.

T JAMES. In a neatly kept churchyard at an equally well kept widening of the High Street. Flint, with a C13 chancel, a higher C15 nave and W tower with big diagonal buttresses and a NE stair-turret, and C19 aisles and N porch. On the inner N and S walls of the chancel tall wide blank arcading with Purbeck marble shafts and moulded capitals. The N and S lancet windows are also original. The chancel is separated from the nave by that rare feature a 'tympanum', that is a plastered partition with the Royal Arms (of Queen Anne), resting on a big beam. The nave roof is of the C15. – PULPIT. Jacobean with strapwork motifs; the tester is preserved. – CHANDELIER. Brass, C17 or C18, in the chancel. – PLATE. Cup and

Paten, 1633; Flagon, 1634; Salver, 1671; Almsdish
Wafer Box and Wine Strainer presented in 1754; Set pre
sented in 1887.

RECTORY, E of the church. C17 but externally much altere
in the C19. Two fireplaces and other details inside ar
original.

COTTAGES to the E and across the High Street to the N c
the church. A pretty group.

High up the High Street to the SE more old houses; none c
special merit. Some are wealthy (BUSHEY HOUSE wit
six-column Greek Doric portico; *c.* 1825, heightened
1900–10; BOURNE HALL opposite, eight-bay three
storey, Georgian, plastered white), some humbler. C
these some are weatherboarded (Fishmongers' Arms
some Georgian red brick (Ivy House), some whitewashe
(No. 75). A number, including some higher up in Bushe
Heath HIGH ROAD and SPARROWS HERNE, are earl
C19 Gothic villas. In the same taste, but larger and muc
later (after 1870), THE CLOISTERS in the High Street.

This lies next to the CONGREGATIONAL CHURCH, 190.
by *Morley Horder*, in the pretty playful style of th
Nonconformist chapels of that moment; red brick wit
an asymmetrically placed tower. The METHODIS
CHURCH, London Road, of 1904 by *Bell & Meredith*,
similar, but less well done.

Schools :

ROYAL MASONIC SENIOR SCHOOL, The Avenue. Ver
large group of red brick buildings by *Gordon & Guntor*
1902. Tudor style. Facing the entrance a centrally place
tall tower in Gothic forms but with an odd Art Nouvea
pavilion roof. The big courtyard in the middle turfe
closed to the S only by a cloister. Large hall with louvre i
axis with the entrance tower. Chapel by *E. D. Webb*.

ROYAL MASONIC JUNIOR SCHOOL, London Road, 1926
9. By *H. C. Smart*, in a much more chastened Ne
Tudor. The main buildings on the sides of a centr
quadrangle. Behind this four double dormitory blocks c
identical design.

ᴛ Margaret's Clergy Orphan Schools, Merry
Hill Road; 1897, by *Alfred & Paul Waterhouse*. Yellow
brick, with Waterhouse's typical abundance of smooth red
indelible terra-cotta slabs; Gothic.

ᴏʏᴀʟ Caledonian Asylum, Aldenham Road; 1902,
by *Sir William Emerson*. Free Neo-Georgian. The central
Neo-Gothic hall recently damaged by fire.

ɪɢʜᴡᴏᴏᴅ Mixed Junior School, Bushey Mill Lane.
One of the new H.C.C. schools (*see* Introduction, p. 28).

C 19 *and* C 20 *houses in the centre :*

ᴜʟᴜʟᴀɴᴅ, Melbourne Road. Of Sir Hubert van Her- 61
komer's, the celebrated portrait-painter's house, only the
entrance survives. It must at all costs be preserved, as it is
the only European work by the best American later C 19
architect *H. H. Richardson*. It was built *c.* 1885. The entrance is eminently typical of Richardson: a big heavy
archway with free acanthus foliage in the door lintel and
tympanum, and two corner turrets. Good solid stone,
white and red.

ᴏᴜʀɴᴇᴍᴇᴀᴅ, Herkomer Road; 1892, by *J. M. Brydon*.
A good example of the picturesque brick and half-timber
villa of that date.

ɪʟᴇʜᴜʀsᴛ, Grange Road; 1903, by *Voysey*. This and
Myholme, Merry Hill Road, 1911, and also, in all probability, the house at the corner of Grange Road and High-
field Road, are characteristic examples of *Voysey's* work
on the least ambitious suburban scale (very suitable for
imitation by anonymous builders). The style has indeed
had most undesirable consequences all over Britain. Yet
Voysey's own houses are happily designed, unpretentious,
unrhetorical, and fitting. Note the batter of the buttresses,
the roughcast, the horizontal windows, and the irregular
stone window surrounds.

Houses farther out (clockwise, starting ɴ*) :*

ᴜsʜᴇʏ Hall, Aldenham Road, *c.* 1880. Large symmetrical Neo-Jacobean brick and stone mansion, with
tower on the l., away from the main structure. Built as a

private house at a cost of £150,000, but soon converte
into that incarnation of Victorianism, a hydrotherapeuti
establishment.

HILFIELD, Hilfield Lane, *c.* 1795, by *Sir Jeffry Wyatvill*
Originally known as Sly's Castle. Castellated, turretec
and cemented house with a gatehouse, complete wit
portcullis. Entrance and s sides both symmetrical. Out
buildings attached to the w.

CALDECOTE TOWERS (Rosary Priory School), Elstre
Road. Obviously Mid-Victorian. A crazy display of com
mercial success with a big asymmetrical square towe:
Much like a hotel at Harrogate or some such spa.

SPARROWS HERNE HOUSE, Elstree Road. C18 with lon
early C19 Roman Doric colonnade on the s front and win
added in 1938.

HARTSBOURNE LODGE, Hartsbourne Avenue. Early Vic
torian lodge with fanciful timber trim including a da
plate 1517.

BYGRAVE

ST MARGARET. Nave and chancel only, with a polygonal v
turret to give access to the bells. Norman s doorway wit
one order of colonnettes and one fat roll-moulding in th
arch. The nave E angles are strengthened by Roma
bricks. The chancel with the chancel arch seems late C14
– FONT. Octagonal with rectangular panels showing th
Instruments of the Passion. – PULPIT. With an attache
C17 iron hour-glass and bits of re-used C15 panelling.
BENCHES. Some with poppyheads. – SCREEN. C15 wit
simple Perp tracery. – COMMUNION RAILS. C17 wit
long sausage-shaped balusters.

CADDINGTON HALL
1 m. NE of Markyate

House of 1804, built of light and dark chequer brickwork
seven bays, two and a half storeys, with semicircular en
trance porch on Tuscan columns. Early Victorian roof.

CALDECOTE

ᴛ MARY MAGDALENE. The stone-built church stands like a miniature model on the grass, N of the barns of a big farm. The W tower starts broad and then, by means of hips, goes narrower. The tower windows seem to be of the late C14. The nave and chancel windows are Perp and of modest dimensions. There is inside no structural division between the two parts. The only more ornamental part of the church is the S porch, embattled and with a unique canopied and crocketed STOUP inside. – FONT. Perp, octagonal, with traceried and cusped panels. – BENCHES. Some in the nave C15, with little decorative buttresses. – STAINED GLASS. In a S window fragment of a kneeling figure. – PLATE. Chalice, 1569; Paten, 1696.

CALDECOTE TOWERS see BUSHEY

CHANDLERS CROSS
2½ m. NW of Watford

ʜANDLERS FARM. Pretty brick and timber-framed farm-house with outbuildings. Restored.

CHESHUNT

ᴛ MARY. Built between 1418 and 1448 by the then Rector of Cheshunt (who was also a Baron of the Exchequer), and important as a dated example of the Perp style in Herts. All-embattled. W tower of ashlar stone with taller SE stair-turret and low buttresses, W door with spandrels decorated with shields and three-light W window. The aisle windows have depressed arches, three lights, and elementary panel tracery. The five-bay arcade inside on piers consisting of four shafts and four hollows in the diagonals. Broad two-centred arches. Two-light clerestory windows. The stencilled and painted decoration of the nave belongs probably to the restoration of 1874 under *Bodley*. – PLATE. Chalice, 1638; Flagon, 1638; Paten, 1672. – MONUMENTS. Unimportant Brasses E end of N

aisle and E end of nave, C15, 1609, and 1449. – Rober
Dacres † 1543, tomb-chest in recess in the chancel, th
superstructure remodelled by Sir Thomas Dacres in 1643
– Henry Atkins † 1638, physician to James I and Charle
I, under arch similar to the previous one, but wit
draperies tied round the flanking columns. – Margare
Watton † 1675, small standing wall monument crowne
by an urn. At the foot an inscription in Greek. – Danie
Dodson † 1747, life-size figure nonchalantly leaning on a
urn, back wall with garlands hanging down to the l. and r
By the younger *W. Woodman*.

The old village lies close to the church. In CHURCHGAT
and CHURCHFIELD some of the village character is sti
preserved, though badly interfered with by CHESHUN
COLLEGE almost opposite the E side of the graveyard
The College was founded by Selina Countess of Hunting
don and transferred to Cheshunt in 1792. When it move
to Cambridge the premises were taken over by the Churc
of England. They consist of two earlier Georgian red bric
houses by the street, the modest original College buildin
of stock brick, and the big and self-assured new building
of 1870–1 (by *Lander & Bedells*). They are of stock bric
in the E.E. style with a tall tower of typically High Vic
torian outline, and detail all kinds of excrescences, eve
bargeboarding. At the E end of Churchfield stand
another educational building, three hundred years olde
and correspondingly modest, the DEWHURST CHARITY
SCHOOL of 1640, of brick with mullioned brick window
and three gables.

Half a mile to the E of the old village a new development too
place along the main road from London, the usual ribbo
development (which came as natural to the C17 and C18
as it comes to ours). The High Street (or combine
Crossbrook Street, Turners Hill, and High Street, th
latter also known as Cheshunt Street) stretches for over
mile. In TURNER'S HILL near the S end of Cheshunt
where it merges into Waltham Cross, a first group con
sisting of Nos 75 (standing with its gable to the street)
77–79 (a fine pair of five-bay brick houses), 88 (early C19

yellow brick with a gently projecting bow window), THE
GRANGE (also yellow brick, also early C19), Springfield,
and Nos 102–104 (with a date-plate 1698). Then, in
Turner's Hill, past the Public Library, the so-called
MANOR HOUSE, early C18, of four bays and three
storeys with two-bay lower wings. The doorcase has
rusticated pilasters; the windows are segmentheaded. A
little to the N on the W side the DEWHURST ALMS-
HOUSES founded in 1642, a row of ten plain one-storeyed
brick cottages. Off Turners Hill lanes lead down on the
E side towards the river Lea. Much of the area is now
covered by the glasshouses of market gardeners and
nurserymen, the dominant motif of the scenery around
Cheshunt.

To the W occasional large individual houses remain along
such streets as COLLEGE ROAD (BROOKSIDE HOUSE
and CHESHUNT COTTAGE, large, early C19, with many
bargeboarded gables and with hood-moulds above the
windows; GROVE HOUSE, C18 brick), CHURCH LANE
(one castellated Late Georgian house with Venetian windows), BLIND MAN'S LANE (CLOCK HOUSE, seven-
bay, two-storey, red brick, C18). Also in Blind Man's
Lane the new JUNIOR MIXED INFANTS SCHOOL (see
Introduction, p. 28).

CHESHUNT GREAT HOUSE lies ½ m. NW of the church. It
is the still impressive remains of a much larger moated
house. What remains is no more than one wing of a courtyard house. The wing incorporates the Great Hall, a hall
40 ft long and still preserving its timber roof with wind-
braces. The roof is now plastered. The date of the hall is
probably late C15. Of the exterior architecture nothing
survives earlier than c. 1600 (the N gable with its blocked
mullioned window). The rest was converted into a house
of more comfort about 1700. Of that time the blocked
segmentheaded hall windows, the plain ten-bay E front,
and the S entrance front which, however, was again
altered later, probably in 1801, when the other ranges of
the house were pulled down. The four-centred entrance
arch and the window above would go well with a date c.

1800. The finest C18 piece in the house is the large stair
case with slim balusters of three alternating shapes, broa
spiral, narrow spiral, and columns.

CHILDWICKBURY
2 m. NW of St Albans

Large and well-kept mansion. Supposed to contain later C1
work incorporated in what was done in 1854 and abou
1900. The building history of the house has not yet bee
elucidated. (Good Rococo overmantels inside.)

Close to Childwick Green, just S of the E end of the churcl
a miniature Jacobean house. Central doorway with foui
centred arch at the top. Canted bays l. and r.; mullione
and transomed windows.

CHIPPERFIELD

ST PAUL, 1837, by *Talbot Bury*. Flint, aisleless nave, tran
septs and chancel; lancet windows. The only remarkabl
feature the timber roof forming a proper crossing wit
diagonal beams at the meeting of nave, transepts, an
chancel.

MANOR HOUSE. C17 brick and half-timbering and
modern extension at the back; the front an extremel
handsome addition of 1716 (date on a cistern); eleve
bays wide, two-storeyed, of red brick, with parapet. Fin
iron gates to the Common.

LITTLE WINCH. On the S side of the Common, close to th
SW corner. 1935, by *Maxwell Fry*. A brick and a weather
boarded part, of different heights. The two parts and th
fenestration show an admirable sense of proportion. Th
result, though entirely of the C20, is as restful as Herts C1
or C18 farm architecture. It should, however, be added i
fairness that the architect had intended a concrete hous
and that the use of local materials was an afterthough
caused by objections from the Council. The large livin
room is on the ground floor on the E (r.) side, the studio o
the upper floor on the W (l.) side.

CHIPPING BARNET

arnet, although the one town in Herts which is not at all
parated from London by open country, yet keeps some of
a urban individuality of its own. This is to a large extent
ae to the position and personality of the parish church.

t JOHN THE BAPTIST. The church points with its E end
towards the High Street which comes up the hill from
London. To its l. and r. the main roads fork to Watford
and to St Albans and Hatfield. The architecture of the
church, which is largely Victorian, makes the most of this
position, more than the medieval church had done. This
was built at the expense of John Beauchamp who died in
1453.* When *William Butterfield* was commissioned in
1875 to enlarge the old building, he decided to keep the
medieval nave and N aisle and to add to it a new higher
nave with its own aisle to the S. He also removed the old
chancel and tower. So the present church seems to have
two naves and two aisles. From the N you see a low aisle
and a nave with a clerestory of three-light windows. These
clerestory windows on the S side look into Butterfield's
nave. His own clerestory has somewhat perverse alternating three-light and circular cinquefoil windows. The old
church was of flint with sparing stone dressings; Butterfield's has plenty of stone-bands and chequerwork to en-
rich the rhythm of the flint work. His W tower is most
impressive, big and broad, a beacon when you come up
from London, and a dominant accent for the town. Inside,
the mid C15 church has an arcade with piers with four
attached shafts, four hollows in the diagonals, and complex mouldings in the two-centred arches. Butterfield's
piers and arches are much more robust. – STAINED
GLASS. N and S windows of the aisles, good Arts and
Crafts style of the 1880s. – PLATE. Small Cup, 1679; Cup
and Paten, 1706. – MONUMENTS. Thomas Ravenscroft 36a
† 1630, excellent recumbent alabaster effigy under canopy.
The details of the canopy an interesting example of

* *See* the inscription in the spandrel of one of the arcade arches.

Gothic Survival: cusped arches, rib-vault, quatrefo
frieze of the top cornice. – James Ravenscroft † 1680 ar
his wife † 1689, two fine small marble busts in an altere
Neo-Gothic surround.

CHRIST CHURCH, New Road.* Flint with stone dressing
1845–52, by *G. G. Scott*. N aisle 1855. The pret
CHURCH HALL (brick, flint, and stone) in a fancy Tud
style, 1907, by *L. W. Ridge & Waymouth*.

The town itself has little of pre-Victorian date. The on
Georgian stretch is w of the church in WOOD STREET:
row of varied cottages (Nos 10–16) on one side of th
street, mostly of brick, and one or two opposite; farth
out a few individual houses, not specially noteworthy.

In addition the following buildings:

QUEEN ELIZABETH GRAMMAR SCHOOL, Wood Stree
opposite the s side of the church. Later C16. Tudor bricl
work, with diapers of vitrified headers, three-windo
front, the windows with wooden mullions, at the angl
two polygonal towers.

RAVENSCROFT ALMSHOUSES, Wood Street, 1679. But
that date now only the central archway and gable.

GARRETT'S ALMSHOUSES, Wood Street, 1731. Ve
simple one-storey row of six cottages.

LEATHERSELLERS' ALMSHOUSES, N end of Union Stree
1843 plus addition of a further eight houses 1865. Thr
ranges; white brick in the typical timid Tudor style of s
many early C19 almshouses.

CHORLEYWOOD

CHRIST CHURCH, 1870, by *Street*. Flint, with low shingle
w spire. The only other feature of interest is the trip
traceried opening from the chancel into the s chapel.

The architectural significance of Chorleywood is connecte
with the name of *Charles F. A. Voysey* who built hir
63a self a house here in 1900–1. It is called THE ORCHAR
and situated in SHIRE LANE. The garden front is esp

* Administratively in South Mimms, Middlesex.

cially characteristic, with two identical gables (with
Voysey's typical tiny ventilation slits), but a gentle, carefully balanced asymmetry in the centre. Some of the trees
in conjunction with which the house was meant to be
seen have been replaced. Inside, the Hall with the staircase
and fireplace is one of the best Voysey designed. The
metalwork such as door-hinges is also in the daintiest
Voysey fashion.

OLLYBANK, the neighbour of The Orchard, also by
Voysey, was built in 1903–4. It is as good in most respects
as The Orchard.

smaller job of *Voysey's* was the r.-hand-side addition to
HILL COTTAGE farther N in Shire Lane.

CLOTHALL

T MARY. The church has a SW tower in which is the
porch. This is C14; so is the S chapel. The latter is the
most interesting part, with an arcade to the nave on unusual piers with semi-octagonal members and a Piscina
characteristic of the period. – FONT. C12, of the table-top
type, Purbeck marble, square with shallow blank roundheaded arches. – BENCHES. Some bench-ends with
poppyheads. – DOOR. In the S doorway, with long iron
hinges, probably C14. – STAINED GLASS. Christ, the
Virgin, and Saints in medallions, only fragmentarily C15,
ornamental quoins with flowers and delightfully drawn
birds; thick canopies above; hardly before 1400 and perhaps later. – BRASSES (in the chancel). Early C16 priest,
c. 3 ft long; John Vynter † 1404, Rector of Clothall, *c.* 3 ft
long; John Wryght † 1519, Rector of Clothall, with scrolls
and the Trinity above the figure; two more brasses
covered by the chancel stalls.

of the church a nice Georgian brick house of the usual
five-bay, two-storey type.

CODICOTE

T GILES. Mostly 1853, but the S aisle has C13 bases to its
arcade, the nave N wall has a C13 lancet window, and the

tower arch is of the C15. – PULPIT. Jacobean. – PLAT
Small engraved Chalice, 1558; Paten, 1568; large Stand
ing Paten, 1772.

At the triangular village centre some pretty half-timbere
(George & Dragon Inn) as well as chequerwork bric
houses.

CODICOTE LODGE. Mainly late C18. Seven bays with r
cessed three-bay centre. Doorway with Ionic column
bulging frieze, and segmental pediment. A specially ri
contemporary fireplace inside.

CODICOTE BURY. Red brick, built c. 1655. Good stairca
with spread tapering banisters, leading up through a
storeys.

NODE DAIRY AND STUD, 1927, by *Maurice Chesterton*. A
extremely odd design. Circular with a circular courtyar
thatched, and with a very fantastically detailed entran
arch. The tower top is no less surprising.

COKENACH *see* BARKWAY

COLNEY HEATH

ST MARK, 1845, in the Transitional Norman style. C
yellow brick. N porch with fat columns and from it a
outer staircase *à la* King's School, Canterbury, leads u
to the starved NW tower. Apsed E end with roundheade
lancet windows. Thin W gallery inside.

CORNEY BURY
1 m. N of Buntingford

Early C17 brick manor house with three straight gables o
the W side, one over the centre, the others over unequall
projecting wings. The porch and the whole S and E side
remodelled later in the C17. A rainwater head gives th
date: 1681.

COTTERED

ST JOHN THE BAPTIST. The outstanding feature is th
spacious aisleless nave with large three-light transome
Perp windows with four-centred heads. It makes th

church appear a palatial Hall. The masonry of the nave is older (*see* the C14 doorways). Of the C14 also the W tower (*see* the W window and tower arch). The tower is unbuttressed and has a lead spire. The chancel is lower than the nave. Its windows are Perp but the chancel arch looks early C14. – FONT. Early C18, of lovely grey Derbyshire marble, with baluster stem and fluted bowl. – DOORS. Nave, heavy oak, C15 (?). Vestry, with Late Medieval ironwork. – PAINTING. On the nave wall large figure of St Christopher with indications of river surroundings and much incidental drama of the medieval highway. – PLATE. Chalice and Paten, 1711.

ORDSHIP HOUSE. Large, irregularly gabled manor house, partly C15, partly C17. The house is surrounded by a moat.

LMSHOUSES. Brick, mid C18, one-storeyed with quoins and three dormers. Altered lately.

CHOOL. Built in 1825. Plain rectangle. Windows with hood-moulds.

CROMER *see* ARDELEY

CROXLEY GREEN
1 m. E of Rickmansworth

LL SAINTS, 1872, by *J. Norton*. In 1907 *Temple Moore* added a new nave to the S of the old (GR). The difference in quality is remarkable. *Temple Moore's* design is original and interesting, with the lancet windows, and the wall-passage carried also along the straight E end. The arches towards the old building are roundheaded and rest on short heavy rectangular piers. Exterior of yellow brick with bands of stone.

he characteristic feature of Croxley Green is its long triangular Green with several pretty buildings, especially towards the N end.

of the N end of the Green in LITTLE GREEN LANE one of the new H.C.C. schools (*see* Introduction).

t the S end of Croxley Green beyond the railway CROX-LEY HALL FARM with a splendid late medieval barn,

101 by 38½ ft, and well preserved inside and out. Nave an
aisles, one entrance transept, kingpost roof, ampl
strutted. At the Hall some C16 panelling and a bric
chimney remain. The Hall belonged to Dr Caius.

DANE END

DANE END HOUSE. Handsome white early C19 house c
five bays and three storeys with lower side wings. In fron
of the centre a one-storey porch of four coupled Ioni
columns.

DANESBURY see WELWYN

DATCHWORTH

ALL SAINTS. Small flint church. Nave to which late in th
C13 a N aisle was added (arcade of four bays on octagona
piers with slightly hollow-chamfered arches). W tower an
chancel C15 (upper stage of the tower 1875, chancel re
modelled C17). The plastered C15 nave roof looks rathe
domestic with its wind-braces. – FONT. Good C15 wor
with panelled stem and panelled octagonal bowl.
STAINED GLASS. E window early C19. – In the N aisle
window good c. 1875 glass in the style of *Walter Crane*
– PLATE. Chalice and Paten, 1569. – MONUMENT. Coffi
lid with foliated cross; c. 1300.

HOPPERS HALL. Timber-framed and plastered gabled C1
building. The plan is L-shaped and the two wings differ
little in date.

DELAMERE HOUSE see GREAT WYMONDLEY

DELROW see ALDENHAM

DIGSWELL

The visual character of this leafy village of houses in thei
gardens is determined by the austere back screen of th
RAILWAY VIADUCT. Forty brick arches (built by *Lewi
Cubitt* in 1850).

ST JOHN THE EVANGELIST. A small church close to Digs
well House. The external appearance much altered i

1811. Cemented. The NW tower small. Inside, a plain arch of *c.* 1200 between chancel and N chancel chapel. The Piscina in the chancel is of the C13. In the N aisle a very curious display of blank geometrical tracery of *c.* 1290, perhaps connected with a founder's monument. – SCREEN. Doors from a former rood screen, *c.* 1540, the earliest example in Herts of the new Renaissance fashions of ornamentation. – STAINED GLASS. Window S aisle (SS Michael and George) by *Kempe*, 1894. – PLATE. Engraved Chalice, 1563; Flagon, 1672; Paten, 1673. – MONUMENTS. Brasses in the chancel. Outstandingly fine brasses to John Peryent, Standard-Bearer to Richard II, and his wife † 1415, big frontal figures. – Small brasses to a Knight, *c.* 1430; to Thomas Hoore † 1495, wife and children; Robert Battyl † 1557, wife and children; to William Robert and wife, both figures in shrouds, *c.* 1480. – Epitaph to Richard Sedley † 1658, large and good, with oval inscription surrounded by a laurel garland, black columns, and fine ornament.

IGSWELL HOUSE, by the church, good early C19 stone mansion of five bays, with a giant portico of unfluted Ionic columns and straight entablature to the garden and a plain Tuscan porch to the drive.

EASNEYE *see* WARE

EAST BARNET

T MARY, Church Hill. Nave walls and three small windows in the N wall, Norman. The rest C19. Tower of yellow brick in a Neo-Norman style, aisle 1868, chancel 1880. – PLATE. Cup of 1636. – Fine graveyard, with old cedar-tree S of the church tower. In the graveyard MONUMENT to John Sharpe † 1756, large urn on big base under heavy arched baldacchino.

APTIST CHURCH, Crescent Road, 1931, by *F. Goldsmith.* Red brick, with a front whose unmoulded verticals reach right up into the gable.

st Barnet is entirely Outer London, rural only in the immediate neighbourhood of the church. Of individual houses only two are remarkable: OAKHILL COLLEG: long white mansion in ample grounds, five-bay centr with lower two-bay wings and an outer four-bay wing o the S side. The house has an Early Georgian nucleus an was altered and enlarged in the early C19.

TREVOR HALL, Stuart Road, built for Colonel Gillum 1860 by *Philip Webb*, the architect of William Morris Red House at Bexley Heath, Kent. Surprisingly fresh an un-Victorian in its plain gables and the broad coving o the W side. Originally called Church Hill House.

MONKFRITH AVENUE INFANTS SCHOOL (*see* Intro duction, p. 28).

EASTBURY
1¼ m. SW of Oxhey Place

FRITHWOOD HOUSE and THE GLADES, both in Watfo Road, are excellent examples of the two main types English domestic architecture in *c.* 1900–5. Frithwoc House is by *Mervyn Macartney*, The Glades probably b *Voysey* (no documentary evidence). The former is Neo William-and-Mary, the latter Neo-Tudor; but bot handled with personality and imagination. Frithwoc House is brick, with brick quoins, white wooden mu lioned and transomed window casements and far projec ing roof. The Glades has *Voysey's* characteristic slopin buttresses, roughcast and irregular stone surrounds to th windows. It is a composition of great charm

EASTWICK

ST BOTOLPH. A short yew avenue leads to the churc which was rebuilt in 1872 by *Blomfield*, except for th chancel arch and the W tower. Blomfield's church consis of nave and chancel only and is of no interest. The chanc arch is an astonishingly ambitious piece of C13 desig with three orders of tall Purbeck shafts and a complex moulded arch, as if for a cathedral (cf. Standon).

PLATE. Paten, 1705; Chalice, 1719; Paten, 1735.

MONUMENTS. Under the tower the best C13 effigy in th

31b

county, a marble Knight in chain mail with long surcoat. His legs are crossed. – Brass to Joan Lee † 1564. – Epitaph to Mary Plummer † 1700, good, of diptych type, with three Corinthian columns. – Epitaph to Walter Plummer † 1746, so good that it may well be by *Rysbrack* (*see* the delightful cherubs' heads and the exquisitely carved classical details of frieze and pediment).

ELSTREE

ST NICHOLAS, 1853, by *P. C. Hardwick*, with the use of the short octagonal piers and capitals of the C15 church. The C19 building rather ugly outside with low SW spire. – FONT. Perp, octagonal, with little decoration. – SCREEN between nave and chancel, very pretty wrought metalwork, designed by *Sir Arthur Blomfield*, 1881. – The stencilling on the N side of the chancel is probably by *George Walton* (*see* below).

CHOPWICK. House N of the church, Georgian, brick, five-bay, two-storeyed house.

COTTAGES S of the church, thoroughly beautified by sham half-timbering about 1920, yet no doubt decidedly pretty.

MILL HOUSE (former Elstree School), farther S. The main school buildings consist of a long, low, whitewashed house to which is added a red brick C18 house with two symmetrical polygonal bay windows and a central Venetian window. Across the road the chapel with a number of *Kempe* windows. The STAINED GLASS dates from 1877 to 1906. The oldest windows are in the apse and the Nativity in the nave. The Angels and Shepherds are 1878, the Charge to St Peter, 1879, etc.

THE LEYS (Middlesex C.C. Home) in Barnet Lane to the E of Elstree was built in 1901 by *George Walton*, a Glasgow architect, friend of Charles Rennie Mackintosh, and one of the most interesting domestic architects of Britain about 1900. The detail betrays the Glasgow Art Nouveau, but the composition is symmetrical and quiet, without the high tensions and *outré* expression of Mackintosh's work. The interior has been altered by the M.C.C., but

enough of the original woodwork remains to give th
South Englander a whiff of Scottish air.

ESSENDON

ST MARY, 1883, by *W. White*. Essendon is worth a specia
visit if only to see the FONT in the church. It is of Wedg
wood's Black Basalt ware, an exquisitely beautiful clas
sical shape and with all the appealing matt sheen of th
Wedgwood body. It was given to the church in 1780.
PLATE. Chalice and Paten, 1569; large Paten, 1692
Flagon, 1769; Baptismal Dish, 1778. – MONUMENT
Brass to W. Tooke † 1588 with wife and children (s aisle
– Large Epitaph to W. Prestley † 1664.
ESSENDON PLACE. Probably early C19.
CHURCH OF ENGLAND SCHOOL (*see* Introduction, p. 28

FANHAM'S HALL *see* WARE

FLAMSTEAD

ST LEONARD. Low w tower of flint and random stone
patched up with brick, also Roman brick. High up trace
of two-light Norman windows. No battlements; thi
spike. The body of the church flint; nave with clerestory
aisles, heavily buttressed s porch, unbuttressed N porch
low much restored C14 chancel, C14 NE vestry. Most win
dows are simple Perp, but the N aisle has one which is De
(ogee reticulated tracery). The interior confirms that th
w tower is Norman. The tower arch is depressed round
headed on the simplest of imposts. Into it, during the C1
a smaller arch was inserted, treble-chamfered on impost
with typical capitals of that century. The Norman nav
was aisleless of the same width as the present nave. Th
six-bay arcades show that aisles were added in the earl
C13. Octagonal piers, the w and E responds (except fo
one) slimmer attached circular shafts. The capitals ar
stiff-leaf, much renewed; the capitals of the respond
have the leaves composed in two tiers. The chancel arc
and the Piscina in the chancel are C14, but one N lance

window goes back to C13. – C15 nave roof on carved stone corbels. – PULPIT. 1698; just framed panels with very little inlay. – COMMUNION RAILS. *c.* 1700 with twisted balusters. – SCREEN. Well preserved C15 work; tall arcades, each division of six lights, with the central mullion running up to the apex of the arch; the individual lights end in round arches, the tracery is elementary Perp. – WALL PAINTINGS. Apart from St Albans the most important series in the county, all revealed only in 1930–2. None well preserved. Between the spandrels of the nave arches lower parts of four Apostles, large figures, C13. – Nave upper wall even larger C15 figure of St Christopher. – Above the chancel arch Christ in Glory C13, with Doomsday scenes C15. In the NE chapel mid C14 series of stories of the Passion in two tiers. Last Supper, Crucifixion, Mocking of Christ, Entombment (the best preserved and hence most readily appreciated scene), Crowning with Thorns, Resurrection. – PLATE. C17 Chalice and Paten; Pewter Flagon, 1675; Flagon, 1690; Breadholder given in 1700. – MONUMENTS. Brass to John Oudeby, Rector, † 1414, with indent above showing that there was a demi-figure of Virgin and Child under a canopy. – Tomb-chest with stone effigies of man and woman under one ogee canopy; early C15, the figures badly preserved. – Sir Bartholomew Fouke † 1604, the usual kneeling figure. – Saunders Children, erected about 1690, large altar tomb 36b of black marble with the figures of five deceased young children in contemporary dress and with praying hands placed on a ledge which could be used as the s aisle altar. The surviving sixth child kneeling on the floor, no doubt not in the original position. The monument is by *William Stanton* and cost £1,500. – Sir Edward Sedbright, by 39a *Flaxman*, 1762. Nobly carved composition with Hope and Faith reclining to the l. and r. of a slender fluted urn.

o the N of the church the SAUNDERS ALMSHOUSES, 1669, of brick, one-storeyed with roundheaded entrances and plain two-light windows. – VINE COTTAGE to their E, a handsome house, timber-framed with brick infilling.

FLAUNDEN

OLD CHURCH, just E of Latimer village in Bucks, in
spinney, completely hidden. Only a few crumbling wa
remain now amidst the trees and undergrowth. The Ro
Commission on Historical Monuments could still in 19
draw a plan and describe the building which dated chie
from the C13 and had the interesting peculiarity of
Greek cross plan. Traces of C13 wall paintings had a
survived until then.

ST MARY MAGDALENE, in Flaunden village; 1838. S
George Gilbert Scott's first building, described by him
his Memoirs as 'the poor barn designed for my unc
King' who was then vicar of Latimer (GR). Flint and bri
dressings. Lancet windows in the Commissioners' trac
tion, timber bellcote. – FONT. Octagonal bowl, Perp, wi
quatrefoil decoration. – PLATE. Chalice and Paten, 157
Salver, 1731.

FROGMORE

2 m. S of St Albans

HOLY TRINITY, 1842. Norman, of flint, with red bri
dressings and stone details: singularly violent and ra
contrast. Bellcote, E apse, nave, and aisles; no galleri
The interest of the church is the name of its architect: S
George Gilbert Scott. He cannot in later life have thoug
with much pleasure of this youthful effort.

FROGMORE HALL *see* ASTON

FURNEAUX PELHAM

ST MARY. A big church, Perp except for the long chanc
whose lancet windows (two with inner nook-shafts) a
Sedilia and Piscina arrangement and details (stiff-le
capitals) date it as middle of the C13. Tall unbuttressed
tower with Herts spike. The nave aisles frame the tow
Two-storeyed embattled S porch with two-light window
markedly higher than the unembattled aisle. Big S chap

coming forward as far as the s porch. The windows Late
Perp. As the chapel was built (by Robert Newport) about
1518 and the N and S aisle windows are of the same shape
as those of the chapel, the same late date may be assumed
for the former as well. Two-light clerestory windows. The
N and S aisle arcades are of a late type too, with semi-
octagonal shafts and hollows (without capitals) in the
diagonals. Low-pitched nave roof with tie-beams, high-
pitched chancel roof with struts and collar-beams. In the
nave the sub-principals are carried on angels. – FONT.
Octagonal, C13, of Purbeck marble with shallow blank
pointed arches. – STAINED GLASS. In the s chapel *Morris*
and *Burne-Jones* windows for the Calvert family, that on
the s with four figures of angels 1866, that on the E with
the Virgin, Gabriel (by *Morris*), and Michael 1873. The
quality is outstanding, especially if compared with other
Victorian glass. – MONUMENTS. Tomb-chest in the s aisle
at the W end with cusped quatrefoils and shields. On it the
exquisite, *c.* 3 ft long brass figures of a man and woman of
the early C15. They lie under a cusped double ogee canopy
with pinnacles to the l. and r. – Brass plate to R. Newport
with kneeling figures, dated 1518, on a marble slab. –
Tomb-chest of Edward Cason † 1624, with black marble
pilasters and top slab. Against the back wall inscription
tablet.

FURNEAUX PELHAM HALL. C16 brick manor house with
stepped gables (cf. e.g. Great Hormead). Mid C17 alterations of those on the W have given them a curved shape.
Good panelling inside.)

GADEBRIDGE *see* HEMEL HEMPSTEAD

GARSTON

ALL SAINTS, 1853, by *Sir G. G. Scott.*
LONDON TRANSPORT GARAGE, 1951–2, by *T. Bilbow.*
LYTES. An Early Victorian red brick house forms the centre
of the recent Colony for men with spine injuries: one-
storey brick cottages, ingeniously equipped; a friendly
group round the lawn; by *Norman & Dawbarn.*

GILSTON

ST MARY. Basically C13; *see* the W doorway of three order
the chancel lancets, and the N doorway and one N windo
of the nave, the latter with elementary plate tracery. T
upper parts of the tower probably late C16 (brick with
stair-turret; cf. Sawbridgeworth). The N aisle is old, t
S aisle C19. The arcades are low and have quatrefoil pie
with later arches. – FONT. Hexagonal, C12, of Purbe
22b marble, with shallow blank arches. – SCREEN. A surviv
of first-rate importance. Evidently late C13 and w
enough preserved to have made reconstruction possib
Tall dado, shafts thin and only 2 ft long, trefoiled point
arches and stylized flowers in the spandrels. Straight to
– PLATE. Chalice and Paten, 1562; Paten, C17; Flago
1697. – MONUMENTS. Two good big mid C17 epitaph
Bridget Gore † 1659, white standing figure in shroud
front of an oval black niche, drapes l. and r., and weepi
putti wiping their eyes with them. The type had be
made popular by John Donne's tomb in St Paul's Cathe
ral. – Sir John Gore † 1659, black and white, with lo
inscription flanked by blank columns; thin curly brok
pediment with small figures on it; signed by *Josh
Marshall.*

GILSTON PARK. Large asymmetrical mansion of rando
rubble in the Early Tudor style with Gothic detail in t
tower and entrance. Mullioned and transomed window
stepped gables. 1852, by *Philip Hardwick.*

GOBIONS

1½ m. NW of Northaw, 2¼ m. SE of North Mimms

The house belonged to the More family, including S
Thomas More, in the C16. It was pulled down in 1836
the owner of BROOKMANS who wanted to add t
grounds to his own estate. All that remains of it is t
50b FOLLY ARCH, a large sham-medieval entrance gate at t
S end, by Hawkstead Road. It was erected by Sir Jere
Sambrooke († 1754), owner of Gobions. It has a la

roundheaded arch and rectangular thin turrets with rectangular windows. Centre and turrets are castellated. Sir Jeremy also erected the Battle of Barnet Memorial at Hadley. The Folly Arch is a very early example of medieval revival, contemporary with *Kent's* and earlier than Walpole's Gothicism. The designer seems to have been *James Gibbs* (Manuscript life of Gibbs, perhaps an autobiography, at the Sir John Soane Museum). Sir Jeremy's grounds also belonged to the early examples of the new picturesque taste. They were laid out by *Bridgeman* (who also planned the grounds of Stowe).

ookmans was built *c.* 1680 in the plain sound style of that date, but destroyed by fire in 1891. Only the stables survive, with an upper storey added and the carriageway through the centre blocked up.

GOLDEN PARSONAGE *see* GREAT GADDESDEN

GOLDINGS

Devey, one of the most successful and least known Victorian domestic architects, *c.* 1870. A vast Neo-Tudor mansion of red brick with diapers. The principal front is broadly symmetrical and of moderate size, but to its r. is a wing attached at an angle which has a turret and a big tall square tower and no symmetry at all. The whole is successful, though undeniably a piece of presumptuous display.

GORHAMBURY

f Sir Nicholas Bacon's mansion of 1568 the porch and masonry of the Hall and one projecting wing survive. The porch is a would-be classical composition with Tuscan attached columns flanking the entrance arch on the ground floor, and Ionic columns and niches flanking the two-light upper windows. It led to the screens passage. The dais end of the Hall is marked by a large window.

1777 a new house was begun by the third Viscount Grimston. The architect was *Sir Robert Taylor*. The house is ashlar-faced and has a grand Corinthian portico raised on a plinth with broad outer staircase and three

H.—4

windows on each side. On the garden site the portico is attached columns. Originally the house had low win; connecting the main building with side blocks. The low wing was replaced by a two-storeyed building in 1816–1 and the outer N block by a more substantial one in 182 (*W. Atkinson*). In the same year the old S wing and S bloc were pulled down.

The interiors have as their most beautiful adornment sever magnificent fireplaces attributed to *Piranesi* who illu trated in his engravings two superb Roman urns belon; ing to the house. Many family and other portraits of valu Terracotta busts of Sir Nicholas Bacon, his wife, an their little son, the famous Francis. Stained glass fro; the old Bacon mansion made up into two large screens.

GRAVELEY

ST MARY. Small flint church. W tower with diagonal bu tresses, nave and long chancel. The latter dates from th C13 (*see* the windows on the N and S sides, the fragmen of E windows replaced by a Perp window, and especial the double Piscina with pointed arches formed by th intersection of semicircular ones just as at Jesus Colleg Cambridge). The chancel N doorway was originally in th nave. Its date is C12, a date which is borne out by th nave Double Piscina. The windows of the nave C14– C1 The N aisle 1887. – SCREEN. C15; nothing special. MONUMENT. Big epitaph to Mary Sparhauke † 1770, b *B. Palmer* (classical with a crowning completely smoo and unadorned urn against a black obelisk).

GRAVELEY HALL, W of the church. C17 brick house.

GREAT AMWELL

The space N of the church is one of the most delightful spo in Herts, thanks no doubt to *Robert Mylne*, architect to th New River Company and a man eager to perpetuate his ow and others' fame. The New River was begun by Sir Hug Myddelton in 1609 to give London better water. He con pleted the great enterprise after only four years in 1613. T

mmemorate this great feat which was indeed after two
ndred years still of some importance to London, *Robert*
ylne erected a MONUMENT TO MYDDELTON, an urn [40a]
Coade stone on a pedestal on which we read in pretty
ters: 'From the Spring at Chadwell 2 miles west and from
s source of Amwell the Aqueduct meanders for the space
XL miles conveying health, pleasure, and convenience to
e metropolis of Great Britain . . . an immortal work since
an cannot more nearly imitate the Deity than by bestow-
g health.' Then it goes on to say that the monument was
dicated by 'Robert Mylne, Architect, Engineer etc. in
oo'. It stands on an island in the New River with four
eping willows and a yew tree and smoothly cut lawn.
ose to it is the source, also embellished by a stone with a
em ('O'erhung with shrubs, that fringe the chalky rock /
little fount pur'd forth its gurgling rill', etc.), and another
t smaller island has a second monument to Myddelton
AMWELL, perpetuated be thy stream / Nor e'er thy
ring be less / which thousands drink who never dream /
ence flow the streams they bless'). The whole is a perfect
cture with the church up the hill, standing in its GRAVE-
ARD, uncommonly well provided with memorials larger
an tombstones. The most striking of these is that built by
ylne in 1800 for himself and his family, a white brick
be, crowned by an urn. Others are the Cathrow Monu-
ent with four short baseless Tuscan columns and a big
recian sarcophagus, and the Plomer Monument of 1728,
obelisk.

JOHN THE BAPTIST. A small church of great antiquity,
distinguished by its Norman apse, a feature very rare
amongst Herts parish churches (cf. Bengeo). Of the same
period the low roundheaded chancel arch, of two orders
on the simplest imposts and one window whose equal
splays outside and inside suggest an CII date. The other
architectural features are of less interest. C15 W tower
with diagonal buttresses and pyramid roof behind the
battlements. The W DOOR is of the same date as the
tower. – PULPIT. Mid C17 with termini caryatids at the
angles. – PLATE. Chalice and Paten, 1620; Paten, 1786. –

BRASSES to a priest (nave), and to a man with two wiv
and children (nave), both C15.

GREAT BERKHAMSTED see BERKHAMSTED

GREAT GADDESDEN

ST JOHN THE BAPTIST. On the hillside in a not very attra
tive village, but well placed against a screen of beech tre
with the E end facing the valley. The E end is the chief i
terest of the church. The visitor sees two gables, the
one of the brick-built NE Halsey Chapel of 1730, the l. o
of the C12 chancel (window C19) with quoins and shall
buttresses strengthened with Roman bricks. In the S w
of the chancel is a small C13 lancet window. The nave h
arcades of four bays, that on the S side with octagor
piers carrying big stiff-leaf capitals said to be origir
early C13 work, but drastically re-tooled if not new. T
arches are hollow-chamfered. The N arcade has the sar
arches and moulded capitals. The N aisle E window la
C13. The building needs renewed study to clarify i
history. S porch, clerestory, tower and nave and ais
roofs are all C15 (tower rebuilt 1861). – PLATE. Chalic
1637.

MONUMENTS. Brass to William Croke † 1506 and wi
(chancel). – Brass to an unknown woman, c. 1520 (N aisle
– John Halsey † 1670, exceptionally good Italian-lookir
epitaph with finely designed cartouche and, on top,
Berninesque bust (chancel). – Thomas H. † 1715, Ann
† 1719, Jane H. † 1725, Henshaw H. † 1739, all four th
same dignified design with busts under drapery ba
dacchinos between pilasters and below open segment
pediments. The sculptor is not recorded. – Charles H
† 1748, white epitaph with bust against obelisk.
Frederick H. † 1762, white epitaph with profile medallic
against obelisk. – Agatha H. † 1782, small epitaph wit
large angel holding a book. By *Flaxman*, and the onl
signed monument of this important series. – Thomas H
† 1788 and wife, with obelisk and on it oval medallic
with Mrs H. taken up to heaven.

ᴏʟᴅᴇɴ Pᴀʀꜱᴏɴᴀɢᴇ, 2 m. ɴᴇ. The original house of the
Halseys. This ᴄ16 house was probably enlarged in 1705
and then, when the family moved away to Gaddesden
Place, the out-of-date old house was pulled down and
only the more modern wing left standing. The wing is of
five by four bays, red-brick-built with angle pilasters and
a plain parapet. The windows are segmentheaded. The
doorway has a fine segmental pediment on richly carved
corbels and between these a frieze rising from both sides
to a point in the centre (a typical early ᴄ18 motif). Pretty
staircase with finely twisted banisters.

ᴀᴅᴅᴇꜱᴅᴇɴ Pʟᴀᴄᴇ. Built by *James Wyatt* for the Halsey
family in 1768–73 (the earlier date scratched into a wall on
the ground floor, very early, it will be noticed, for *James
Wyatt*). Five-bay centre with portico (rebuilt after a fire
of 1905) with one-storeyed semicircular galleries and
outer two-storey wings with central Venetian windows.

GREAT HORMEAD

ʀ Nɪᴄʜᴏʟᴀꜱ. Away from the village street, on a hill behind Great Hormead Bury. The church is much restored
(1874), the chancel rebuilt, and the s porch an addition. w
tower with diagonal buttresses (late ᴄ14 to late ᴄ15),
nave, and two aisles. Three bays with octagonal piers,
moulded capitals, and double-chamfered arches. The
date may be *c.* 1300. The last much shorter arcade bays
were added, probably later in the ᴄ14. The w tower arch
still later, say *c.* 1400 (shafts with capitals and, in the
diagonals, hollows without capitals). – ꜰᴏɴᴛ. Norman,
undecorated, on thick circular stem and eight shafts set
around. – ᴘʟᴀᴛᴇ. Two Chalices, 1740, 1748. – ᴍᴏɴᴜ-
ᴍᴇɴᴛ. Lt-Col. Stables, killed at Waterloo 1815, Grecian
sarcophagus with the word Waterloo on it in an oval
laurel wreath. By *Kendrick*.

ʜᴇ Vɪʟʟᴀɢᴇ Sᴛʀᴇᴇᴛ is uncommonly charming. No
house of special importance, but thatched cottages with
narrowly spaced exposed upright timbers and with
Gothick windows (in chronological order: Tudor Cottage, Judds, Milburns, The Cottage).

GREAT HORMEAD BURY. Simple Georgian but with Tudor centre still recognizable.

BRICK HOUSE, 1½ m. NE of the church. Quite on its ow and at the time of writing in a neglected state. An interesing rather tall and gaunt early C16 small manor hous with stepped gables and some brick mullioned windov under brick hood-moulds.

GREAT MUNDEN

ST NICHOLAS. Unbuttressed W tower of the C15 wi spike. The body of the church with much restored wal and windows. The masonry goes back originally to th C12: see the simple Norman N doorway (an order of colo nettes, and roll moulding in the arch) and one small No man N window in the chancel. At the E end of the S ais one fine Dec three-light window, at the W end a simil one of two lights. The interior bears out the exterior in pression. Of the Norman chancel arch the N side surviv with one primitive volute or rather spiral capital and or with a face either with fingers pulling the mouth open with sprays of foliage growing out of the mouth.* The side of the Norman chancel arch was destroyed when th arch was widened in the C15. The S arcade is of three ba and has C14 detail, and there are besides in the aisle tw ogee-headed recesses and a fine stone reredos at the S en also with little ogee niches. The top is castellated. PULPIT. Jacobean, with two tiers of the usual blar arcades. – CHANCEL STALLS with a few rather starve poppy-heads. – PLATE. Chalice of 1696.

HIGH TREES see p.

GREAT WYMONDLEY

ST MARY. Small flint and stone church. Its most remar able feature is its apsidal chancel. Nave and chancel a Norman as proved by the S doorway (colonnettes wit rudely carved faces on capitals, star ornament of the abac

* A Norman arch in the N side of the chancel was found at the re toration in 1865 but not left exposed.

and star ornament all over the tympanum) and the chancel arch (shafts with primitive volutes at the angle of the capitals). The Double Piscina also has waterleaf capitals. The windows are C13 lancets (chancel) and C14 and C15 designs in the nave. The W tower with diagonal buttresses and a pyramid roof behind the battlements is C15. The nave roof also belongs to the C15. It rests on primitive head corbels.

ELAMERE HOUSE. The three-storeyed brick building of *c*. 1600. The N front has two straight gables, the E and S fronts curved gables of the later C17. Good staircase of *c*. 1600 and some contemporary fireplaces.

GRIMS DYKE *see* BERKHAMSTED

GROVE, THE, *see* WATFORD

GUBBINS *see* GOBIONS

HADHAM HALL *see* LITTLE HADHAM

HADLEY *see* MONKEN HADLEY

HAILEYBURY COLLEGE
1 m. SE of Little Amwell

he college was opened in 1809 as a training school for the 59a East India Company. The original buildings were designed by *William Wilkins*, the architect of Downing College, Cambridge, begun in 1807, and of University College, London. The arrangement chosen for the buildings is a representational stone-faced façade to the S and behind it a quadrangle of yellow brick ranges. The façade is one-storeyed and has a central six-column portico, intermediate accents of four columns, and outer accents of pilasters. The whole is of forty-two bays and (Wilkins's usual fault) not sufficiently pulled together. In the quad also the individual parts appear somewhat scattered. Access from the S front is through the intermediate porticos which were originally open towards the quad. The E one still is. The main *point de vue* in the quad was the N side with a pediment and cupola. But even that is no more

representational than, say, the Barracks of Woolwich
the same time. The appearance of the quad was rude
dramatized with the erection of a big new chapel in 187
Until then the chapel had been the present library with i
gently coved ceiling, and there had been no dome pressin
on Wilkins's long horizontal façade. The new chapel, de
signed by *Sir Arthur Blomfield*, is a hefty building in
kind of Byzantine or some such *Rundbogen* style, ar
stretches out arched cloisters to the l. and r. The style di
not suit the elder Blomfield who was a Gothicist by con
viction. Its coarseness was mitigated in 1936 when *S
Herbert Baker* added an impressive apse extending ver
sheer into the quadrangle. The interior also was chaste
classicized. Other additions to the original scheme are, i
chronological order: Bradby Hall, 1887, by your
Reginald Blomfield. He cannot in his later Franco-Cla
sical manner have looked back with approval to th
gabled Neo-Jacobean design with its red brick walls, thic
wooden galleries, and open timber roof. *Reginald Blon
field* also designed the African War Memorial (1903), a
obelisk on a scrolly Baroque base. The Lodge and Form
Rooms facing the memorial are by *Sir J. W. Simpson* &
Maxwell Ayrton (1905–8) who are also responsible for th
Big School (New Hall) with its Ionic façade on the E sid
of the quadrangle.

HAMELS
1½m. WSW of Braughing

A Late Elizabethan mansion of some fame was replace
about 1720 by a big plain Early Georgian one. This in i
turn was made sham Elizabethan in the C19. Of the late
C18 a number of exquisite fireplaces, one having as it
central relief a representation of Shakespeare and hi
Muse.

HARE STREET
2 m. E of Buntingford

Typical of many hamlets in Herts. Developed along a mai
road with notable houses, both of the C16–C17 timber
framed overhang type (e.g. former SWAN INN near s end

nd the more formal Georgian brick type (HARE STREET
IOUSE, five bays, two storeys, parapet and hipped roof.
Doorcase with pediment on Roman Doric pilasters. Nice
ron gates to the street. The chimney stacks show that the
tructure of the house is older and the front a later re-
nodelling.)

HARESFOOT see BERKHAMSTED

HARPENDEN

e chief attraction of Harpenden is the way in which the High
eet has a broad, turfed and sloping, tree-planted band in
 middle, with the houses standing higher on one side
n the other, and the way in which at the E end the High
eet opens out funnel-wise into the Common. Otherwise
re is not much of interest, only a few old houses of note as
inst the hundreds of phoney half-timbered residences of
l-to-do Londoners which have grown up in the last
ty years.

NICHOLAS, 1862 by *W. Slater*, except for the w tower
flint and stone, diagonal buttresses, SW stair-turret, spike).
n the N aisle on window ledges C12 scalloped capital from
he former chancel arch and C12 capital with upright
tylized leaves. – FONT. *c.* 1200, polygonal bowl of Pur-
eck marble with two blank pointed arches on each panel.
– MONUMENTS. Brass to William Anabull † 1456 and
wife, very decayed figures (close to pulpit). – Brass to
William Cressye † 1559 and wife, kneeling figures in stone
urround (N transept wall; cf. Wheathampstead, Hey-
vorth). – Godman Jenkyn † 1746, standing wall monument with bulgy sarcophagus and obelisk with scrolly
hield.

R LADY OF LOURDES, Rothamsted Avenue, 1905, by
F. *A. Walters*.
ETHODIST CHURCH, High Street, 1929, by *A. Brace*.
Broad, symmetrical, free Neo-Tudor stone front.
 the village proper just one house: BOWERS HOUSE,
early C18, two-storeyed, eleven-bay, grey brick with
ertical strips of rubbed bricks and aprons to the upper

windows. Older parts behind. The whole house is n(
hidden by a new parade of shops.

Towards the Common on the w side the former BULL IN(
an excellent C15 half-timbered house with the origin
Hall, half-timbered additions of the Tudor age, especia(
a barn at the back, and a Late Georgian bow-front
addition at the front next to the C15 gable. – Opposite (
the E side two good houses: HARPENDEN HALL, the (
side early C17 with porch, some brick and flint chequ(
and a brick cornice on the ground floor, the r. side of
1700 with six bays (originally seven?) and a doorway wi(
curving up cornice and broken segmental pedime(
Corinthian pilasters and a charmingly carved vase wi(
garlands under the pediment. C18 red brick also Nos (
and 17–18.

The ROTHAMSTED EXPERIMENTAL STATION has (
Neo-Georgian main building of 1914–16 on the w side (
the Common (by *Freeman & Hodgson*).

CROSS FARM, 1 m. SE. C17 gabled brick front and an a(
tached timber and brick block.

48a MACKERY END, 1½ m. NE. Fine stately symmetri(
brick front dated 1665, still with 'Dutch' gables wi(
pedimented tops. Central porch with brick pilasters a(
segmental pediment. The back proves that the body (
the house goes back to *c.* 1600 or earlier.

LAWRENCE END *see* p. 153.

HATFIELD

About the year 970 Edgar, King of Mercia, gave Hatfield (
the Benedictine monks of Ely. In 1109 the monastery of E(
was converted into a bishopric, and Hatfield becam(
Bishop's Hatfield which is its administrative name to th(
day. The bishops had a residence at Hatfield which was (
41 built on a palatial scale by Bishop Morton towards the end (
the C15. Of this Bishop's Palace substantial remains su(
vive, close to the parish church, which is dedicated to (
Etheldreda, the patron saint of Ely. The palace becam(
Crown property after the dissolution, and in it Mary Tud(
and Queen Elizabeth I spent years of their childhood, bo(

ider conditions close to imprisonment. King James I,
uch impressed by Robert Cecil's palace of Theobalds on
e occasion of a visit suggested he should exchange it for
atfield, and Robert Cecil hastened to accept and took over
atfield in 1607. However, the old palace was gloomy and
t of date, and so Robert Cecil also hastened to pull down
ost of it and use the materials to build for himself a new
ouse as palatial as Bishop Morton's had been four genera-
ons before. This is how Hatfield came to possess its two
laces and its church of St Etheldreda.

The church lies on a hill which, though not high, rises
fficiently above the Great North Road to give shape to the
hole cluster of houses which forms the old town. A new
atfield has grown up within the last fifty years or less on
e other side of the railway. It has been known as the New
own long before the Ministry of Town and Country Plan-
ng (now of Housing and Local Government) decided to
ake it the site of one of its projected 'new towns' or satel-
e towns of London. Its planning is now a joint enterprise
th that of Welwyn Garden City.

r ETHELDREDA. The parish church and its churchyard
lie on the top of an eminence. Down the hill run the main
streets. Behind the church to the E is the entrance to Hatfield Palace and one of the entrances to Hatfield House.
The W tower makes an impressive show from the high
road below. It is of four stages, with set-back buttresses,
a broad W door with quatrefoil decoration in the spandrels, and a four-light W window. The exterior of the nave
is a disappointment after this first impression. It looks
strikingly Victorian and was indeed rebuilt by *David
Brandon* in 1872. He changed the windows from Perp to
Dec, raised the roof, removed box pews and three-decker
pulpit, and (strangest alteration of all) narrowed the chancel arch. In spite of all this the general impression of the
interior is interesting, with its broad nave and the vistas
through into the various openings of the E parts. These
are in a more genuine condition and architecturally very
remarkable. The church possesses a transept with the

unusual adjuncts of two W chapels, and a chancel with
C15 S and a C17 N chapel. The chancel, transepts, and
transept chapels are the oldest surviving portions. The
date from the C13, as can be seen from the inner jambs
the chancel E window with nook-shafts, the chancel Pis
cina, the blocked E lancet window in the S transept, an
the blocked trefoil-headed larger opening to its N, and th
surprisingly splendid arch between S transept and
chapel. This has trefoil responds with big dogtoot
decoration between the shafts, large stiff-leaf capitals, an
a complex arch section. The C15 added the W tower an
the S chapel. Its arcade towards the chancel is unusual
ornate. Instead of the customary four-shaft-four-hollo
section the pier has four triple-shafts and above the ho
lows of the diagonals demi-figures of angels holdin
shields. The arch from the S chapel to the transept (whic
cuts into the C13 trefoil opening) is triple-chamfered an
has no capitals between jambs and voussoirs. It looks as
it belonged to the C14, in which case a S chapel prior
the one now existing must be presumed.

Finally in 1618 William, Second Earl of Salisbur
built the N chapel as a mortuary chapel to hold his father
tomb. The SALISBURY CHAPEL is the only part of th
church which is stone-faced. Its windows are still entirel
in the Perp tradition, but the three-bay arcade to th
chancel has tall Tuscan columns (cf. Watford, 1595). Tw
bays are original, the third was added in the C19. Th
columns are of Shap granite, a material which was on
coming into favour at the end of the Tudor era. The in
terior of the Salisbury Chapel was lavishly adorned by th
third Marquis in 1871. The artists employed were Italian
(cf. Hatfield House). There is plenty of Salviati mosa
and of alabaster used (the latter notably for the blin
arcading of the N and E walls). The W and S openings a
filled by exquisite iron gates of early C18 Flemish wo
which were brought by the third Marquis from Amie
33   Cathedral. In the chapel stands the MONUMENT T
ROBERT CECIL, First Earl of Salisbury, † 1612. It wa
ordered by the second Earl from *Simon Basyll*, and th

sculptures on it are by *Maximilian Colt*. The monument is
entirely in the Dutch tradition, established by *Tommaso
Vincidor* in the Nassau Monument at Breda. The Earl
lies on a black marble slab supported by four kneeling
allegorical figures: Faith, Justice, Fortitude, and Pru-
dence. One of these has her breasts bare, a reminder
of the distance which European civilization had travelled
between the time when the church and when the chapel
was built. But behind the four Virtues, below the effigy
of the Earl in his full State dress, lies a skeleton on a
rough straw mat, and that rude reminder of the vanity
of worldly glory takes one back to the late Middle Ages. –
In the same chapel are, moreover, the following MONU-
MENTS: A knight in armour, his chest covered by his
shield, C13. – A body in a shroud on the floor; he lies
relaxed, the attitude and the mastery of handling might
be Italian. It is the effigy of Sir Richard Curle, by
Nicholas Stone, 1617. Stone wrote in his notebook:
'I mad a pector lieng on a grave ston of gre marbell
for Mr Corell of Hatfield for which I had £20.' – The
Third Marquis of Salisbury † 1903, Prime Minister to
Queen Victoria, bronze by *Sir William Goscombe John*,
replica of the monument in Westminster Abbey.

OTHER FURNISHINGS. PULPIT. By *A. E. Richardson*, 1947. Polygonal, with plain wooden panels with
coloured shields. – ORGAN GALLERY. By *W. H. R.
Blacking*, 1927. On Tuscan columns, arranged so as to let
the light from the w window come in unimpeded. – COM-
MUNION RAILS. C17 with broadly twisted balusters. –
CHANDELIER. Brass, given in 1733 (s chapel). – STAINED
GLASS. Nothing medieval, but a good cross-section
though Late Victorian glass. Infinitely the best the s
transept window by *Morris & Co.*, designed by *Burne-
Jones*, 1894. It has a purity of glow, with its typical prevalent green and its peacock blue and rose-colour, never
achieved by any other glass before the early C20. – Chancel E window and N chapel E window by *Clayton & Bell*,
c. 1870–2. – The N windows of the N chapel and the E
window of the s chapel by *Burlison & Grylls*, the former

1881, 1894, 1899, the latter, to the design of *Temp.
Moore*, 1902. – PLATE. Two Chalices and Patens, tw
Flagons, two Almsdishes, and a Spoon, all dated 1684 an
all made for the Coronation of James II. – Cross an
Candlesticks in the S chapel, designed by *Temple Moore*.
Processional Cross in the same chapel designed by *A. I
Richardson*. – MONUMENTS (other than those in Salisbur
Chapel). Brass to Fulke Onslowe † 1602, inscriptio
on stone tablet (chancel, N wall). – Sir John Brocket
1598, very simple standing wall monument, withou
figures. Sir John was a merchant; yet his helmet i
suspended above the tomb. – Dame Elizabeth Brocke
† 1612 and his mother. Big standing wall monument wit
the two ladies stiffly reclining, propped up on thei
elbows, one behind and above the other. The backgroun
architecture flat and not too costly. – Sir James Reade an
his son John, by *Rysbrack*, 1760. Two busts, and above
portrait medallion against the usual obelisk. By the side
two big beautifully carved adult cherubs with large wings
– Thomas Fuller † 1712, standing wall monument wit
inscription on drapery and two putti l. and r.; not of hig
quality. – Several late C18 to early C19 epitaphs high u
in the nave, particularly fine the Heaviside Monument b
Thomas Banks, 1787, the side pieces later. In the centr
two female allegories of Death (a reversed torch) an
the Caduceus, the symbol of Medicine.

CHURCHYARD GATES. Magnificent ironwork taken t
Hatfield from St Paul's Cathedral. They were mad
about 1710.

BISHOP'S PALACE. What remains of Bishop Morton'
Palace is the foremost monument of medieval domesti
architecture in the county and one of the foremost monu
ments of medieval brickwork in the country. It is no mor
than one wing of a palace built round a courtyard and i
addition the gatehouse range to its W. The palace wa
built in this form *c.* 1480–90. It is known in the form i
had immediately before its destruction from a drawing o
c. 1608. It had then the surviving hall range as its W range
and N, S, and E ranges with exterior details and interna

arrangements clearly no earlier than the Elizabethan age.
The hall range is a brick building *c.* 230 by 40 ft with projecting porches on the W and E near the centres of the
sides and buttresses of the C19. The windows are of two
lights under hood-moulds; not large. The original tall
bay window at the dais end is blocked up. The dais was at
the S end of what now appears to be the Hall. This went
originally only as far as the porches. To the N of these
were the Kitchens and Offices. The porches have four-
centred entrances, and that of the W front a stair-turret
rising higher than the porch itself. At the top of the
porches are parapets on brick corbel-tables. The roof of
the hall is a splendid specimen of late medieval timber
construction, with the principals resting on carved stone
corbels, the arched braces moulded, the collar-beams
cross-trussed, and with ogee-shaped wind-braces in two
tiers between the principals. The rooms adjoining the
Hall on the N and S are gathered under large cross-gables.
The gatehouse range is simpler, with stepped end-gables
and brick windows similar to those of the hall range.

The hall range was converted into stables in 1628 and
remained in use for that purpose until the C20. To its N
an early C19 Gothick range, similar in style to the contemporary work at Hertford Castle.

ATFIELD HOUSE. Hatfield House was built by Robert
Cecil, first Earl of Salisbury in 1608–12. The W wing was
gutted by fire in 1835 and redecorated by the second Marquis († 1868). He also did much redecoration in other
parts of the house and was followed in this by the third
Marquis (the Prime Minister, † 1903). The house is the
most important mansion in the county and one of the four
or five most important Jacobean mansions in England.

In plan Hatfield House does not at first sight seem to
be anything out of the ordinary. It keeps to the Elizabethan tradition of the E-shape. In size, however, it is
unusually large for that plan type (*c.* 300 by 150 ft). The
wings are thus designed to have a thickness of two and at
their ends even of three rooms. These ends are emphasized by square angle turrets. The wings face what

was originally the approach road from London. Recesse‹
between them along the front of the main range lay a›
open loggia, closed by the second Marquis in 1846 an›
converted into an Armoury. Such loggias were becomin›
fashionable in England just in those years in which Rober‹
Cecil built Hatfield. Other examples are at Cranborne i›
Dorset and Holland House in London. Neville's Court a›
Trinity College, Cambridge, can also be regarded as
parallel. There is in fact documentary evidence to sugges›
that the loggia was an afterthought conceived while con›
struction of the house went on. The loggia has round›
headed arches separated by Roman Doric pilasters busil›
decorated with strapwork as are also the spandrels. Abov‹
it runs the Great Gallery with mullioned and transome‹
windows separated by pilasters and a crowning strapwor›
balustrade. In the centre of the loggia rises the three›
storeyed porch with coupled free-standing superimpose‹
columns of the Roman Doric, Ionic, and Corinthia›
orders. There is again a lavish display of strapwork an‹
similar fanciful decoration, finishing on the top with ›
balustrade with squashed bulgy pilasters and a larg‹
carved date, 1611. The wings have larger mullioned an‹
transomed windows for their various bays. Entrances int‹
the wings are also roundheaded, though those to th‹
turrets and some in the loggia still use the four-centre‹
form (one of the few survivals of Perp traditions).

In contrast to the sumptuous display on the s side, th‹
N side is surprisingly bare and matter-of-fact. Save for th‹
central doorway and the fine, tall, square, stone cupol‹
above the centre there is practically no decoration, jus›
the smooth brick walls with large many-mullioned an‹
transomed windows on two floors and an attic floor abov‹
with small low windows. The squareness and horizon›
talism of all this strikes one as curiously modern in th‹
c20. While the N and s fronts are not strictly symmetrica›
in the E and W sides the designer has made an attempt a›
compositions complete in themselves.

We are in the fortunate position at Hatfield to kno‹
who the designer was. His name is *Robert Lyminge*. H›

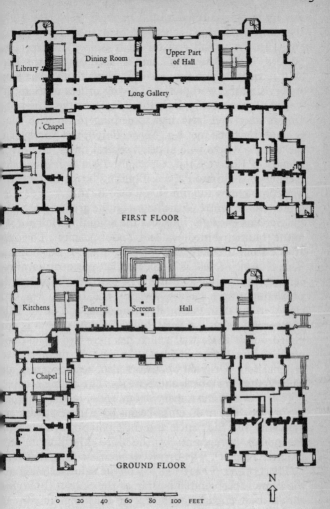

FIRST FLOOR

GROUND FLOOR

N

HATFIELD HOUSE

was by trade a carpenter, and he went from Hatfield t Blickling in Norfolk, where he died and was buried i 1628. In the parish register he is called 'architect an builder' of Blickling Hall, and as according to the Hat field records he also provided drawings there apart from supervising the workmen and giving orders to them, h was in all probability the creative work on the elevation: Others may well have had something to do with mor general decisions too, e.g. *Simon Basyll*, the Surveyor the King's Works who appears several times, and diver friends of Robert Cecil, especially *Thomas Wilson*, late Keeper of the State Papers. Building began in 1608 an was complete by the time Cecil died in 1612.

Across the centre of the house on the ground floor run the Screens Passage. This and the adjoining Hall are sti in the traditional medieval and Tudor position. The ope arcade from the Screens Passage to the l. is not origina The SCREEN itself is a spectacular piece of Jacobea carving, immensely skilful and of barbaric profusion. I projecting upper gallery towards the HALL was onl closed in the C19. Facing it, at the other end of the Hal is a second gallery, a very unusual feature. This is co belled out of the E wall which has here two stone door ways to the Great Staircase. In one of them still a original door. Original woodwork also, besides screen an gallery, the long tables, and benches. The ceiling is cover not, as was still customary about 1600, of the hammer beam type. The main cross-beams have fine fretwork an pendants, but the panels and their painting are the wor of Italians brought in by the third Marquis in 187 (painter *Taldini*). The fireplaces also date from that tim

The GREAT STAIRCASE is of the same richness an the same superb craftsmanship as the Screen. In style should be compared with that at Blickling. It runs u on three sides of a narrow rectangular open well and ha elaborate tapering banisters and newel posts covere with strapwork and pretty figure decoration (one who: post has trophies with garden tools and a little figure of gardener in relief). The posts are crowned by lion sup

porters and naked putti carrying musical instruments and
other objects. The staircase ceiling belongs to the remodelling campaign of the second Marquis. E of the
Staircase is the SUMMER DRAWING ROOM, specially
well preserved, except for the C19 fireplace. The Organ
was bought for the Chapel from a Dutchman in 1609 at
the enormous price of £1,084. S of the Drawing Room are
the YEW ROOM and the MORNING ROOM with an
original fireplace. The ARMOURY, originally open to the
s (*see* above), has a set of important tapestries not belonging to the Jacobean house. It represents the four seasons
and was made by *Sheldon* in 1611. The ceiling is C19 but
the stately stone doorway to the Screens Passage is
original. – At the other end of the Armoury lies the
CHAPEL facing the courtyard with a large E window with
two transomes, the only one which has still rounded heads
to its individual lights. The window is filled with the
original Flemish stained glass; and the biblical pictures
presented by Sir Henry Wotton to Cecil are also original.
They are of the Venetian school. As for the rest, only the
arcading of the Chapel Gallery is Jacobean, everything
else was redone by the third Marquis and his Italian men
between 1869 and 1880.

The w part of the main range contains serveries and
gives access to the KITCHENS which are in the basement,
not a unique but an unusual position in Elizabethan and
Jacobean times. The secondary staircase here, called the
ADAM AND EVE STAIRCASE, was remodelled in the C19
but retains a fine door surround of *c.* 1700 on the first
floor. The largest room on the first floor is the LONG
GALLERY, about 180 ft long. Halfway down a branch
leads off at right angles running across the centre of the
house and opening towards the Hall. It is doubtful
whether this has always been part of the Long Gallery or
whether it was not originally divided off, as were indeed
the two ends of the Gallery which are now marked by
columns. It is also not certain, it seems, how far the ceiling and the fireplaces are original. The rooms to the w of
the S–N branch of the Gallery are the DINING ROOM

(C19, with a C17 big fireplace brought to Hatfield fro[m]
Quickswood, another Cecil house) and then, beyond th[e]
Adam and Eve Staircase, the LIBRARY (very restraine[d]
marble fireplace with a mosaic portrait of the first Ea[rl]
made in Venice, 1608). At the E end beyond the Gre[at]
Staircase is KING JAMES'S DRAWING ROOM, with [a]
new or much renewed ceiling and a magnificient fir[e]
place no doubt by *Colt*. The large figure of the King [is]
not of bronze; it is painted to look bronze. The idea [of]
such a standing figure above a fireplace is taken fro[m]
Blondeel's grander composition at the Greffe at Bruge[s.]
The fireplace from the Summer Dining Room on th[e]
ground floor is now in KING JAMES'S BEDROOM. The[re]
are several more original fireplaces in other rooms.

The gardens were begun at the same time as the house, an[d]
that to the E, though completely redone in the C19, co[n]
veys a good idea of the design of a Jacobean garden. Th[e]
original fountains were devised by the celebrated *Solom[on]
de Caus*, and plants were bought by the equally cel[e]
brated *John Tradescant*. The terrace on the S side has [a]
handsome brick balustrade. To the W of the house in th[e]
gardens is a large C18 RELIEF of Queen Elizabeth I an[d]
her Courtiers which comes from the Royal Exchange. T[o]
the N the C19 approach drive connects the house with th[e]
railway station. At the station end is a decorative GATE [of]
terracotta and wrought iron and a seated STATUE of th[e]
third Marquis († 1903) by *Frampton*.

Farther away in the Home Park is the RANGER'S COT[]
TAGE, timber-framed, early C17, but refaced with bri[ck]
later in the century. The whole of the park is 530 acres i[n]
size, the largest in the county.

THE TOWN

From the churchyard start the main streets down the hi[ll]
towards the Great North Road: Church Street and Fo[re]
Street. At the beginning of CHURCH STREET, ove[r]
looking the churchyard, Nos 2–4, a group of half-timbere[d]
late C16 houses with the upright timbers exposed. Th[e]
other houses in the street are of minor interest. FOR [THE]

STREET is a perfect example of the self-respecting street 6b
in a small Georgian town, with its visual charm considerably increased by the stepping down of the houses to
follow the descent of the street. Nos 2–4 are one mid C18
composition of fifteen bays, almost entirely plain and thus
ideal as a foil to the church which it faces. Then a gap and
at the corner THE EAST INDIAN CHIEF, five-bay,
earlier C18. After that the Georgian procession marches
on without a hitch: No. 12, late C18, with an Adamish
doorcase, and so on to No. 20. Nos 16 and 18 are of
chequered purple and red brick. Meanwhile an accom-
paniment has set in on the opposite side: No. 3 with a
door-hood on lushly carved brackets; No. 7, still entirely
in the same tradition yet dated 1826, etc. Towards the
foot of the hill the houses are smaller and humbler, and at
the corner of PARK STREET appears the first of the
timber-framed and gabled type of the C17, the EIGHT
BELLS INN. In Park Street are more early houses, e.g.
Nos 9–11 with overhanging upper floor and symmetrical
outer gables. The old street ends soon, and the C19 sealed
it first by the fine Late Georgian house No. 38 which is
entirely in the country, not in the town style, and then by
the Viaduct arches of the third Marquis's station approach
to Hatfield House (with its Neo-Jacobean balustrade).
ttle else of interest in the old town. In the GREAT
NORTH ROAD No. 52, Late Georgian, of five bays and
two storeys with a porch displaying clustered Gothic
shafts, and No. 69, Late Georgian, with a door surround
in *Coade* stone *à la* Bedford Square, London. Off the
Great North Road in BATTERDALE the COLONELS'
HOUSE (the colonels of the Herts Regiment), late C17
brick, and the cottage at the back (in FRENCH HORN
LANE) which was the Herts Regiment's Armoury.
AST HYDE *see* p. 175.

THE NEW TOWN

atfield New Town had already developed to the NW,
before it was established as one of the 'New Towns' in
the sense of to-day. It had first grown in conjunction

with the de Havilland Factory (1935, by *J. M. Munro*
A little earlier still, the COMET, by *E. B. Musman*, 193
one of the earliest inns in England, built in the style of th
C20, without borrowings from the past. Of the new Ne
Town one neighbourhood is growing up in 1951–2: Rc
GREEN, just s of the Comet. The plans and most house
by *Lionel Brett* and *Kenneth Boyd*. So far about one-thir
of the new population lives in four-storey flats, the rest i
terrace houses. Density *c.* 16 dwellings to the acre. We
calculated vistas, and nice contrasts of yellow and re
brick with a certain amount of white plastering. Ma
it stay white. Also flats by *Hening & Chitty*.

H.C.C. TECHNICAL COLLEGE, Roe Green Lane. B
Howard Robertson, 1951–2. A large group of building
facing the Barnet by-pass road. The main block, inco
porating Hall, offices, and library is at the N W corner. Th
has a tall entrance motif to the w with the fashionab
projected and canted-out frame, which gives the gener
view from the s an odd outline. The block has a pitche
roof and a large s window running with a triangular hea
right up to the roof-pitch. The roof of the canted porc
is continued into the roof-pitch without any break. Th
classroom wings are arranged round courtyards with a
attractive connexion between them by a long straigl
N–S promenade across the courtyards and below the cros:
wings. Construction was with the aid of prefabricate
units with hardly any wet processes on the site. A larg
extension is going up to the s of the main group. Th
will be a Secondary Modern School. A piece of sculp
ture by *Barbara Hepworth* at the s w angle of the con
pleted buildings. Inside two decorative panels by *Be*
Nicholson.

HEMEL HEMPSTEAD

One of the most attractive towns of Herts, with its Hig
Street running up along a hillside so that on part of i
course one side lies several steps lower than the other, an
the church appears at a broad opening considerably belo

e street level. It is to be hoped that the development of the
ellite town (*see* below) will be carried out so that this
ecific character of the town and its many good Georgian
ouses will be preserved, as was indeed intended by the
anning consultant *G. A. Jellicoe*.

r MARY. A large church essentially Norman, the only one 10
in the county with the exception of St Albans. Nave and
aisles, transepts, crossing tower, chancel, and a small
room N of the chancel. The outer walls of flint are all C12,
though windows have in the C14 and C15 been enlarged.
The earliest part is the relatively low chancel. This seems 16b
to date from *c.* 1150 and is (a rarity in England) rib-
vaulted. The ribs and transverse arches have the simplest
roll mouldings and rest on wall shafts with scalloped
capitals. The narrow room to the N (had it originally an
apsidal E end, or was it a sacristy?) is also rib-vaulted. The
chancel N window is Norman with double nook-shafts. The
transepts and nave were built after the chancel. The
nave can hardly be earlier than *c.* 1175. It has six bays
with circular piers with shallow bases and capitals of
many varieties or ornamented scalloping. Little stylized
leaves occur and also the so-called water-leaf motif. The
arches are simply of two steps. The clerestory is contemporary, a rarity. The windows have nook-shafts inside,
and a billet-frieze runs all along the outside and around
the window arches. The W end of the nave has a doorway
of two orders with zigzag and leaf motifs in the voussoirs.
The crossing tower is extremely simple on the lower
stage, but opens in large shafted twin windows on the
upper stage with decorated voussoirs. The staircase turret
on the SE is circular in its upper stages. The tower is
crowned by a fine big leaded spire rising to nearly 200 ft.
In the S transept the W window is also Norman. Otherwise the windows are mostly Perp, except for those in the
S wall of the chancel which are Dec.
On its W side the church faces scenery still completely
rural. The E end lies below the High Street.
   The interior of the chancel was repainted in 1888 to

Bodley's designs. – The only early roofs are those of th
transepts. They are C15 and have arched braces wit
traceried spandrels. – STAINED GLASS. S chancel win
dows, 1858, by *Clayton & Bell*; S aisle, 1870, by *A
Gibbs*. – PLATE. Covered Chalice, 1563. – MONUMENT!
Brass (W end S aisle) to Robert Albyn and wife, very goo
work of the late C14. – Sir Astley Paston Cooper † 184
Neo-Gothic epitaph by *S. Manning*.

FRIENDS MEETING HOUSE, St Mary's Road, off the Hig
Street. Early C19; plain rectangle of purple and red bric
The front half domestic, the back with arched window
for worship. The burial ground lies by the side.

TOWN HALL, High Street. Neo-Jacobean, red brick wit
stone dressings. The centre 1851 by *George Low*, addi
tions of 1861 and 1868.

SOUTH HILL JUNIOR MIXED AND INFANTS SCHOO
(*see* Introduction, p. 28).

The HIGH STREET is one of the most agreeable streets o
Herts. It rises in a gentle curve, skirting the hillside an
opens about halfway to reveal the churchyard and churc
with its spire. The most characteristic element of th
street is its early C18 houses with their typical segment
headed windows. Most of these houses are of purple bric
with red dressings, but some are whitewashed. The bes
examples are on the E side: Nos 33–39, dated 1728 on
rainwater head; No. 51, dated 1725; Nos 65–69, date
1714; No. 71, dated 1730; and No. 81 (The Sun), date
1726. Earlier buildings are the group of rambling cottage
on the W side (Nos 60–68), and lower down No. 41, th
King's Arms, with half-timbered premises going far bac
into the side alley. These side alleys running up the hill t
the E are characteristic of Hemel Hempstead Hig
Street. To follow them means to realize how near th
countryside still is to the town. Of houses of later Geor
gian date the best is No. 1 with stone façade and an Adam
ish door surround.

To the N the town comes to an abrupt end at the N end of th
High Street. Big trees to the l. and r. indicate a change o
scene, and the best houses farther N are indeed right ou

in the country: MARCHMONT HOUSE on the road to Piccotts End and the Gaddesdens (early C19 with Greek Doric doorway *in antis*, and four pediments to street and garden sides), and GADEBRIDGE in its own grounds off Gadebridge Lane (*c.* 1800 with portico of giant Ionic pilasters; the whole front is eleven bays wide). s of Gadebridge, i.e. to the w of Hemel Hempstead in Bury Hill, LOCKERS COTTAGE (pretty, of timber-framing, brick, and plaster, with a weatherboarded extension) and LOCKERS (of two parts, the l. one C16 with gables, the r. one C18 with fine doorway). In Bury Road s of Bury Hill a late C16 two-storeyed stone porch with columns, known as CHARTER TOWER, is attached to a C19 building.

Only to the s does the High Street continue in an urban way. The MARLOWES running parallel with Bury Road is a street proper. Its architecture is chiefly early C19. The best individual houses are a little earlier: LITTLE MARLOWES HOUSE and OLD MARLOWES HOUSE, both three-bay, two-storey cottages. The rich doorcase of the latter is, however, Early Georgian. Near the s end of the Marlowes is CORNER HALL, a good timber-framed house with close-set uprights in the overhanging upper storeys; C15 or C16.

Further s, the new OFFICES for SIR ROBERT MCALPINE & SONS, by *H. J. Bebb*, 1951–2, are the first introduction to the New Town. They stand close to what is going to be the Town Centre; but of that not an indication can yet be seen. That is a matter for regret, here and in other New Towns; for only the urban character of a centre would endow the housing with a corresponding urban character. Without such a centre it tends to look suburban and indeed to be suburban. The office building for McAlpine's is an interesting, if a little mannered design, with a display of just too many unexpected motifs. Parallelogram of light brick. Three storeys with a recessed and shorter fourth ending to the s in a deep sun canopy with concave south edge. The s side of the storeys below with large window strips with concrete mullions and transomes. In contrast to this the long (w)

entrance side has lower window strips and above each
them slanting panes of a different shape related
curiously sloping ceilings inside. Concrete porch wi
canted supports.

Of the domestic quarters of the New Town one has so f
been specially developed: ADEYFIELD. The architect
H. Kellett Ablett. First house April 1949, thousand
April 1952, not a spectacular rate of growth. Density i
tended to be 20 persons to the acre, but still considerab
less. The terrace houses are nothing special. The mo
remarkable thing is the Shopping Centre. It is crosse
diagonally by a road with large pedestrian spaces in th
angles. Arcaded shop-fronts of simple design and fla
above. The E side is broken up into smaller detache
buildings which so far seems no advantage. But the Soci
Centre which is going up in 1952 to close the square
the S may alter that impression. S of it one long, tall
block of flats with weird, somewhat perverse details, a lo
zigzag parapet wall in the front, pram sheds with pebble
or cobbled fronts between this and the main doorway
and a centre balcony – just one – in the middle of th
whole composition, very Tecton in style. E of this grou
is the future recreation ground, and E of this a tw
storeyed H.C.C. SECONDARY SCHOOL (*see* Introdu
tion, p. 28). A PRIMARY SCHOOL a little way to the S
the Shopping Centre.

The beginnings of an INDUSTRIAL AREA (Addressograp
Multigraph, Ltd., by *Fuller, Hall, & Foulsham*, Alford
Alder, by *W. Leslie Jones*, etc.). 1½ m. E of the old churc
and ¾ m. E of Adeyfield, extending northward.

LEVERSTOCK GREEN *see* p. 155.

HERTFORD *

The county town, and all that the centre of a predominant
rural county should be, not too big (14,000 inhabitants
1951), with much of its visual traditions left and yet not
all a museum piece. The only architecturally unfortuna
thing is that of the five medieval parish churches of Her

* I have to thank Mr G. E. Moodey for many valuable contribution

rd, three have completely disappeared, and the other two
e without medieval remains.

ANDREW, St Andrew's Street, 1869, by *J. Johnson*; the
steeple 1876. The style is, according to Kelly, 'transitional between Early English and Decorated with some
intermixture of French Gothic'. Of the church preceding
Johnson's only the N doorway survives: C15, with hood-
mould on demi-figures of angels and the usual quatrefoil
decoration of the spandrels. – PLATE. Elaborately chased
C16 Chalice (Spanish?); C18 Chalice and Paten.

LL SAINTS. Off Fore Street to the S. To the S of the
church the open country seems to begin, with plenty of
fine trees. The church was designed by *Paley, Austin, &
Paley* of Lancaster in 1895, and completed in 1905. The
penalty of going to a Northerner for the design is that the
church, built of red Runcorn stone, is completely alien in
Herts. It is of good conscientious design and impressive
size, with Perp detail, a tall tower with taller stair-turret,
and some original features such as the hexagonal NW
porch. – STAINED GLASS. A vast seven-light E window by
Kempe, 1900 ('I am the vine, ye are the branches'). –
PLATE. Flagon, 1680; Chalice and Paten, 1696; Paten,
1725.

APTIST CHURCH, Cowbridge, 1906, by *G. Baines &
Son*. Neo-Perp with Art Nouveau licences.

RIENDS' MEETING HOUSE, Railway Street, 1670. Red
brick with two front gables and originally no doubt mullioned windows. On the ground floor there seem to have
been two doors towards the street. Well preserved woodwork inside.

HIRE HALL, 1768–9, by *James Adam*, Robert Adam's
brother. Large yellow brick block in the middle of the
town completely unadorned, unless the two curved projections on the N and S are accepted as ornamental. The
arcades at the back were originally open and gave access
to a covered market. Plain three-bay entrance on the E,
above which there was originally a grand Venetian window.
Fine top-lit rotunda on the upper floor in the centre.

COUNTY HALL, 1939, by *James & Bywaters* and *Rowla[...]
Pearce. Large group of Neo-Georgian buildings, the d[...]
tail with the freedom which England learned from Sca[...]
dinavia about 1930. Scandinavian are the precedents [...]
the slender cupola, the portico of fluted, not pilasters b[...]
pilaster strips, the ornamental motifs sparingly used a[...]
the cloister arcading to the r. of the portico.

CORN EXCHANGE AND PUBLIC HALL, Fore Street, 185[...]
by *Hill* of Leeds. The stone-faced front is like that of [...]
ambitious Methodist Chapel: three bays with gia[...]
Corinthian pilasters, large, tripartite, and arched, debas[...]
Cinquecento window between, and a big pediment. I[...]
mediately behind it the

COVERED MARKET, Market Street, 1889, by you[...]
Reginald (later Sir R.) *Blomfield*. That is the only rema[...]
able fact about it. One-storeyed, red brick with arcadi[...]
and glazed, raised centre.

CASTLE. Not much is left of the once renowned castle: t[...]
mount, about 22 ft high, some of the C12 flint curtain-wa[...]
of the Bailey with a postern gate and octagonal tower [...]
the SW angle, and on the N side of it a late C15 gatehou[...]
of brick with angle turrets on both sides. Its only decor[...]
tion is friezes of round arches on corbels, subdivided in[...]
twin arches. The gatehouse was much altered about 18c[...]
when the gateway was blocked, a porch made, a s wi[...]
added, and the fenestration regularized. So the buildi[...]
is now typical Gothicism of that date. Moreover t[...]
lawns and nice sited trees stretch down to the river [...]
make a picture of gentle arcadian charm.

HALE'S GRAMMAR SCHOOL, NE of All Saints. Early c[...]
building of brick with a porch on one front and a proje[...]
ing staircase opposite on the other. Gabled and wi[...]
brick windows under hood-moulds originally no dou[...]
with brick mullions.

CHRIST'S HOSPITAL SCHOOL FOR GIRLS, Fore Stre[...]
Founded as a school for the younger children of Chris[...]
Hospital, Newgate Street, London, in 1683. The origi[...]
buildings were completed in 1695. Of these the followi[...]
remain: The Gateway in Fore Street with lead figures [...]

Bluecoat boys, given in 1721, and at the N end of an avenue
of trees the Steward's House and attached to it on the w
the School Hall, formerly the Writing School, refaced
and embellished in the C20 but inside still with its original
coved ceiling.* Originally cottages or wards ran along the
l. and r. sides of the avenue, but these have been replaced
by larger buildings of 1900–2, at the time when the school
was converted into a school for girls. A hundred years
before (in 1800) an addition had been built to the w of the
School Hall, the Dining Hall, also much altered. It is a
large room on the upper floor with arched windows, and
in it are the wooden corbels and frieze from the Hall of
the original London Christ's Hospital which was pulled
down in 1902. The words and figures date from 1829. By
the entrance a fine Rococo bust of Thomas Lockington,
Treasurer of Christ's Hospital in 1707–16. It was brought
to Hertford from St Mary Magdalene, Great Fish Street,
London. More recent new ranges towards the NW: 1901
and 1906 by *A. R. Stenning*. The new library was built by
S. Tatchell in 1935. Facing Fore Street a long range of
red brick with pediment and niches containing figures of
Blue-girls. This is the original girls' school of 1778. To
the r. of the Entrance Gates the Grammar School and
Schoolmaster's house, both of 1783.

MORGANS ROAD JUNIOR MIXED AND INFANTS
SCHOOL (*see* Introduction, p. 28).

HERTS COUNTY HOSPITAL, North Road. The centre,
1833, by *Mr Smith* (probably Thomas). Stuccoed front of
seven bays and two and a half storeys with a three-bay
pediment embellished with carved statuary.

PERAMBULATION

The centre of the town is now Parliament Square, an open
space made only in 1821. From here streets run in three
directions: Fore Street E, the Wash, leading to Mill
Bridge, and St Andrew's Street N, Castle Street S and
then w. In PARLIAMENT SQUARE, as a characteristic

* The Bluecoat boy in the niche over the entrance comes from the
other Bluecoat School at Ware.

beginning, side by side Nos 12 and 14, the former C1
plastered with a big twin gable, the latter early C1
severely classical with good bold capital lettering in
Egyptian type. FORE STREET, the main street of Hei
ford, carries on this contrast. At its start, No. 1, thre
storeyed and stuccoed, with Italian Renaissance tri
c. 1850, like London city buildings of the same date. Th
at once Nos 3–13, a long C17 house with an exceptiona
richly pargetted façade, the motifs chiefly thick folia
scrolls. Some of it redone skilfully in the C20. Opposi
BELL LANE leads past an overhang storey on the l. anc
'manufactory' of the early C19 on the r., to BAILEY HAL
a stately early C18 mansion of five bays and two and a ha
storeys with parapet and giant angle pilasters. The thi
middle bays slightly projected and also flanked by gia
pilasters. Originally there was a big curved pediment
top. Pedimented doorcase with Tuscan columns agair
a rusticated background. An arched window above. T
entrance side has a doorcase with a segmental pediment
fluted Corinthian pilasters, and inside a staircase wi
delicate twisted and columnar balusters. E of all A
Saints churchyard the BRITISH SCHOOL OF INDUSTF
and the HARRISON ALMSHOUSES of 1850 and 185
both red brick, in a villa Tudor style. Also the ABF
SMITH MEMORIAL SCHOOL, of yellow brick, with r
brick and stone, 1861, and the COWPER MEMORI
SCHOOL, red brick Tudor of 1841. Back in Fore Stre
at the corner of Church Street, the SALISBURY ARM
late C16 to early C17, much restored and wholly r
pargetted, but with a good original Jacobean stairca
and an overhanging upper floor towards Church Stre
At the s end of Church Street, on the r., the OLD VICA
AGE, timber-framed and plastered, the front-door dat
1631. The Shire Hall faces the small MARKET PLAC
this, Salisbury Square, and another street widening
the N of the Shire Hall form a pretty, varied group
squares. Off Salisbury Square to the N, the short BUI
PLAIN leads to the gates of LOMBARD HOUSE, the hou
of Chauncy, the Herts historian of c. 1700, with an irre

ular, roughcast C17 back overlooking the river and weatherboarded storehouses, barns, and cottages, and an early C18 brick façade. A Jacobean overmantel in the Hall. On the way to Lombard House on the r. Nos 16–20 also of the late C17 and early C18. – Back to Fore Street and on the E. The keynote is plastered early C19 fronts, little (except the Post Office) jars acutely. The most interesting houses No. 42, an Egyptian front of 1825 with Egyptian shop window, Nos 76–78 of *c.* 1830, Nos 88–96, a typical early C18 brick house of six bays, and the Regal Café which looks Early Victorian but has original Jacobean panelling inside. The continuation of the Christ's Hospital buildings in Fore Street comprises the Blue Boy Inn on the corner of South Street and the former Brewery adjoining it. This has a semi-hexagonal front with a semi-hexagonal porch, rising to a height of 3 storeys; tiny flanking wings.

CASTLE STREET has a number of worthwhile timber-framed and plastered cottages, e.g. Nos 14–18, then No. 20, Georgian brick, and then LONGMORE'S of yellow and red brick, castellated, built probably *c.* 1840–50 (w half 1904). Opposite THE WALNUTS, mid C17 with C18 alterations. At the end facing us Nos 55–61, one composition with Nos 1–3 WEST STREET. Also one composition Nos 4–16 WATER LANE, off Castle Street, formerly, the MHLG suggests, outbuildings of the Castle. The N front of this group is Gothick of *c.* 1800, like the remodelled Castle gatehouse. Castle Street is continued by WEST STREET. Here No. 6, one of the usual two-storey, five-bay brick houses. The second and fourth upper windows have brick aprons. The house is dated 1719. It was the Brewer's house of a Brewery still operating behind. Next to it the weatherboarded maltings and then, No. 10, the maltster's house, reported late C18. No. 17 West Street has a carved door dated 1654 in the yard, No. 37 a Jacobean porch and door.

ANDREW'S STREET runs to the w. It begins with Nos 2–6, Georgian brick of different heights and designs, then cottages with overhangs, No. 22 with Early Victorian

bargeboarding, and No. 28, an ambitious design dat
1726: five bays, with giant Ionic angle pilasters and abo
the cornice an attic storey. The broad doorway has Io
brick pilasters, the window above a segmental pedime
reaching up into the cornice. This and the houses in t
immediate neighbourhood of St Andrew's Church are t
best of Hertford. To the w No. 51 of the later c17, timb
framed with broad plaster panels. Modillion frieze; la
c18 doorcase with pediment. To the E of the church t
OLD VERGER'S HOUSE, No. 43, with overhanging upp
floor and broad narrowly spaced vertical timbers. To t
N CECIL HOUSE, No. 52, with a charming elaborate c
Gothic porch. Off St Andrew's Street to the N O
CROSS with a FOUNTAIN composed of fragments
the demolished church of St Mary the Less. The cent
motif is a c13 lancet window with two nook-shafts a
dog-tooth ornamentation. The continuation of Old Cro
is COW BRIDGE, where on the l. is a Neo-Jacobean co
tage with a middle loggia. This is a replica of one o
signed by *H. Roberts* for the 1851 Exhibition as
example of the improved working-class housing dev
loped at the request of Prince Albert (cf. Abbots Lan
ley). At the corner of Cow Bridge and PORT HILI
group of early c19 yellow brick houses designed as o
composition, with central pediment and raised an
blocks. Another such example of early c19 planning
NORTH CRESCENT, or North Road, the N continuati
of St Andrew's Street. This is a row of semi-detach
houses, the whole row connected by lower links. At
beginning, opposite, stands NORTH ROAD HOUSE, w
a Greek Doric porch, which dates the composition a:
1825.

HERTINGFORDBURY

ST MARY. All 1890 in outer and largely c19 even in in
appearance. w tower with diagonal buttresses and reces
spire. Chancel, nave, and N aisle, c19 N chapel. The ch
cel actually dates from the c13, and the group of th
lancets with the middle one higher than the others, no
shafts and elaborate inner arches is the best piece

Roman Remains: St Albans, Sea-God mosaic

Scenery: Broxbourne and the river Lea

(a) *Scenery:* Ashridge Woods

(b) *Scenery:* The village green at Westmill

3

4

Scenery: Village street at Much Hadham

(a) *Town Scenery:* St Michael's Street, St Albans

(b) *Town Scenery:* Fore Street, Hatfield

6

(a) *Scenery:* Gazebos, Ware, overlooking the river Lea

(b) *Scenery:* Burton's Mill, Sawbridgeworth

Scenery. The railway viaduct, Welwyn.

Church Exteriors: St Albans Cathedral; Norman transept and crossing tower, Early English Chancel, Decorated Lady Chapel

Church Exteriors: Hemel Hempstead, Norman crossing;
the spire later

(a) *Church Exteriors:* East Barnet, a Norman village church

(b) *Church Exteriors:* Ware, a prosperous Perpendicular town church

Church Exteriors: Aldenham, a Perpendicular village church

Church Exteriors: Ashwell, an exceptionally ambitious Perpendicular village church (*Copyright Country Life*)

(a) *Church Exteriors:* Buntingford, 1614–26, the apse of 1899

(b) *Church Exteriors:* Ayot St Lawrence, 1778–9, by Nicholas Revett

(a) *Church Interiors:* St Albans, St Michael's church,
tenth and early twelfth centuries

(b) *Church Interiors:* St Albans Cathedral, Transept triforium,
late eleventh century

15

(a) *Church Interiors:* Weston, Crossing, twelfth century

(b) *Church Interiors:* Hemel Hempstead, Chancel, twelfth century

Church Interiors: St Albans Cathedral, Nave, late eleventh century and *c.* 1220–30

(b) *Church Interiors*: Baldock, early fourteenth century

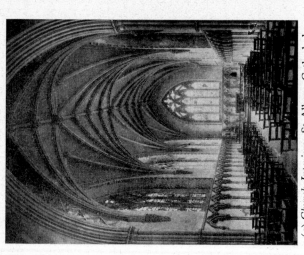

(a) *Church Interiors*: St Albans Cathedral, Lady Chapel, c. 1300–20

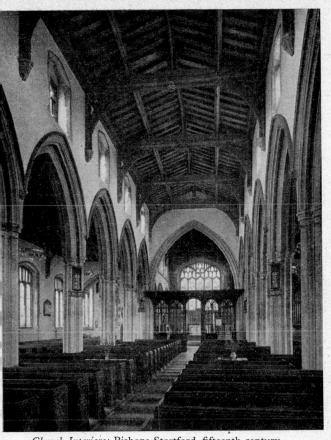

Church Interiors: Bishops Stortford, fifteenth century

(a) *Church Interiors:* Wyddial, Chancel chapel, 1532

(b) *Church Interiors:* St Paul's Walden, Chancel, 1727

(a) *Church Details:* Offley, thirteenth century capital

(b) *Church Details:* Ippollitts, Corbel head, probably
early fourteenth century

21

(a) *Church Details:* Stanstead Abbots, Porch, fifteenth century

(b) *Church Furnishings:* Gilston, Screen, late thirteenth century

Church Furnishings: Sandridge, Chancel arch and screen, *c.* 1100, late fourteenth century, and 1886

Church Furnishings: St Albans Cathedral, Iron Grille of the chantry
chapel of Humphrey, Duke of Gloucester,
late thirteenth century

Church Furnishings: St Albans Cathedral, Vault of the chantry chapel of Humphrey, Duke of Gloucester, † 1447

Church Furnishings: St Albans Cathedral,
Ramryge chantry chapel, *c.* 1515–20

Church Furnishings: Wyddial, Screen, early seventeenth century

Church Furnishings: Essendon, Font, of Wedgwood's
Black Basalt ware, 1780

Church Painting: St Albans Cathedral, Crucifixion, thirteenth century

(a) *Church Sculpture:* Sandridge, Reclining figure from the chance screen, late fourteenth century

(b) *Church Sculpture:* Ware, St John the Baptist, from the Font, fifteenth century

(a) *Church Carving:* Bishops Stortford, Misericord, fifteenth century

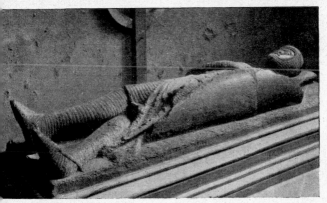

(b) *Church Monuments:* Eastwick, thirteenth century

31

(b) *Church Monuments:* Sawbridgeworth, John Chauncy † 1479

urch Monuments: Hatfield, Robert Cecil, first Earl of Salisbury
† 1612, by Maximilian Colt (*Copyright Country Life*)

Church Monuments: Watford, Sir Charles Morrison,
by Nicholas Stone, *c.* 1630

Church Monuments: Knebworth, Judith Strode, † 1660

(a) *Church Monuments:* Chipping Barnet
Sir James Ravenscroft + 1680

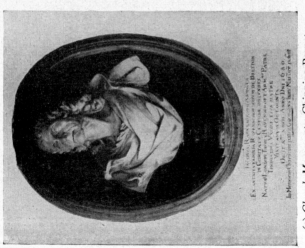

(b) *Church Monuments:* Flamstead, Saunders
Children + 1690, by William Stanton

(a) *Church Monuments*: Knebworth, Lytton Lytton, † 1710

(b) *Church Monuments*: Offley, Sir Henry Penrice † 1752, by Sir Robert Taylor

Church Monuments: Abbots Langley, Lord Raymond † 1732,
by Sir Henry Cheere

(a) *Church Monuments:* Flamstead, Sir Edward Sedbright † 1782
by John Flaxman

b) *Church Monuments:* Hatfield, John Heaviside † 1787, by Thomas
Banks ; the side pieces are later

(a) *Monuments:* Great Amwell, Memorial to Sir Hugh Myddleton, 1800, by Robert Mylne

(b) *Church Monuments:* Little Gaddesden, John William seventh Earl of Bridgewater † 1823, by Sir Richard Westmacott

Country Houses: Hatfield, Bishop Morton's Palace, *c.* 1480–90.
(Copyright Country Life)

(a) *Country Houses:* Shenley, Salisbury Hall, *c.* 1540-5

(b) *Country Houses:* Little Hadham, Hadham Hall *c.* 1575

(a) *Country Houses:* North Mimms House, *c.* 1600
(*Copyright Country Life*)

(b) *Country Houses:* Hatfield House, 1608–12
(*Copyright Country Life*)

Country Houses: Hatfield House, Frontispiece of the former entrance front, 1611 (*Copyright Country Life*)

Country Houses: Hatfield House, Staircase, *c.* 1612

(a) *Country Houses: Hatfield House, Screen, c.* 1612
(Copyright Country Life)

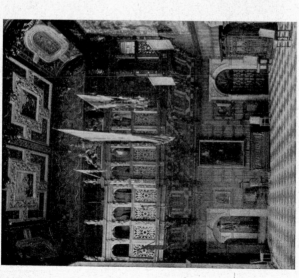

(b) *Country Houses: Balls Park, c.* 1640–5,
Porch c. 1720

46

Country Houses: Balls Park, Plaster ceiling, c. 1650 (Copyright Country Life)

(a) *Country Houses:* Mackery End near Wheathampstead, front 1665

(b) *Country Houses:* Tyttenhanger, *c.* 1655–60
(*Copyright Country Life*)

Country Houses: Tyttenhanger, Staircase, *c.* 1660
(*Copyright Country Life*)

(a) *Country Houses:* Beechwood, 1702 *(Copyright Country Life)*

(b) *Country Houses:* Gobions, Folly Gate, *c.* 1730, by James Gibbs

Country Houses: Moor Park, 1720, by Giacomo Leoni or Sir James Thornhill (*Copyright Country Life*)

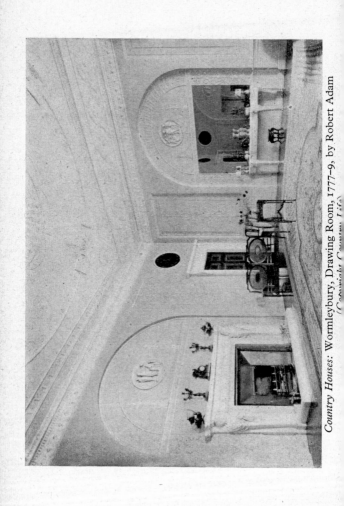

Country Houses: Wormleybury, Drawing Room, 1777–9, by Robert Adam
(Copyright Country Life)

Country Houses: Woodhall Park, 1777, by Thomas Leverton
(Copyright Country Life)

54

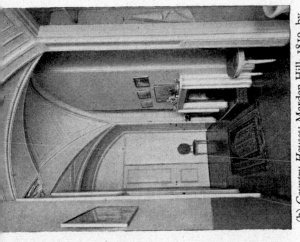

(b) *Country Houses*: Marden Hill, 1819, by Sir John Soane (*Copyright Country Life*)

(a) *Country Houses*: Ashridge, Chapel

Town Buildings: Thirlwall's Bank Tower, Derry, with St Columb's the first Protestant cathedral to be built in these islands

(b) *Town Houses:* St Albans, Ivy House, early eighteenth century

(a) *Town Houses:* Bishops Stortford, the Black Lion

57

(a) *Town Houses:* St Albans, Romeland House, *c.* 1710

(b) *Schools:* Berkhamsted, *c.* 1544

(a) *Schools:* Haileybury College, 1809 by William Wilkins, the dome by Sir Arthur Blomfield, 1876

(b) *Schools:* Old Hall Green, St Edmund's College, Chapel, by A. W. N. Pugin, 1845

(a) *Almshouses:* Buntingford, Bishop Ward's Hospital, 1684

(b) *Almshouses:* St Albans, Duchess of Marlborough's
Almshouses, 1736

Late Victorian and Edwardian Architecture: Bushey, entrance to 'Lululand', 1885 by H. H. Richardson

Late Victorian Architecture: London Colney, All Saints Convent, 1899 by Leonard Stokes

(a) *Late Victorian Architecture:* Chorleywood, The Orchard, 1900, by C. F. A. Voysey

b) *The twentieth century:* Welwyn Garden City, begun *c.* 1920, by Louis de Soissons and A. W. Kenyon

The twentieth century: Primary School at Boreham Wood
by the Hertfordshire County Architect's Department

medieval architecture the interior has preserved. –
BENCHES with carved ends in the Rococo taste by the
celebrated *Joseph Mayer* of Oberammergau. – PLATE.
Covered Cup, standing Paten and Flagon, 1675; Cup and
Paten. 1706. — MONUMENTS. Lady Calvert † 1622,
standing wall monument with recumbent effigy and a
kind of overmantel back. – Sir William † probably 1637,
and Lady Harrington, both recumbent, in shrouds. One
daughter kneels at their feet turned towards the altar.
Attributed to *E. Evesham*, but not of any striking quality.
– Spencer Cowper, a judge of the Common Pleas, † 1727,
an early work by *Roubiliac*; only a smallish epitaph but
the relief with Cowper in his judge's robes and the graceful figures of Faith and Justice standing to his l. and r.
are of great fluency and charm. – William Early Cowper
† 1764. A seated life-size allegorical figure with wings,
dull in her face and classical in her draperies, points to
cherubs and rays up against a pink marble obelisk. To the
r. a putto holds the Earl's portrait on an oval medallion. –
Thomas Francis de Grey Earl Cowper † 1905. Tomb-
chest with recumbent effigy, by *Henry Poole*, 1909. – The
high iron railings of the Cowper (N) Chapel are dated
1891. – In the churchyard big plain raised sarcophagus to
Sarah Lady Cowper † 1719.

OOLMERS or WOOLMER PARK *see* p. 279.

HEXTON

T FAITH. Early C19, except for some details of nave and w
tower. The latter has recently partly collapsed. The nave
piers are circular on the s, quatrefoil on the N side. Can
that be a capricious C19 invention, as the Royal Commission seems to believe, or must one assume a nave and
aisles of *c.* 1300? Box pews and a reading desk placed
symmetrically. The s chancel chapel is nice pre-archaeo-
logical Neo-Gothic, complete with vault and the Com-
mandment Boards, etc. – PLATE. Pieces of 1818–27.
which probably dates the restoration of the church. –
MONUMENTS. Plain tablet to Peter Taverner † 1601 and
his wife, who 'was a grave, prudent, provident, above her

H—7

sexe learned, and religious matron'. – One epitaph
1845 by *Gaffin*.

RAVENSBURGH CASTLE, 1 m. SW, on Barton Hills. Ir
Age hill-fort on the summit of the Chilterns, naturally c
off on three sides by steep slopes. It is oval, 22 acres in e
tent, 1,435 by 695 ft. The ditch around the camp measur
40 to 60 ft, while the bank is 16 to 18 ft high. On the
side is a double ditch, and in the NW corner is an entranc
marked by the bank on one side curving inwards, on tl
other outwards.

HIGH BARNET *see* CHIPPING BARNET

HIGH CANONS *see* SHENLEY

HIGH CROSS

ST JOHN THE EVANGELIST, 1846, by *Salvin*. Grey stor
with a SE steeple and a red brick Vicarage behind. Arch
tecturally not specially interesting, but exhibiting an in
teresting contrast between the STAINED GLASS of the
and W windows. That in the E by *Kempe*, an early work
1876, with his typical full forms and rather overdor
yellows. That on the W was designed by *Selwyn Image* an
dates from *c.* 1893. It is most extraordinary for that dat
evidently with knowledge of what Burne-Jones had dor
for Morris & Co. windows, but entirely original in tl
sombre glowing colours and the rather mannered, Raver
nesque central figure of Christ. The diagonal trails
leaves above and below the figures are charming, as ar
all the decorative features. The window might easily t
mis-dated as modern English work of *c.* 1930.

HIGH DOWN *see* PIRTON

HIGH TREES
1½ m. S of Great Munden

HIGH TREES FARM. Timber-framed and plastered hous
of two storeys, probably of *c.* 1600. Inside the Hall Scree
is preserved, not a frequent thing in Herts. Its approx
mate date is 1650.

HIGH WYCH

JAMES, 1861, by *Pritchett* (GR). A perversely ugly church, but as original in its handling of Gothic forms as anything in the Art Nouveau of forty years later. Flint, with red brick and stone dressings. Asymmetrical circular turret, polygonal above and ending in a spirelet. Very big, low-starting roof. S porch with an apsidal W bulge. Interior of yellow brick with red brick trim and much surface decoration at the E end. Thin circular aisle piers with big, square, richly and naturalistically foliated capitals. Pointed arches. The School next door also by *Pritchett*. Even the churchyard wall rises oddly at the gates.

HILFIELD see BUSHEY

HINXWORTH

ST NICHOLAS. Nave without aisles, low W tower with angle buttresses, chancel of C18 brick. The rest is mixed stone and flint. S porch with three-light windows as at Ashwell. Inside the church two niches for statues, one on the E side of a N window, the other in the SE corner of the nave. – BRASSES. Man and woman, mid C15 (chancel N wall). – Man and woman, nearly 4 ft long with, below, individually cut and mounted figures of six children. Late C15, unusually good, believed to be John Lambard † 1487, Alderman of London.

INXWORTH PLACE. One of the best preserved C15–C16 stone (clunch) manor houses of Herts. Rectangular block with SW wing. Originally perhaps H-shaped. Several C15 doorways and two to four-light straightheaded windows with the individual lights pointed and cusped at the top. In addition later mullioned and transomed three-light and four-light windows. – Elizabethan improvements.

HITCHIN

Hitchin is without doubt, next to St Albans, the most interesting and visually most satisfying town of Herts. It has not only plenty of good timber-framed and gabled as well as

C18 brick houses, but very little to spoil the harmony of these two types. There is indeed not a shop nor an office building in the centre of the town which seriously jars, especially nothing on a wrong scale. Moreover the town has kept its medieval plan virtually without interference, a real market square (rare in the county) with parallel streets running off at the angles to the N and S. The church lies back with its E end to the river, and one street runs parallel with the other on the other side of the river terminating the town on that side.

ST MARY. The church is different from all other Hert parish churches in that it is evidently a building representing the commercial wealth of a late medieval town. As in most English towns the source of the wealth was wool. The building has a nave and aisles of five windows and chancel and chancel chapels of five windows, the chancel chapels projecting exactly as far as the chancel. Thus the E view, from where the town has opened it up to the nicely landscaped river, is of three parts with their large 5-light windows, the aisles low-pitched with battlements, the chancel flat-topped with angle pinnacles and battlements. The church is in fact embattled all round, one of the usual ways to express importance and money spent. The most spectacular piece is the S porch, two-storeyed with an staircase turret, two bays, window openings on the W and E sides, an elaborate lierne-vault inside, an inner doorway of six orders of thin colonnettes, and an outer doorway with above it a three-light window and four niches with brackets for statues and a relief of the Trinity in the central battlement. The arms of the Staple of Calais prominently displayed on the S wall. This porch was probably paid for by Nicholas Mattock, a rich merchant of Hitchin. The N porch is also two-storeyed. The N and S windows of aisles and chancel chapels are all Perp, large, and of three lights. There are, however, other differences between nave and chancel. The nave is flint, the chancel chapels stone, the nave battlements are flint, those of the chancel renewed in brick. Much brick has also gone into repair work of the relatively low W tower (with spike) which

1 spite of its angle buttresses, was begun in the C12 and
ompleted in the C13. Under the angle buttresses early flat
uttresses have been found. The W door is obviously
.E. (two orders of shafts with moulded capitals and
oussoirs of complex section), the windows on the bell-
tage are also E.E., the stair-turret starts rectangular,
efore it becomes polygonal, and the treble-chamfered
ower arch towards the nave can well be of the C13 too.

The general impression of the church from outside is
ne of comfortable spaciousness, an impression which the
nterior bears out. Nave arcades of octagonal piers with
ouble-chamfered arches, early C14, with a clerestory
regularly added in the C15, four-centred chancel arch
rected at that time above the responds of an earlier one,
nd chancel of four bays with stone piers with shafts in the
nain axes and hollows in the diagonals. Irregularities at
ne E end of the chancel (where a charnel-house is built
nderneath) and at the junction of nave and chancel.
)ddly enough the nave has four bays but the aisles four
·indows and the porches, that is five bays, and the
hancel has also four bays and the chancel chapels five
·indows. No building dates are recorded.

Uncommonly fine series of ROOFS. The flat ceiling in
ne N aisle with its broadly and beautifully cusped panels
)oks early C14, the S aisle and S chapel, nave, and chancel
oofs are all C15. That of the S chancel chapel has prin-
ipals resting on stone angels and sub-principals with
)ng wooden angel-figures at their feet.

Uncommonly fine series of SCREENS. N and S chancel
hapel to N and S aisles and Parclose Screens to the chan-
el. The latter are, of course, simple, but the W screens
re richer than any other in the county and differ from
ach other in design. No standardization of tracery design
n the Parclose Screens either. – FONT. Stone, C15, with
nutilated figures under ogee canopies. – PULPIT. With
ngle buttresses and restored C15 panels. – BENCHES.
;ome with poppy-heads in the chancel. – DOOR. Impres-
ive S door with cusped panels, C15. – PAINTING. Adora-
ion of the Magi, Flemish, C17. – PLATE. Patens, 1625

and 1634; Salver, 1635; two Chalices and two Flago
1705. – MONUMENTS. Many, but none of great imp
tance. They will be given here topographically. Chanc
Brass to a priest, largish, late C15. – Brass to a man a
woman in shrouds with children, late C15. – Brass t
man † 1452, wife and children, large frontal figures
Brass to a woman, late C15, the figure much rubbed of
Brass to a man with three wives, late C15. – N Chan
Chapel: Three C15 tomb-chests with quatrefoil a
heraldic decoration, on two of these brasses (John Pul
† 1485; civilian and wife). – Brass to a shrouded you
woman with hair let down. – N Aisle: On window s
three defaced stone effigies, one mid C13, the other t
late C14. – Epitaph to Ralph Skinner † 1697, with scro
pediment, flowers and garlands, but no figures (by St.
ton, according to Mrs Esdaile). – S Chancel Chapel: Ma
epitaphs, notably to four Radcliffes, c. 1660. – S Ais
Brass to a shrouded woman with children. – Brass t
man with indent of wife. – Nave, w end: Mid C15 br
to a civilian and wife. – S. Aisle: Epitaph to Rob
Hinde † 1786, by *Chadwick* of Southwark, with a fem
standing under a palm tree.

HOLY SAVIOUR, Radcliffe Road, 1865, by *Butterfield*, a
in every way a full-blooded example of his style: E.E.
red brick with stone and blue brick dressings; no tow
only a w bellcote, the w front with two windows a
three buttresses so that one runs up the centre of
façade. Interior rather dark, as all windows have stair
glass. Short rectangular piers without capitals, and wa
decorated with sgraffito, white brick, red brick, and b
brick in complex diapers. Twice as many clerestory w
dows as arcade arches. Thin iron Screen with tre
arched tops to the sections.

For NONCONFORMIST CHAPELS and PUBLIC BUIL
INGS (Town Hall, Library), *see* Perambulation.

PERAMBULATION

The best plan will be to start at the MARKET SQUARE a
fan out from there. The Square itself has no specia

oteworthy old houses. The best are Nos 2–4, later C18
nd three-storeyed. On the w side the former CORN EX-
HANGE, Italianate of 1851, with big Venetian window
nd lantern turret and next to it one of the few houses at
itchin which look somewhat out of place: Burton's, the
ailor of Taste, with a façade à la suburban shopping
arade. The most interesting corner is at the NE end,
here a street seems to start like the others but there is
stead only a passage through to church and church-
ard. Here lie Nos 10–12 Market Place, a C15 timber-
amed house of eight windows width (with shop windows
n the ground floor), with gables and originally a court-
ard at the back. The CHURCHYARD is surrounded by
odest two-storeyed houses, the prettiest being the
eorgian terrace Nos 24–28. To the E of the church nicely
ept lawn with willow trees, the river made into a rec-
angular pool and behind it a raised terrace and a square.
ll this was done in 1929 (architects *Bennett & Bidwell*).
n the s side of this new square lies a long terrace of eight
hequer-brick cottages, and behind this, by the river, are
he BIGGIN ALMSHOUSES, early C17, on an unusual
lan, round a narrow irregular courtyard with, on one
ide, a Tuscan colonnade. On the E side of the Square
uns QUEEN STREET, the easternmost street of the pre-
ictorian town. In it mostly Victorian houses (No. 40, a
ice villa) and also two Nonconformist chapels and a
chool: BETHEL 1869 (style still like 1845), BRITISH
CHOOLS 1857, CONGREGATIONAL 1855 (yellow brick
ith alternatingly rusticated giant pilasters and pediment).
t the s end, facing what used to be called The Triangle,
he LISTER HOUSE HOTEL, a four-bay, three-storeyed,
tuccoed Early Victorian building in the Georgian tradi-
ion (after 1845).

IDGE STREET leads towards it from the w. In it at the
E end Nos 20–21, a C15 house (altered) with overhangs
ontinued into Queen Street, and original chimney-stacks.
n the s side Nos 30–40 a completely preserved row of
15–C18 houses, with Nos 31–33 the best: timber-
amed, with overhangs also towards the river, crossed

here by a small bridge. The streets leaving the Mar
Place towards the s run into Bridge Street.

These are Bucklersbury and Sun Street. BUCKLERSBU
is on the whole of minor interest (Nos 29–31, the WHI
HART, C16, with overhang on the l. and carriagew
higher overhang, and gable on the r.), but SUN STRE
has several houses of far more than local quality. On
E the ANGEL (overhang, renewed plastering between
timbers, carriageway on one side), then the SUN, an
cellent three-storey, nine-bay front of blue brick w
rubbed brick dressings with segmentheaded windo
and central carriageway. In the courtyard on the r. a l
half-timbered range, on the l. the Assembly Room (w
a Venetian E window) added in 1770. Between the t
unfortunately rises the glass roof of the hotel garage. N
to the Sun follows the CONSERVATIVE CLUB, La
Georgian of dark and rubbed bricks with a three-b
pediment. Opposite this group on the other side Nos 3
25 of c. 1700 (central first floor window with ornament
brick lintel), c. 1800 (with very pretty two-window sho
and c. 1820 (stuccoed, with wreaths to decorate the fri
of the cornice). On the E side follows Roslyn House,
early C19 adaptation of an overhang house (below t
overhang two bay windows on the ground floor). An a
nexe on the r. has an ogee-headed Gothick central wi
dow. The s end of Sun Street is on both sides of pleasa
quiet brick terraces. At their s ends both Sun Street a
Bucklersbury meet Bridge Street and its w continuati
Tilehouse Street.

TILEHOUSE STREET again is worth careful study. Only t
high lights can here be mentioned: No. 3 timber-fram
with herringbone pargetting; Nos 4–5 early C19, stucco
Nos 8–10 C17, with a gabled l. end and the rest of t
front recessed; Nos 11–12 C16 or C17, with a l. gable a
an overhang raised above the carriageway; Nos 13–17
later C18 brick, No. 19 C17, pargetted. Opposite No. 8
three-bay stuccoed early C19 house with doorcase wi
two wreaths in the frieze; Nos 83–84 Early Georgia
Nos 81–82, eminently interesting C15 survival. The

side had originally a canted bay window of three three-light Perp windows with four-centred arches, and one-light windows in the sides. The w end of the street is a very good start for anybody coming from Luton into Hitchin: Nos 70–75 on the l. (N) with a half-hipped end to the long mansard roof of the low cottages, and No. 35 on the r. (S), Late Georgian brick of four bays. In fact Tilehouse Street continues still a little into the Luton Road, and here lie No. 42, a more ambitious Late Georgian house with five bays and Ionic doorcase, built when there was no urban congestion, and then the BAPTIST CHAPEL of 1844 with two giant angle pilasters and four attached giant Tuscan columns. Metope frieze and pediment.

om the Market Place to the N runs the HIGH STREET, less attractive than the other principal streets of Hitchin. It is more affected by C20 shop intrusions, and such houses as Nos 22–23 of c. 1700 do not get their due. Nos 9–10 of the early C18 shows the coming of the three-storeyed façade. But three-storeyed buildings remained rare at Hitchin right down into the C19. The High Street is continued into BANCROFT, an early ribbon development far out of the confusion of the medieval town. It is one of the best streets of Herts, as wide as St Peter's Street, St Albans, and the High Streets of Berkhamsted or Stevenage. In it Nos 18–19 with a Late Georgian brick front with unpedimented doorcase on Tuscan columns. No. 21 a largish Late Georgian brick house of five bays and three storeys, No. 22 of white brick, early C19, and then Nos 26–27 of the early C18 (segmentheaded windows) with an amazingly grand doorcase displaying fluted Corinthian pilasters, and a decorated segmental pediment. The MHLG suggests convincingly that the doorcase may come from a bigger house. No. 34 is mid C18, two-storeyed, five bays. The doorway has a Gibbs-surround. The front is finished by a one-bay pediment. Opposite, Nos 114–116 are of the C15 or C16 with closely spaced vertical timbers and two gables (ground floor shop window, alas!); No. 107, late C18 with doorcase with fluted

Ionic columns, and Nos 105–106 with carriageway ar
asymmetrical gables. Then Nos 99–100, early C19 whi
brick with Greek Doric porch, and Nos 68–83, tl
SKYNNER ALMSHOUSES of two one-storey ranges alor
the street. They are dated 1670 and 1698.

Off the N end of the High Street turns BRAND STREET wi
the dignified stuccoed front of the OLD TOWN HAL
1840, by *Bellamy* (Italian Renaissance of the Bar
brand), and adjoining it the SUBSCRIPTION LIBRAF
(also 1840 with a small temple front and a closed Tusc:
porch) Opposite the NEW TOWN HALL, 1900–1, l
Mountford and *Geoffrey Lucas*, Neo-Georgian wi
lantern turret.

Individual houses: THE PRIORY, 1770–1. A mansion
stone with a noble Palladian S front with small centr
semicircular porch and two projecting wings, each tur
ing a large Venetian window towards the garden. The
side looks on to a courtyard which represents, and inco
porates fragments of, the cloisters of the Carmelite Prio
of Hitchin, founded early in the C14. On the W side a
two arches (without capitals to the piers) and on the upp
floor three small cusped one-light windows and two c
mullioned brick windows. On the N side four mo
cloister arches. The N front of this N range has an interes
ing façade of 1679, with a ground floor arcade on octagon
brick piers with round arches. The church lay probab
where the S range of the house now is. The whole house
still surrounded by a moat.

About 1900 outer suburbs began to spread with well-to-c
houses in gardens. They represent the usual Late Vi
torian and Edwardian styles. Two specially goc
examples of the red brick free Tudor version are by *Fr*
Rowntree: WHITEHILL CLOSE, Whitehill, and LAVEN
DER CROFT, Wymondley Road, the latter of 1906.

STRATHMORE AVENUE PRIMARY SCHOOL (*see* Intr
duction, p. 28).

HODDESDON

ST PAUL. Of the building of 1732 nothing will be notice
externally. But the interior of the nave can still give a

idea of it, a plain rectangle with flat ceiling and arched windows. The W front red brick with pediment. All the rest now appears in the form given to it in 1865 (chancel and chancel chapels) and 1888 (s steeple).

he centre of Hoddesdon is the triangle S of the church with the CLOCK TOWER of stock brick erected in 1835 (by *T. Smith*). From here streets run NW and NE (in the latter a five-bay, two-and-a-half-storey house of yellow brick, mid-Georgian with all the windows tripartite), and the High Street runs S towards London, part of that long ribbon which was already by about 1800 flanked by houses for a good deal of the way. The following deserve notice: the WHITE SWAN on the W side, long and low, with overhanging upper floor and a central bay resting on Tuscan columns to form a porch, and the BULL with a yet bolder overhang on pillars, and a big pediment. No. 76 opposite is a house of considerable historical importance, as its back wing is dated and shows the characteristic mid C17 motifs of one-storeyed pilasters along the whole front, and of a pedimented shaped gable. The date is 1637. On the same side No. 68 (MONTAGU HOUSE) is a big early C18 building. Five bays with quoins and the central three bays flanked by rusticated pilaster strips. No. 70 may have been part of the composition. HOGGIS HALL, No. 64, has remains inside of its C15 Hall (shaped beams, doorway). No. 56 is RATHMORE HOUSE, *c.* 1740, purple and red brick, of six bays, and with a doorcase on Roman Doric pilasters. The GOLDEN LION of *c.* 1600 has many exposed oak beams inside.

T MONICA'S PRIORY a little farther S was originally no doubt outside the village. It was the manor house of Marmaduke Rawdon, built in 1622. It has tall and stately brick E and W fronts with shaped gables. Five gables face w; in the middle is a two-storeyed porch, and to its l. and r. are two-storeyed bays. On the E front the centre is a tower which used to carry a cupola. Of interiors the most important are the Hall with plaster ceiling and the large staircase. A wing was added in 1880 in the style of the original building by *George & Peto*.

More Georgian houses farther s (Nos 48–50) with Gibbs su
rounds to the windows; THE GRANGE, early C18 b
altered, with segmentheaded windows and a semicircul
porch; YEW HOUSE with Cedar House and Brickwoo
House; LOWEWOOD (Public Library), mid C18 house
five bays and two storeys with pedimented doorcase an
C17 remains at the back.

1 m. NE of Hoddesdon quite on its own and in neglecte
surroundings the remains of RYE HOUSE, famous from
the Rye House Plot of 1683. What remains is the Gate
house of c. 1443: red brick with blue brick diapering. Th
doorway has a two-centred arch with quatrefoil decora
tion in the spandrels. The windows have brick hood
moulds. Upper projections on a corbel-table of inter
sected arches and two corbelled out oriel windows. To th
SW of the moat of Rye House the RYE HOUSE INN, wit
two bargeboarded gables and beneath them two com
pletely glazed bow windows with extremely pretty Gothi
glazing bars, part of a Victorian scheme of converting th
whole neighbourhood into a pleasure garden à la Vaux
hall and Ranelagh.

Close to Rye House a new POWER STATION is being buil
to the design of *Sir Giles Gilbert Scott* who establishe
himself for that kind of work with his Battersea Powe
Station. It is large, of pale pink brick and a little busy i
the details, of a style by now quite typical of Englis
power stations.

HOLWELL

ST PETER. Mostly by *Ewan Christian*, 1877 (GR), but ap
parently with the use of old materials. – Brass to Rober
Wodehouse † 1515 with no effigy but a chalice with wafe
and at the top instead of a coat of arms two wodehouse
or wild men.

OLD RAMERICK, 1 m. N. Handsome seven-bay, two-store
front of c. 1700 with parapet and hipped roof. The tilin
in a zigzag pattern.

HOPPERS HALL *see* DATCHWORTH

HUNSDON

﹍use and church lie close together and at some distance
﹍m the small village. For several reasons the church ap-
﹍rs indeed an appendix of the house.

﹍NSDON HOUSE. What remains, and is attractive neither
﹍n shape nor in decoration, is of the greatest historical in-
﹍erest. It is one-quarter or less of a great Tudor house. A
﹍ouse had in fact been built here by Sir John Oldhall
﹍bout the middle of the C15; but of that no visible traces
﹍xist. Then, about 1525, Henry VIII owned it and apparently rebuilt it. Engravings show the prior extent of
the buildings, and the Early Tudor brickwork in the
present structure shows what is preserved of Henry
VIII's time.* It is the following parts the: gatehouse at an
odd angle and surprisingly close to the main building,
some walls in the neighbourhood, and a small raised
summer-house or plaisance (cf. Hampton Court), and of
the house itself the V-shaped angle buttresses and much
of the masonry. The house was the projecting N wing of a
mansion of that E-plan so usual at the time of Queen
Elizabeth I and later, but still very rare under Henry
VIII. The main range ran N–S at the W end of the remaining wing, and at the S end another wing corresponded to
it. The Engravings show the house with big scrolly end-
gables and a cupola, so that one might say that perhaps
the extension to E-shape was due only to the C17. But Bar-
rington Court, Somerset and the outer front of Hampton
Court are both pre-Elizabethan and yet of the same plan
as the Hunsdon of the engravings. So Hunsdon must be
added to these early attempts at getting away from the
asymmetry of Perp house-planning. The central and S
wing were pulled down in 1804. Since then the interior
has been much altered, and the exterior also unfortunately has window surrounds, a new Jacobean veran-

* Mr Salzman quotes documents according to which bricks for the
﹍use were burnt in 1525 and the brick chimneys were completed in
﹍28.

dah, and other features which are evidently mid-Vi
torian.*

ST DUNSTAN. A small village church with interesti
Tudor and later additions. The church has a small u
buttressed W tower (with recessed spire), and a nave a
chancel. The windows are Late Perp, the tower arch
Perp too, though earlier. The best part of the church
the N porch, of heavy coarse timbers like a lychgate a
with elementary bargeboarding (cusps ending in an og
at the top). Of a pre-Perp building the re-used N chape
window gives evidence. It is early C14. The N chapel is
addition of the C16, and a S chapel followed about 16c
Both chapels are brick-built, with all window details al
of brick. – Not much need be said architecturally of t
interior; but the furnishings deserve close notice. – PU
PIT. Jacobean, with tester. – SCREEN. The rood scre
was Perp but only the dado survives. But early in the C
a bigger and more sumptuous screen was erected betwe
the nave and the new S chapel. It is the best example
the county of a Jacobean screen: with a panelled da
with Roman Doric pilasters, sturdy baluster columns ca
rying little arches, a broad cornice and a big pierced stra
work achievement on top. Behind the screen hi
FAMILY PEWS also with some Jacobean decoration.
COMMUNION RAILS, c. 1700, with twisted balusters.
STAINED GLASS. C15 bits in the tracery of the E windo
– PLATE. Chalice and Paten, 1660. – MONUMENTS. Bra
to Margaret Shelley † 1495, shrouded figure nearly 3
long, representation of the Trinity above (chancel).
Small recess with four-centred arch at top and cant
panelled sides and arch. The top is straight and crested.
is the monument to Francis Poyntz † 1528. The inscri
tion is in the newly revived Roman lettering, but the d
tail otherwise is still all Perp (chancel). – Brass plate
James Gray, park-keeper, † 1591, showing him aiming
a stag, while Death is aiming at him. Death says *Sic per*

* Mr W. Branch Johnson has drawn my attention to a diary en
of Mrs Calvert, wife of the then owner, who in April 1805 write
hear there is hardly a bit of old Hunsdon House left standing'.

(So I proceed; i.e. I do as you do) (nave N wall). – Big standing wall monument of alabaster to Sir John Carey † 1617 and wife. Black double columns to the l. and r. of a coffered arch. Achievements on top. The effigies lie side by side with folded hands. The sculptural quality is of the highest then available in England. The work may well be by *Colt* (s chapel). – Equally outstanding the standing wall monument to Sir Thomas Forster † 1612 (chancel), recumbent in Judge's robes under a low six-poster with scale-adorned ogee-shaped cupola. The ornamental detail, especially ribbon-work, etc., is exquisite. – The C18 added some good epitaphs. Felix Calvert † 1713 (nave). The only figures are two small putti on the curves of the broken pediment and two brilliantly carved cherub's heads at the foot. – Opposite, Robert Chester † 1732. The same composition, also only with small figures. At the top what seems a fine relief. – Mrs Jane Chester † 1736 (chancel), medallion with lively head in semi-profile, the inscription below on a hung-up drapery.

HYDE HALL
1 m. NE of Sawbridgeworth

remodelling of 1806 of a square Tudor courtyard house. The remodelling is said to be by the younger Wyatt, that is *Sir Jeffry Wyatville*. The present fronts show nothing older than the C18. The five-bay, two-storey centre of the garden side seems to be the core to which in 1806 stuccoed additions with their giant pilasters with palm capitals were made. This latter style is clearly that of the s and the entrance sides. The courtyard was roofed in in 1806 and a staircase hall built which belongs to the finest of the period in the country. Extremely delicate design clearly under some *Soane* influence. Who was the architect? The name *Wyatt* has been given, but does not seem convincing. The Entrance Hall has a semicircular end screened by Greek Doric columns (and few but Soane used these in England in 1806? They repeat in the gate lodges). The Hall is square. The staircase is an uncommonly excellent addition in the style of the original. It

was done in 1920 by *H. S. East*. It goes up behind th
Hall starting with one central flight, turning into two, an
ending at right angles to the beginning on the galle
above the Hall. The gallery has sky-lit saucer domes an
an arched opening into the Hall. The Hall itself has a sky
light balancing on flat thin Soanian arches which rest c
pilaster strips (just as at Soane's Pitzhanger of 1805). Th
staircase continues with a second identical run from th
first to the second floor and then is covered by a segment
tunnel-vault.

In the garden, used as flower pots, some of the original Ion
capitals from the portico of *Smirke's* old General Po
Office in London.

ICKLEFORD

ST KATHERINE. Nicely placed amid cedar trees. Not ver
attractive plastered exterior. The interesting history c
the church becomes more evident as one enters. The
doorway and a blocked N doorway are C12 with inner zig
zag arches. The S doorway has in addition three orders c
scalloped columns outside and three orders of zigza
voussoirs. The W tower has one lancet window on the
side, the chancel one on the N side. The chancel arch
also clearly C13. Nave roof on stone corbels and S porc
C15; S aisle and S chapel 1859 (by *Sir G. G. Scott*).
STAINED GLASS. W window, 1898, by *Kempe*. – PLAT]
Cup, 1798. – BRASS. Thomas Somer and wife, late C1.
demi-figures (nave, E end).

IPPOLLITTS

ST IPPOLYTS. On an eminence above the houses of th
village. Rebuilt in 1879 with careful re-use of the ol
materials. Low W tower with much set-off angle bu
tresses. Nave and aisles with gabled N porch wit
decorated outer doorway (niches to l. and r. and above
and S porch of brick and timber. Windows in the chance
and S aisle and a doorway in the N aisle are clearly of th
early C14 (*see* the Dec window). The nave arcades belon

to the same date. They are cut into a much older wall*
and have double-chamfered arches. The inner voussoirs
rest on remarkable broad-faced, broad-haired C14 heads. 21
The chancel arch is C15, but the Piscina shows that the s
wall at least must be E.E. – SCREEN. Only bits are old. –
PLATE. Chalice, 1634; Paten, 1639. – MONUMENTS.
Brass of 1594 with small kneeling figures (chancel). –
Effigy of a priest, C14 (recess in s aisle).
house to the w of the church with C17 gable and to the r.
of it a four-bay early C18 brick façade. The OLIVE
BRANCH INN has closely set timber uprights and an
overhanging upper floor.
VENUE FARM, Gosmore, ¾ m. w. five-bay brick front of
the C18.)

JULIANS *see* RUSHDEN

KELSHALL

ST FAITH. Perp, much restored in 1870. All embattled.
Quite a big w tower (diagonal buttresses, Early Perp w
window). Big two-storeyed s porch with NW turret. Aisle
and largish clerestory windows of Late Perp shapes. The
arcades to the aisles (four bays) have their piers with four
main shafts and four hollows in the diagonals, the latter
without capitals. The arches are two-centred. The tower
arch has compound responds with semi-octagonal shafts
with concave panels. In the E wall modern window and
two old brackets l. and r., an angel and a bearded face. In
the NW corner of the N aisle a curious niche 12 ft high and
only 1½ ft wide with hinges for a door. What can it have
been? The nave and aisle roofs are old and painted. The
painting is supposed to be based on old traces and gives a
good indication of the colouring of such roofs. – SCREEN.
Only the dado survives with four painted figures of saints,
C15, poor quality. – DOOR. The s door is probably
original including its lock, key, etc. – STAINED GLASS. E
window, 1868, good, under *Morris* influence. – PLATE.

* An C11 window with stone surround has been exposed in the s
wall.

Paten, 1685. – MONUMENTS. Brasses to Richard Ada
and wife, 1435; the figures *c*. 2 ft long (E end of nave).
Epitaph to E. Franklin † 1617, the usual kneeling figure
but to the l. and r.; instead of columns two figures
Faith and Charity; very Flemish.

RECTORY. Late Georgian five-bay front, stuccoed, adde
to an older house.

KENDAL'S HALL see RADLETT

KIMPTON

SS PETER AND PAUL. Large flint church standing to th
NE of the village. The exterior seems Perp, the interi
tells of earlier history. Low W tower with spike, nave wit
clerestory and hipped roof at the E end (when was this ur
usual feature introduced? In the C18?). N and S aisles,
porch of two storeys with outer stair-turret, S chanc
chapel, and lower chancel. Of all this nothing revea
motifs earlier than the C15 except the chancel E window
three cusped lancet lights under one two-centred arc
This is a motif of *c*. 1300 (renewed). And the masonry
the chancel must date back further still in the C13; fa
inside, the E window can be seen to have replaced simpl
lancet windows. Even they, however, are not the olde
evidence in the church. Directly one has entered, one se
that the whole of the long even N and S arcades of si
bays are of Transitional or E.E. date. Which of the two
it? There is no answer to the question. The truth a
proved by this village church is that the Transition
overlap into the E.E. style was more considerable an
important than is realized. All piers are circular, all arche
of the same complex moulding which must be later tha
1200, but of the capitals of piers and responds eight ar
scalloped with little bits of abstract decoration in th
individual flutings and six have fully developed stif
leaf, ranging from upright to diagonal. – The S chanc
chapel opens into the chancel with finely moulded arche
and a slim pier with the usual C15 section of four shaf
in the main axes and four hollows in the diagonals. Th

s aisle roof is also *c.* 1500. – SCREEN. C15, broad divisions
of four lights each, with simple Perp tracery. The coving
seems much renewed. – BENCHES. Some with poppy-
heads. A few of them have little faces at the lower lobes
of the poppy-head. – PAINTINGS. Remains of early C13
figures of angels in the jambs of the chancel lancets. –
STAINED GLASS. S chancel chapel, Lord Chesham
Memorial, 1885, with *Morris* influence. – PLATE.
Chalice, 1635. – MONUMENTS. Brass to a woman with
open hair, early C15 (chancel). – Thomas Brand, twentieth Baron Dacre, † 1851 : an E.E. blank arch with stiff-
leaf and dog-tooth decoration ; no doubt the design of a
notable architect.

KINGS LANGLEY

he village owes its name to a ROYAL PALACE on the hill to
e w, of which no more than a fragment of a flint wall with
ick quoins remains. It was here that Edmund of Langley,
th son of Edward III, was born in 1341. He was buried in
e adjacent DOMINICAN FRIARY, founded *c.* 1312. It was
dward II's favourite friary, and in it Piers Gaveston was
uried in 1315. Of the Friary a two-storeyed rectangular
uilding 76½ by 18 ft survives, incorporated in a private
chool. It was divided into two rooms and possesses a
umber of plain original windows and doorways. The
mb of Edmund of Langley was, at the time of the dis-
lution, transferred to the parish church.

LL SAINTS. Flint and stone dressings. Thick short w
tower with diagonal buttresses, battlements, and a spike.
Short nave with aisles and clerestory, lower chancel. C15
arcades with octagonal piers with finely moulded capitals
and double-hollow-chamfered arches. C15 tower arch.
The S chancel chapel has an arcade like the nave, the N
chapel a somewhat later arcade with stone pier of four attached shafts with four hollows in the diagonals. The
only indications of pre C15 architecture are the C13
Piscina in the chancel wall and the Dec two-light w window of the N aisle. – PULPIT. First half C17, with book

rests on three sides of the hexagon and tester. Elaborate carved panels and even more elaborately carved back. SCREEN. In the tower arch, C15, much renewed. – RERE DOS. Alabaster, designed by *Joseph Clarke*, 1878. STAINED GLASS. W window *Clayton & Bell*, 1894; aisle Queen Victoria Memorial Window, 1901, *Clayte & Bell*; W window *Powell*, 1908; in the S aisle one win dow (Mary and Martha), *Ward & Hughes*, 1876. MONUMENTS. Edmund of Langley, late C14 tomb-che with a display of heraldry instead of artistic genius. The are thirteen alabaster shields in all. – Sir Ralph Verne and wife (?), *c.* 1500, recumbent effigies on a tomb-che decorated with shields in richly cusped fields. – Brass John Carter † 1508 with wives and children. – Unname Brasses to two ladies, *c.* 1500 and *c.* 1600. – Large epitap to Mary Elizabeth Crawford † 1793, signed by *Bonor* (*inv.*) and *Westmacott* (*sculp.*). Long inscription and abov small medallion with weeping putto and garlands.

The High Street has a number of pleasant old brick house starting promisingly at the S end with the ROSE CROWN INN on the one side, the BLUE COURT HOTE on the other, the one brick with a pretty iron verandah the other a neat symmetrical three-bay early C19 villa stock brick.

BARNES LANE ESTATE. Cottages by *Yorke, Rosenberg, & Mardall*, 1950.

KINGS WALDEN

ST MARY. Flint with stone dressings. Externally, includin the W tower with angle-buttresses and a SE stair-turre mostly C15 and C19 restoration (by *Eden Nesfield & Norman Shaw*, 1868). The only remarkable exception the NE vestry of brick with three-light Perp window. This belongs to the early C17. But inside the N and arcade reveal a much older age. They are of the early C13 proof (just like those at Kimpton) of the long survival Transitional forms into the E.E. style. For the shor circular piers have capitals with slightly decorated sca lops as well as a variety of water-leaf and also with stif

eaf in two tiers. The arches are double-chamfered. The
chancel arch looks late C13. The chancel windows are all
renewed. – SCREEN. Two two-light sections on each side
of the entrance. Each light has as its tracery an ogee
arch and tiny Perp panelling above. – STAINED GLASS,
window by *William Morris*, 1867. Three arch-angels,
wonderfully clear and fresh in the design; none of the
mannerism of most Burne-Jones figures yet. The memorial tablet which goes with the window also evidently by
Morris. How noble and susceptible to the nature of the
glass-painter's material does such a window appear, if one
compares it with other Victorian stained glass, even the
work of a man like *Kempe* (*see*, for example, his E window
of 1901). – PLATE. Tankard, 1736.

NGS WALDEN BURY. Neo-Elizabethan, chiefly 1889–90,
by *Burmeister & Beeston*.

KNEBWORTH

MARY AND ST THOMAS. The church stands in the
grounds of Knebworth House, everywhere surrounded by
fields but within a stone's throw of the front terrace of the
mansion. The exterior attractive owing to its position but
architecturally insignificant: nave, chancel, C15 tower
(diagonal buttresses, SE stair-turret higher than the tower,
and spike), N chancel chapel (Lytton Chapel) added *c.*
1705 to house the new sumptuous family monuments.
The interior has a low Norman chancel arch with one
order of scalloped colonnettes and a blocked Norman
chancel N window. – ALTAR TABLE. C18 on classical
columns. – PULPIT. C18 with carved panels of Flemish
origin; one of them dated 1567. – BENCHES. C15, of plain
solid profile. – IRON GATES to the Lytton Chapel designed by *Lutyens*, also one of *c.* 1705 under the tower
arch. This was originally in the arch between chancel and
Lytton Chapel and is of excellent quality. – STAINED
GLASS. Three-light window in S wall by *Clayton & Bell*,
c. 1875. – PLATE. Chalice, C17; Paten, 1668. – MONU-
MENTS. The Lytton Chapel contains the most remarkable display of family pride in the county. The chapel is

really far too small to hold the three marble tombs put
in it between 1705 and 1710. On the N and S walls
William Lytton † 1705 and Sir George Strode † 17
These two are both by *Edward Stanton* whose signat
on the former is almost too prominent. Both men are
presented semi-reclining; they are stout and wear wi
and their clothes are meticulously portrayed. They tel
much self-confidence and worldly success. Both mo
ments have reredos backgrounds, the former with
tached columns, the latter with pilasters. The form
moreover, has life-size allegories standing outside
columns, which carry a coffered segmental arch. On the
37a   wall is the monument to Lytton Lytton † 1710, obviou
by a different hand and the sign of a change in taste (M
Esdaile suggests *Thomas Green*): more classical and a li
less Baroque (e.g. fluted pilasters instead of columns).
Lytton stands in the centre, a more than life-size por
figure, against an arched niche. – In the same chapel
Brasses to Roland Lytton † 1582 and his two wives, a ta
let to Anne Lytton † 1601, with pretty thin ribbon-w
on pilasters and frieze, and the epitaph to William Rob
son Lytton Strode † 1732 and his wife, two stiff kneel
figures facing a sarcophagus with a relief of allegori
putti, and another relief above. – This monument is sig
by *John Annis*. – But the highest aesthetic quality and c
tainly the most discriminating taste is not to be found
35   the chapel but in the chancel: the epitaph to Judith Str
† 1662: a surprisingly Roman-looking frontal bust wi
out any frills and furbeloes of dress, set against a ba
ground of black marble as noble in shape and soph
ticated in detail as any by the Florentine Mannerists
the C16. – Also in the chancel Brass to Simon Bac
† 1414, priest, frontal with figures of saints in the orphr
of his cope.

E of the church in rather neglected surroundings MAUS
   LEUM erected by Mrs Bulwer Lytton in 1817. Cha
   with curved pediment in the front and crowned by a
   sarcophagus. The architect is unrecorded.

ST MARTIN. In New Knebworth, on the A1 road. One

Lutyens's most remarkable churches. Red brick with stone dressings. No tower, but excessively far projecting roof eaves. So far of the three bays of the nave only one has been built. The aisle separated from the nave by little arches on Tuscan columns, three arches per bay. Big and high transepts, two bays deep. Between the two, separating the transepts from the crossing, one colossal Tuscan column on each side, deliberately dwarfing those of the arcades of the aisles. Similar small arcades on the outer sides of the transepts. Bare chancel and apse. The interior is all white with a timber ceiling supported by the walls and the two giant transept columns.

) the *Lutyens* fan Knebworth has more to give than the church: the GOLF CLUB HOUSE, 1908, indifferently Neo-Georgian, and HOMEWOOD, 1900, an eminently characteristic example of the architect's early style. Low ground floor with cottage windows and big weatherboarded gables, two to the garden, a group of three to the entrance. That in its feeling is not so different from, say, Voysey or Baillie Scott. But the entrance door has a rusticated surround carried up across the lintel, and above the lintel is a pediment with the tympanum between lintel and pediment simply left open, an extremely capricious effect.

NEBWORTH HOUSE. The house, as it now appears, is essentially the work of the first half of the C19, partly *c.* 1815–20 and partly the work of Bulwer Lytton, the novelist, done *c.* 1840–45. The body of the house is one range of a two-storeyed courtyard house of *c.* 1500. The other three were pulled down in 1811. Fragments of original work have been re-erected in 1816 in the brick West Lodge, the composition of which is, however, also C19. The Great Hall is still in its original position, but what pre C19 work it contains is of the C17: the plastered ceiling with rectangular panels and the elaborate Screen with caryatid termini are Jacobean.* The magnificent panelling of the Hall culminating in the reredos behind the dais with its Corinthian columns and pediment across the whole width of the room is later still, about 1675

perhaps. The E front is of E-type with angle turrets
the projecting wings and a central porch. This is Tudor
outline and *c.* 1815–20 only in the details. The W front
the other hand is frankly a romantic paraphrase of
Gothic palace, unrestrained by archaeological conside
tions. In 1883 the E front was unfortunately enlarged b
third storey. In the same year a new office wing v
erected. This has recently been removed and replaced
a new, very tactfully and soberly designed range (arc
tect *Philip Tilden*).

KYTES *see* GARSTON

LANGLEYBURY
2¾ m. NNW of Watford, 1½ m. WSW of Abbots Langley

ST PAUL, 1865, by *H. Woodyer*. The exterior is unprom
ing, though ambitious for so small a parish. Flint. Na
chancel, S chapel, and W tower with short spire. The det
rather coarse. Inside a most ornamental chancel arch, t
very beau ideal for the pious and sentimental Victoria
musician angels on each of the two capitals and angels
ranged radially on the arch. Otherwise also handsome
decorated. In the S chapel MONUMENTS of William Jo
Loyd of Langleybury House † 1885 and of Caroline Ge
trude Walker Loyd † 1893, the former with marble pu
holding a portrait medallion, the latter with a seate
nearly life-size angel with raised arm in the cemeteri
style.

LANGLEYBURY HOUSE (H.C.C. Secondary Mode
School). Nucleus plain Early Georgian. Brick, two and
half storeys, with parapet, seven bays wide. The dat
1727 and 1729 on rainwater heads of the servants' blo
no doubt refer to the house as well. Good Later Georgi
stable block with cupola and clock. Additions were ma
in the later C19 on all four sides.

* But the panels inserted in the side parts of the Screen with ca
touches and arms must be a mid C17 addition.

LAWRENCE END
3½ m. N of Harpenden

even-bay, two-storeyed house of brick with purple brick chequer pattern, hipped roof, one-storeyed porch. Completed 1841 but still Late Georgian in character.

LAYSTON
1 m. NE of Buntingford

r BARTHOLOMEW. Derelict at the time of writing. C15 W tower; big, with diagonal buttresses and a Herts spike, nave, and chancel. The nave details all C15, the chancel clearly C13 (big lancet windows on all three sides). The chancel arch, however (shafts and hollows in the diagonals), C15. The S porch also C15 (partly renewed). – Furnishings partly removed, partly neglected.

LEMSFORD

r JOHN THE EVANGELIST, 1850, by *David Brandon* (GR). In the E.E. style (even the W tower, in spite of its Perp outline). Stone, not flint. Interior with naturalistic leaf capitals. Added in 1930 a S chapel for the Hall-Cain family. Perp with rich lierne-vault, by *F. E. Howard.*

LETCHWORTH

etchworth, to nearly all those who know the name in ritain and abroad, means a garden city, in fact the first garen city ever built. The adventure began in 1903, several ears before the Hampstead Garden Suburb and seventeen efore Welwyn. The idea of the garden city came from benezer Howard's book of 1898. To translate the idea into sual terms *Barry Parker* and *Raymond Unwin* had to make a organism out of a diagram. In this they succeeded. The ampstead Garden Suburb makes that even clearer than etchworth. For Letchworth, as the first exploratory pioneer b, suffered from some initial faults which it has never quite ercome. The principle of the garden city is one of

controlled social and architectural structure and controll
growth. Number of inhabitants, type and location of hous
type and location of factories has to be kept in a certain re
tion to each other, with the result that the town should be
independent and self-sufficient unit. At Letchworth it to
long to attract industry, and population consequently c
not grow fast enough to justify an architectural display
public buildings as the plan had foreseen them along t
large central square or green. In fact the visual failure
Letchworth is that very square, laid out in axis with t
station and at right angles to another main axis. Comi
from the station one has, as one should have, an initial fee
ing of urban bustle (a few shopping streets of tallish buil
ings). But then the square is reached, and the public buil
ings are mostly small, architecturally indifferent, and do n
seem to be related to each other (Council Offices by *Benn*
& *Bidwell*, Grammar School by *Barry Parker*). The large
of them, St Francis' College (by *Morley Horder*; new exte
sion by *L. H. Shattock*) stands in no comprehensible positio
and represents no scale echoed anywhere else. The domest
architecture of the early years, on the other hand, is eminent
convincing. It is very similar to that of the Hampstead Ga
den Suburb, except that exposed brick is rarer. The style
mostly a free and comfortable Neo-Tudor with gables. T
houses are detached or in groups of four. The streets curv
except for the main axes, existing trees are preserved,
garden walls since cut up for green – all principles adopte
since for municipal estates. To the younger generation the
have thus become a matter of course, but it should not
forgotten that they were for the very first time systematical
followed at Letchworth. The old village of Letchworth li
outside the garden city, and it seems a pity that the *Parke*
Unwin plan did not choose to make use of the churc
and hall as a centre or sub-centre. It would have mea
a welcome break in the architectural uniformity of th
small-scale housing (cf., for example, Oxhey).

ST MARY. Flint; nave and lower chancel; no tower, only
timber bell turret. C13 windows in the chancel. – DOO
with C13 iron hinges. – PLATE. Late Elizabethan Chali

and Paten. – MONUMENTS. Stone effigy to a Knight, only
2 ft long, on a window sill. He holds his heart in his
hands. – Brass to Thomas Wyrley † 1475 (chancel), to a
husband and wife (later C15; nave).

ETCHWORTH HALL. Jacobean brick house with C19 and
C20 additions. The tower especially, needless to say, is
Victorian. The house should be approached not from the
present front but from the NE. There lies the porch which
gave access to the Hall. In the Hall the Screen is preserved, contemporary and not very elaborate. More
elaborate the fireplace in the Parlour which lies in a wing
projecting to the NW. The house has a variety of straight
gables. The original plan was probably H-shaped.

ILBURY HILL, 1 m. W. Part of an Iron Age hill-fort, on
the S side of the road, opposite the cemetery. The single
rampart and ditch of the camp originally enclosed about
14 acres, with an entrance in the S bank. Stotfold Road
runs along the bank on the W, and the line of the E rampart of this almost oval camp is probably followed by a
hedge. The N part of the camp is skirted by the modern
road (coinciding partly with Icknield Way). The fort was
constructed c. 500–300 B.C.).

LEVERSTOCK GREEN
2 m. ESE of Hemel Hempstead

OLY TRINITY. Designed 1846 by *Raphael Brandon*, consecrated 1849. A small flint church with double bellcote.
The window tracery is Dec. – Original STAINED GLASS
in the chancel windows. – ROOD SCREEN, STOLLS, and
ALTAR by *Sir Walter Tapper*, 1932.

o the N WOODLANE FARM, C17 with C18 Gothick windows and other alterations. Original staircase.

LILLEY

T PETER, 1870–1, by *Thomas Jekyll*, the Japan enthusiast
who designed the woodwork for Whistler's Peacock
Room. Of this un-Victorian sense of romance and delicacy
the E.E. exterior of Lilley church betrays nothing (except

perhaps for the brick and stone chequerwork parapet
the SW tower). On entering, however, one is puzzled b
the fact that the porch under the tower is red-brick line
The church itself is flint. Otherwise only a few indication
of anything out of the ordinary run of churches. Th
chancel, for example, is not paved with red and yello
Minton or *Maw* encaustic tiles, as one might expect, bu
with tiles in two shades of soft green with an occasion
sang-de-boeuf. The chancel ceiling is handsomely painte
Of the medieval church one feature remains: the plai
Norman N arch in the chancel. It is of red stone, un
moulded, on the simplest imposts.

PUTTERIDGE BURY. Large Elizabethan-style mansion b
Sir Ernest George & Yates, completed as late as 1911.

LITTLE AMWELL

HOLY TRINITY, 1863, by *Ewan Christian*.
HAILEYBURY COLLEGE, *see* p. 103.

LITTLE BERKHAMPSTEAD

ST ANDREW. Essentially 1857 and 1894. Of the churc
built in 1647 no telling features remain. – PLATE. Chalic
and Paten, 1684; Paten, 1701; Paten, 1721; Almsdish
1791; Flagon of Sheffield Plate, *c.* 1790.

Pleasant Georgian houses close to the church, especiall
LITTLE BERKHAMPSTEAD HOUSE, five bays, thre
storeys, with (later?) Greek Doric porch. Farther NE an
belonging to The Gaze a high red brick Folly Towe
erected in 1789, perhaps with the bricks from an olde
house. It has tall blank arches, classical cornices, an
battlements.

LITTLE GADDESDEN

SS PETER AND PAUL. Quite on its own outside the village
Architecturally less important than for its monuments
The W tower is not high. It is of flint and has diagona
buttresses. The rest of the church is cement-rendered, th
treatment dating probably from the time when *Jame
Wyatt* and *Sir Jeffry Wyatville*, busy with the rebuildin

f Ashridge, rebuilt the s aisle and porch in 1812 and
dded the s chancel chapel in 1819. The s arcade is of
876, the N arcade, with octagonal piers and hollow
hamfered arches, as well as the tower, C15. – SCREEN.
Much renewed. – BENCHES. Some with poppy-heads. –
TAINED GLASS. Two *Kempe* windows of 1895 at the SW
nd. – PLATE. Mid C17 Chalice; Flagon, 1635; Paten,
781. – MONUMENTS. An exceptionally full and varied
eries, especially important for the very progressive and
Mediterranean style of those of the later C17 (*see* also
Nettleden). Earlier only Elizabeth Dutton † 1611, the
sual epitaph type with kneeling figure, removed to Gad-
esden from St Martin-in-the-Fields, London, when that
hurch was rebuilt in the C18. – Elizabeth Countess of
Bridgewater † 1663, large classical monument without
gures except for two small mournful putti. – Elizabeth
Viscountess Brackley † 1669, epitaph with an inscription
n a delightfully scrolly writing-master's script. – Henry
Stanley † 1670 *aet*. 14, epitaph with two putti. – Dr H.
Stanley † 1670, stately urn on pedestal.* – Third Earl
f Bridgewater † 1701, good epitaph. – Jane Countess of
Bridgewater † 1716, similar to the monument of 1663.
Ann Norton † 1796, by *Ashton*, Grecian, with mourning
emale figure. – John William, seventh Earl of Bridgewater, † 1823, a masterpiece of *Westmacott*, with a *tondo*
with a labourer, his wife, and child, a dog and tools and
wheat-ears, very Raphaelesque. – Francis Henry, eighth
Earl of Bridgewater, † 1829, with seated female. An in-
cription notes specially that 'He bequeathed £8,000 as a

40b

In the floor of the Vestry memorial to the infant son of Dr Stanley
n an inscription which runs as follows:

TIBI GNATE USO
LUCIS BREVI FUSO
CITO QUE HIC CONCLUSO
(MISERO ME DELUSO)
HOC MEMORIALE
BREVE ET CORDIALE
CARMEN TRIPEDALE
SAXULUMQUE QUALE
CURTO NON STET MALE
LONGUM NISI NIHIL VALE

reward for literary men for writing essays to prove benevolence of God as displayed in the Works of Creation.'

JOHN OF GADDESDEN'S HOUSE, opposite the NE entran to Ashridge. Well restored and enlarged timber-fram C15 house with overhanging upper floor. The timb roof of the Hall is original. If the date is indeed C15, as Royal Commission assumes, then the house cannot that built by John of Gaddesden who was Physician to King from 1335 onwards and retired to his native vill later in the C14.

MANOR HOUSE, 1576. Stone house with front of two t rets with stepped gables and a lower centre with a tw storeyed bay window. Mullioned and transomed w dows. In the centre on the ground floor the Hall w a large fireplace and some C15 panelling brought fr Ashridge.

54   ASHRIDGE (now Bonar Law College). Ashridge, in its v
3a   park high on a ridge of the Chilterns, began its exister as the earliest English College of Bonshommes, found by Edmund Earl of Cornwall, Henry III's nephew, 1276. After the Dissolution it was in royal hands, a Princess Elizabeth lived here during Mary's reign. 1604 it came to Sir Thomas Egerton, and that family mained in possession to the time when the pres mansion was built. It is the largest of the roman Gothic palaces near London and was designed by Ja Wyatt in 1808. His son Sir Jeffry Wyatville added 1814–20 the N porch, the E wing with the staircase hall a the stables. The gardens and grounds were landscap by Capability Brown c. 1760 and again by Repton in early C19. To Repton the pretty, highly dressed featu near the house are due, although they are not executed conformity with the elaborate plans which he m and published. In the sun rose garden, for example, intended to fill up a conduit; but the structure stand there now is by Wyatville. One of the few remain fragments of monastic buildings faces the garden : BARN, much altered by Wyatville who set the front b

o form a rustic verandah out of the original oak posts
nd added dormers and turret. Otherwise an UNDER-
ROFT survives below parts of the Dining Room and
Drawing Room (octagonal piers without ribs, and single-
hamfered ribs).

e House is, no one can deny, a spectacular composition.
The way in which *Wyatt, Jnr* has entered into the spirit
f *Wyatt, Snr* is wholly admirable. The result is equally
uccessful from the drive and from the garden. On both
ides the chief accents are the twice stepped-back tower of
he chapel with its two tiers of angle turrets and its tall
lender spire, and the big heavy square tower above the
taircase. The chapel projects towards the garden with
all Perp windows and an apse. It is connected with the
main building on the r. by a Perp arcade now closed with
brick and converted (by *Clough Williams Ellis* in 1929)
nto the Dining Room of the college. The main building is
ymmetrical with two bay windows and a narrow three-
arched loggia in the middle with an oriel above. The E
ront is also symmetrical, with a central five-bay loggia.
The entrance side is quieter. The main emphasis lies on
Wyatville's porch, tall entrance hall windows, and stair-
ase tower behind. It has four plain bays of two and a
half storeys to the l. and four to the r., and then on the r.
ollow nine further buttressed bays of only one and a half
toreys. On the l. an Orangery wing branches off at a pic-
uresque angle. The whole building is of Totternhoe stone.
the INTERIORS the most impressive are the Chapel and [55a]
he Staircase. The CHAPEL consists of the apsed chapel
proper with tall windows with two-centred heads and a
an-vaulted coving carrying a canted panelled ceiling, a
pretty, typically C19 motif. The wooden fittings are by
Wyatville. The ANTECHAPEL opens up into the tower,
n effect as striking as any that *Wyatt's* more famous Fonthill may have afforded. In fact, in the absence of Fonthill,
Ashridge is the best example of *Wyatt's* truly romantic
nandling of the Gothic style.

atville's STAIRCASE HALL is perhaps a little drier, but
certainly just as dramatic, very high, with a staircase start-

ing in the middle with one short flight of stairs, turning
right angles against the back wall into two, and turn
again and leading up in two long flights against the s
walls to the first floor landing. The railing is of cast ir
On the first floor the hall is surrounded by arcades of fo
centred arches with figure niches in the corners. Th
are more tall niches above, then a thickly corbelled-
gallery with a fine iron railing, and more arcading beh
it carrying a fan-vaulted coving on which the lant
stands. This has a fan-vault with the fans surroundin
circle with a sun dial. The whole is designed with gr
elegance. The impression is one of dizzy height. The E
TRANCE HALL N of the Staircase Hall is also excessiv
tall, or seems so because it is relatively narrow, and ha
hammerbeam roof.

In 1860 *Sir Matthew Digby Wyatt* redecorated the DRA
ING ROOM, gave it a copy of Guido Reni's Aurora ceil
and delicate Italian ornamental painting around, t
colossal fireplaces with caryatids and door surrounds
colossal aedicules with free-standing columns and pe
ments. He also built a FERNERY in the garden.

Thirty years ago, it is said, the whole house had only t
bathrooms.

LITTLE HADHAM

ST CECILIA. The church lies on its own to the N of the
lage Street and to the W of the outbuildings of Hadh
Hall. It is a small church, of nave and chancel with
tower, N transeptal chapel, and S porch. The tower
diagonal buttresses and a spike. The tower arch dates i
c. 1400 or a little earlier. The nave has Perp windows. T
chancel windows are renewed. The interest of the chu
lies in the S porch and the transept. The S porch is of
C15, lightly built of timber with wide open sides trefo
cusped along the tops. The gable is bargeboarded, a
with a simple trefoil cusping, ending on top in an og
The N transept is supposed to date from the late C16. I
of brick with elementary posthumously Perp thr
light W and E windows and intersected tracery in the fo
light N window. Inside, the transept opens in a wide fo

centred arch. The PULPIT bears the date 1633. It has small-scale strapwork decoration, and a contemporary back and a big tester. Its decoration is the same as that of the PANELLING of the pew to its E and also some panelling in the N transept. The church has later box pews and the pulpit which is a three-decker (a rarity in Herts) is in its lower parts also later. – SCREEN. C15, of five one-light openings at each side of the entrance. – STAINED GLASS. A few C15 fragments in a S aisle window. – BRASSES to a Knight in armour (perhaps Thomas Baud) and his Lady, elegant, somewhat mannered figures, c. 1480; and to R. Warren, a priest, late C15, much rubbed off (chancel, S wall).

ADHAM HALL. Excavations have proved the existence of [61] a C15 house not on the exact spot or in axis with the present house. The brick outbuildings to the W are not in axis either and may partly be older than the house. They consist of the Gatehouse, added to an older building to its E, and originally no doubt higher than it is now, and a large brick barn (cf. Upp Hall). The mansion itself was built c. 1575 by the Capel family. It was much larger than it is now. All that survives is the W range with the main entrance and half the S range. Originally there were four ranges round an inner courtyard with the Hall probably in the E wing. E of this a later C17 Banqueting House was built, and yet further E the still existing terrace and a sunk formal garden with two pavilions at its NE and SE corners. Of all this traces and often foundations have been found. The house is of brick. The W range has the gateway between polygonal towers. The windows are all mullioned and the large ones transomed, and all have pediments, a feature which gives the building a somewhat classical air. Between the towers is a straight gable. The S wing has a low ground floor with brick arches, but the front and the upper floor inside have been entirely remodelled at about the time of Queen Anne. At the same time a wider staircase was built out close to the S end of the E side of the W range. To the N and NE is a late C19 addition in keeping with the rest. Not much of importance inside.

H—8

In and around the village many worthwhile timber-fram
farmhouses and cottages. By the main crossroads a gro
with dates from 1672 to 1732. Good houses near Lit
Hadham also at FORD HILL and BURY GREEN.

LITTLE HORMEAD

ST MARY. The fame of this small and lonely church is its
DOOR, with the most lavish display of C12 ironwork, tv
large interlaced quatrefoil patterns in the centre, and be
ders of scrolls and trails. The door belongs to the N doc
way which has one order of colonnettes with scallop
capitals and an arch with a thick roll moulding and a th
unusual triangular moulding. The same capitals ar
mouldings grouped inside in the awkwardly depress
chancel arch. The S doorway is also Norman and simple
In fact the whole nave is Norman (see also one deep
splayed small roundheaded N window), the chancel E.
(the S lancet windows are original). – The roofs are of th
late Middle Ages, with rough tie-beams in the nave, wi
diagonal wind-braces in the chancel. – FONT. Early C1
octagonal, with very pretty blank tracery. – ROYAL ARM
Dated 1660, small but nicely carved; above the chanc
arch.

BALLON'S FARM, SE of the church. Timber-framed C1
house with two symmetrical gables to the street. Thatche
roof.

LITTLE MUNDEN

ALL SAINTS. The exterior is not very promising. Tl
usual unbuttressed W tower with spike, the usual fli
nave and chancel, and a N aisle with N chancel chapel, a
much restored. The interior much more interesting. Tl
first bay of the N arcade has imposts with capitals of tl
C12, if not the C11, of three projecting rolls with herrin
bone hatching (cf. Walkern). In the chancel S wall is a c1
doorway, very plain and much renewed. That proves
nave and a chancel eight hundred years old. Next con
the C14 contributions, the N arcade of two bays wit
octagonal piers and double-chamfered arches and the

arch into the chancel chapel. In the E respond of the arcade three pretty little ogee niches for statuettes. Half a statuette is still *in situ*. The w arch between chancel and chapel has a big crocketed ogee gable and serves as the canopy to a MONUMENT for an unknown Knight and Lady (tomb-chest with shields in quatrefoils and little mourners between). The costumes are clearly of the later C14. To the E of this arch, early in the C15, another was opened to house a second monument. The tomb-chest here is plainer, the costumes indicate the date suggested. The arch of ogee shape and panelled inside with a row of lozenges with quatrefoils. In the apex the figure of an angel. Also of the C15 the chancel arch and w tower. – SCREEN. From N aisle to N chapel. Plain C15 panel tracery.

LITTLE WYMONDLEY

ST MARY. Chancel, nave, and only slightly higher w tower of the C15. The rest 1875.

WYMONDLEY BURY, s of the church; surrounded by a moat. Brick, gabled, the N side symmetrically gabled.

WYMONDLEY HOUSE, near the w end of the village. Late Georgian five-bay, two-and-a-half-storey cemented front with a porch with unfluted Ionic columns.

WYMONDLEY HALL, to the r., on the way to the Priory. Early C17. Handsome timber-framed six-gabled front, the third to fifth symmetrical. Of these the third and fifth have bay windows below, while the fourth and sixth have only upper floor oriels. Good group of chimneys.

WYMONDLEY PRIORY, $\frac{1}{2}$ m. N. Of the Augustinian house founded in the C13 no more remains than a few odd C13 arches inside a farmhouse and one big aisled barn, supposed to be also of pre-Reformation date.

The village street is specially attractive.

LOCKLEYS *see* WELWYN

LONDON COLNEY

ST PETER. By *George Smith*. A lean, cemented façade in the *Rundbogenstil*, with vaguely transitional Norman detail.

The date is 1825, that is remarkably early for a Norma[n] Revival. Aisleless interior. w gallery on thin cast-iro[n] columns with Norman capitals. The STAINED GLASS [of] the E windows was designed by Ruskin's friend th[e] *Dowager Marchioness of Waterford* and made by *Hugh[es]* in 1865. It represents the Ascension in a broad pictoria[l] somewhat Raphaelesque, style.

62 ALL SAINTS CONVENT. Begun in 1899 by *Leonard Stoke[s]*. A fine, very freely Neo-Tudor front, with much pic[-] turesque, original detail and yet strong and honest. Re[d] brick, purple brick, and stone. The centre motif is a gate[-] house with a figure frieze above the door. The l. and [r.] halves are only broadly symmetrical. They have sever[al] bay windows. To the r. the main front ends with a turre[t] and after that follows the lower Refectory with a large da[is] window. The style is similar to *Stokes's* later work fo[r] Emanuel College, Cambridge. – There is an equally fin[e] cloistered garth inside. The CHAPEL was added in 192[0] by *Comper*. It is yet unfinished. It consists so far of thre[e] bays of pale brick with tall pointed windows in whic[h] Perp and E.E. motifs are mixed. The interior is whit[e] with the large baldacchino as the one all-dominating ele[-] ment (tall golden columns with curious little flower[s] painted on and a crocketed ogee top), a most surprisin[g] combination of the Italian and the English. The cho[ir] stalls also have slim Tuscan columns and yet little bu[t-] tresses. Tree of Jesse glass in the E window. The extra[-] ordinary harmony of the interior is due to the fact tha[t] *Comper* directed everything from the baldacchino to th[e] candle sconces on the walls, the candlesticks on the alta[r] and even the size and type of the candles.

LONG MARSTON

Of the medieval church only the w tower remains, hidde[n] by trees. It is of flint and stone-chequer work and has n[o] buttresses. The date is C15.

The new church of ALL SAINTS is by *Carpenter [&] Ingelow*, 1882, without a tower, quite modest, but we[ll] designed with Dec details. In it a large number [of]

edieval fragments are re-used or displayed. The aisle
ers are those which stood in the parish church at Tring
ntil 1880 (a fine late C15 design). In the N wall is an
rly C14 window, then a Norman arch with shafts and
og-tooth ornament of the voussoirs, then a C13 window
f two lancets, and then various small fragments. The
ULPIT is ordinary early C17 work, the very renewed
CREEN at the E end of the S aisle dated originally from
e C15.

MACKERY END see HARPENDEN

ARCHMONT HOUSE see HEMEL HEMPSTEAD

MARDEN HILL
¾ m. SW of Tewin

It c. 1785–90 as a plain nicely proportioned block of 55b
ellow brick with a bow window on the garden side. The
nteriors were discreetly stuccoed. Had the house re-
ained like that it would have been a pleasant but by no
eans a remarkable building. In 1819, however, *Sir John
oane* was called in. He added an Ionic four-column
orch and made small alterations (his typical shallow in-
sive segmental arches) to the Entrance Hall and Dining
oom. He altered the staircase and gave it a beautiful
mooth and tense flow in a relatively narrow space. It
tarts with one middle arm and turns backwards in two to
 each the upper floor. The handrails run on without any
ewel posts. The ironwork is classical and extremely
imple. The skylight is an oval dome most sparingly
ecorated. The first floor room above the Entrance Hall,
oane's only other addition, is one of his masterpieces.
oane was specially ingenious in small spaces (*see* his own
ouse, or the Dulwich Gallery, or Pitzhanger, Ealing). At
Marden Hill he has divided the room into an oblong main
art and a smaller part by the windows, also oblong but
t right angles to the first. The two parts are separated
nly by a slight canting of the walls and by the design of
he ceiling. The large oblong consists of a short seg-
entally vaulted bay, a square bay with a kind of cross-

vault and a large rosette in the middle, a medieval boss
it were, and another segmentally vaulted bay. The part
the window has the same rhythm but turned by
degrees and on a smaller scale. The centre here is a sh
low saucer dome, and l. and r. of it are again shallow s
mental vaults. The composition is so original as to
almost perverse, but the effect, although complex, is
at all confusing.

MARKYATE

ST JOHN THE BAPTIST. Below the A5 road in the SE c
ner of the grounds of Markyate Cell, reached from th
by an avenue of elm trees. Thin embattled w tower of
brick with blue brick chequer, and nave of 1734, enlar
by aisles with arched windows in 1811; chancel 1892. T
arcades inside have roundheaded arches. The octago
piers look decidedly later than 1811. Curved w gallery
thin iron columns.

MARKYATE CELL. Large Neo-Elizabethan brick mans
of 1825–6 by *Robert Lugar* (*see* his *Villa Architecture*),
corporating remains of the mansion built by Humph
Bourchier in 1539–40. He had taken over the building
a nunnery founded early in the C12.

MEESDEN

ST MARY. Away from the village. The nave dates from
C12 (*see* the s doorway). The short transepts were add
(or renewed) in the C13 (*see* the narrow two-bay arca
from the nave with octagonal piers and moulded capita
but rebuilt in 1877. The chancel is of *c*. 1300 (*see* the
newed E window of three cusped lancets under one tw
centred arch). The pretty timber bellcote with its shing
spire is C19. All this is in no way out of the ordina
What, however, makes the church worth a special visi
the s porch, entirely built of brick, probably *c*. 1530
Wyddial). The two-light windows are of brick, the mu
moulded doorway is of brick, and so are the diagonal b
tresses and the crenellation with angle turrets and a ni
under a stepped gable. Below the battlements trefoile

orick corbel-table (cf. Rickmansworth Rectory and Red-
ourn). – TILES. In the chancel a whole series of early
:14 tiles in dark green and yellow with circles, quatre-
oils, etc. – PLATE. Chalice and Standing Paten, 1621. –
1ONUMENT. Robert Yonge † 1626, with bust in circular
niche.

CTORY (former Manor House). Five-bay, two-storey
orick house with hipped roof.

MINSDEN

1APEL. In ruins. The antiquarian will not find much to
nstruct him, but the picturesque traveller much to de-
ight him. Situated in a coppice, completely surrounded
oy trees and undergrowth. The fragments of nave and
chancel stand irregularly to a height of 10 to 20 ft. They
ire of flint and all details have decayed so much that outlines, door, and window holes now appear like designs in a
Henry Moore or Hepworth style. Inside the building and
closely around it is lawn. The ivy has been removed to
bare the wall surfaces.

MONKEN HADLEY*

ne combination of Hadley Green and Hadley Common
ults in one of the most felicitous pictures of Georgian
ual planning which the neighbourhood of London has to
er. It is elusive to the descriptive word and eminently
iglish in character. The elements are the wide rather
apeless Green to the N, by the Great North Road, and the
angular Common farther S with the church between,
ocking the direct communication between the two. Both
reen and Common converge towards the church, the
reen funnel-wise, the Common less dramatically.

r MARY. Built probably in 1494, the date appearing in an
inscription on the W tower. Flint and iron-stone with
white stone dressings. W tower with diagonal buttresses,
battlements and higher SW turret. C18 copper BEACON

* Parts of Hadley belong to the Urban Districts of Chipping Barnet
d East Barnet.

on top, a great rarity. Nave and aisles of two bays;
tower opens in a further bay into the aisles. In addit
chancel aisles of one bay. Their arches have the simpl
mouldings (concave double-chamfers). The nave pi
have capitals only towards the arches, not towards
nave. The arches are four-centred. Squints from b
chancel chapels to the chancel. – STAINED GLASS. E w
dow by *Warrington*, 1846 (signed); s transept E wind
by *Wailes*; other contemporary glass. – PLATE. An u
usually fine collection. Cup, 1562; Standing Cup a
Cover, 1586; Flagon, 1609, of coffee-pot shape; Cup a
Obelisk Cover, 1610; another, 1615, especially han
somely decorated; Paten, 1618. – MONUMENTS. U
usual number of small brasses: Lady, C15 (in front of
altar); two ladies (s transept E wall); man and woma
C16 (chancel s wall); woman in demi-profile, *c.* 1504
transept w wall); William Turnour † 1500 and wife a
children (s aisle). – In addition the following later mon
ments: Sir Roger Wilbraham † 1616, by *Nicholas Sto*
epitaph with two busts of outstanding quality in o
niches, the attitudes of exquisite Mannerism. – Ab
Stamford and her son, 1626, epitaph with painted p
trait of the son, and painted decoration. – Elizabe
Davies † 1678, epitaph without figures, signed by *W*
liam Stanton. – Richmond Moore † 1796, epitaph w
female in mournful attitude by a broken column; u
signed.

Of the houses along the sides of Hadley Green and Hadl
Common only a few are of high individual merit. It
their universally satisfying standard and their variety
scale, texture, and juxtaposition that makes them so e
joyable.

On the w side of HADLEY GREEN, OLD FOLD MAN
HOUSE, five-bay, two-storey Georgian, and OLD FO
MANOR GOLF CLUB HOUSE, originally two cottag
now connected by an early C19 gateway with fo
columns and a broad parapet with Soanian incised li
ornament. On the SE side of Hadley Green from s to
OSSULSTON HOUSE, three-bay, red brick, with Gib

surround to the arched door; then two Georgian cottages, then a wide gap; then HADLEY HOUSE, good mid Georgian five-bay red brick house with pediment and Roman Doric porch, with stables to the r., the most ambitious property along the Green; then FAIRHOLT, also mid Georgian, MONKENHOLT, Late Georgian, two cottages, two more houses, and the WILBRAHAM ALMS-HOUSES, 1612, six one-storey red brick cottages with two-light brick windows with arched tops to the two lights. The Almshouses mark the beginning of the funnel-like access from the Green towards the church and the Common.

om the N the beginning of the Green is the BATTLE OBELISK, erected in 1740 by Sir Jeremy Sambrooke (*see* Gobions*); Portland stone. It records the Battle of Barnet of 1471. Then farther S DURY ROAD with on the r., on an odd island site, a Victorian brewery in the middle of all this Georgian domesticity (weatherboarded sheds at the back towards E), and on the l. Georgian houses: THORN-DON FRIARS, Early Georgian, and HADLEY BOURNE, with a seven-bay red brick façade.

o the N of the church THE PRIORY, with a few C16 re-mains but mainly early C19 Gothic Revival; a sym-metrical front to the street. Then GROVE HOUSE, late C18, very thoroughly Neo-Georgianized by *H. A. Welch*, and BEACON HOUSE (with C17 remains). To the s of the church WHITE LODGE with a good though somewhat embellished Early Georgian doorcase. Two pretty Gothic cottages between White Lodge and the church.

he church closes the vista completely and only after one has passed it does the view open on to the Common with Hadley Wood as the background. The church is not much visible from the Common. The CHURCH HOUSE, C17 brick, stands as a partial screen in front of it; that is, E of the E end of the church. On the N side of the Common only MOUNT HOUSE, the individually best house of Hadley, mid C18, five-bay, red brick, with pediment and pedimented doorcase. On the s side quite a chain of nice houses: HADLEY LODGE, irregular with a handsome

four-column Ionic porch placed asymmetrically; GLAD
MUIR HOUSE, five-bay, red brick, with Victorianize
front; HURST COTTAGE, five-bay, two-storeyed, ear
C18 with an attached gabled Tudor cottage on the r
HADLEY HURST, good large house of c. 1710 wi
stables. Curly broken pediment above the central doo:
magnificent cedar tree in front.

MOOR PARK

51 The grandest C18 mansion in Herts. Built for Benjam
Styles, a merchant who made a large fortune out of tl
South Sea Bubble. It was said that he spent £130,000 c
the house. In fact it was not even a complete rebuilding
Styles probably used the walls of the Duke of Mo:
mouth's house, which existed on the site. Nor was his th
first building there. This was, it seems, George Neville'
the Archbishop of York's, built late in the C15. The
Cardinal Wolsey made Moor Park his chief country sea
before he got involved in the development of Hampto
Court. Dorothy Osborne's Sir William Temple becam
so enamoured of the gardens of the house as he kne
them that he called his own country house Moor Park.

Styles was principally advised by *Sir James Thornhill*. H
or more probably *Giacomo Leoni*, designed the house
1720. It is of five by nine bays, all cased with Portlar
stone, with two and a half storeys and a top balustrad
very classical. Its chief adornment is the four-colum
portico on the entrance side. The giant columns are in tl
Corinthian order with splendidly detailed capitals ar
entablature; the coffering inside the portico is equal
splendid.

The garden side has an attached portico; the two side ba
at each side are emphasized by giant pilasters. The grou:
floor has banded rustication and arched windows, moti
more French than Italian.

Inside, all the display is concentrated on the ENTRANC
HALL, of cubical shape, running up the whole height
the house, with a gallery on first floor level, just as Inig

Jones had done it at the Queen's House, Greenwich. But instead of Jones's chasteness there is here every device of magnificence. The ceiling has panels in feigned perspective, the centre one imitating the inside of a dome. The walls have large, brilliantly painted pictures by the Venetian *Jacopo Amigoni* who lived in England from 1729–36. They were much lighter originally than they are now. Their subject is the story of Io. The paintings are surrounded by putti and garlands. The front doorcases have the richest columns and pediments, putti by their sides, and allegorical females on the pediments, all this probably done by the two Italians *Artari* and *Bagutti*.

Through the Hall one goes straight on into the SALOON much less accomplished in its decoration of painted architecture and mythological stories. This work is attributed to *Thornhill*. The painting of the STAIRCASE is signed by 'F. Sleker Venetie' and dated 1732. The oval dome, however, is no doubt of the time when the house belonged to Lord Anson (1755–62) or to Sir Laurence Dundas, for whom *Robert Adam* added side wings in 1763–4 (demolished in 1785). To Adam's style belongs the former BALL ROOM running the whole depth of the house. Its delightful ceiling decoration is by *Cipriani*.

The gardens were landscaped by *Capability Brown* c. 1755–60. The formal portion on the NE side dates from c. 1830–40.

The S Entrance Gates towards Batchworth Heath have a central Roman Doric archway.

In the grounds streets of private houses have been erected in the last thirty years or so. No. 6 TEMPLE GARDENS is by *Connell, Ward, & Lucas*, 1937, in the typical International Modern style of these architects. The curved outer staircases and the curved canopies should be noted. With the general rectangularity of blocks and windows they form the sort of contrast which abstract painters and sculptors of the twenties and thirties relished and which Le Corbusier introduced into architecture.

MERCHANT TAYLORS' SCHOOL (*see* Rickmansworth).

MUCH HADHAM

5 Of its own kind Much Hadham is visually probably the mos
successful village in the county. Its kind is that of th
wealthy, in a way almost urban, village, with big Georgia
houses in contrast with the more varied C16 and C17 cot
tages. The main street is long and of very high architectur
quality. It has in its course two mansions big enough to pos
sess proper ranges of stables and at its s end one in larg
grounds. The church stands away from the street, and clos
to it the Bishop of London's palace and the Rectory.

ST ANDREW. Quite a large church, all embattled, and on
of complicated history. A C12 church can be surmised bu
has left no visible traces. About 1220 the chancel was re
built (blocked N lancet window). About the middle of th
century a s aisle was added to an older nave, three bay
long, with octagonal piers, plain moulded capitals, an
double-chamfered arches. As building went on to the w
taste changed and the last bays have slightly more com
plex capitals and arches. The N aisle is of two dates. Its
bay, wider than the others and probably originally open
ing into a Norman transept, is late C13, the other bays ar
early C14 (see the capitals of the octagonal piers, and th
arch mouldings). The arches are sparsely studded wit
fleurons. Amongst the s aisle windows one original one i
in the Dec style. The same style appears in the s aisl
Piscina. The W tower followed under the aegis of Bisho
Braybrooke of London (1382–1404). It is of three stages
embattled and has a tall spike. The buttresses ar
diagonal, the w window is tall. The tower arch has an in
teresting moulding. The C15 added the s porch, inserte
the big five-light E window with panel tracery in two tier
and several other windows, and put in new roofs. The
all survive and are worth study. The nave wall-posts res
on figures, the nave and chancel tie-beams are a littl
decorated on their undersides, the nave braces carr
tracery, etc. – SCREEN. C15 with 'panel' tracery. –
CHANCEL STALLS. With panelled back walls and poppy
heads. – DOOR to N vestry. With big C13 ironwork. –

CHAIRS. Two big chairs of *c*. 1400; of uncommon interest. – PAINTING. On the N wall remains of ornamental Early Tudor wall painting. – TILES. A few C14 tiles inside the N chancel recess. – STAINED GLASS. In the head of the E window, unfortunately too high to be seen properly, two figures of male saints and a row of female saints, C15, apparently well preserved. – E window by *Burlison & Grylls*, *c*. 1875–80. – S aisle last window from W designed by *Selwyn Image* and executed 1891. – PLATE. Two Chalices and a small Paten of 1576; Paten of 1811. – MONUMENTS. Brass with demi-figure of a man, C15 (chancel floor). – Brasses to a man and woman, *c*. 1500; to Clement Newce † 1519, wife and children; and to William Newce † 1610, wife and children (nave E end). – Epitaph to Judith Aylmer † 1618, wife of the Bishop of London, with the usual kneeling figure. – Joane Goldsmith † 1569 (nave E end). – Dionis Burton † 1616 (next to the Goldsmith brass).

To the N of the churchyard stands THE PALACE, the Much Hadham residence of the Bishops of London, a long brick house with a many-gabled front. The brick casing of the later C17 covers a timber-framed structure of earlier date. The shape is that of an H. In the centre was the Hall, originally open to the roof. The old tie-beams can still be seen. Except for one C15 beam on the first floor, the old details, such as the staircase rail and newels, and some panelling, are of Jacobean type. To the S of the churchyard is the RECTORY of the early C17, but much altered.

The main street of Much Hadham is a delight from beginning to end, more sustainedly so perhaps than any other in Herts. The beginning in the N is THE LORDSHIP, an ambitious gentleman's house of *c*. 1740–5, with a stable block at r. angles to the l.; the house has nine bays and two storeys (originally three but converted into two about 1830), a three-bay pediment, a later Tuscan porch, and good iron railings and gates. At the back one wing survives of what was probably originally a much larger Tudor mansion. The wing opposite was re-cased in the C19. Outer S wing of 1912 by *Sir Reginald Blomfield*.

Inside a fine mid C17 staircase (not in its original po
tion).

More or less opposite The Lordship are some gabled c
houses, and then NORTH LEYS, of chequered brick, f
bays wide, with straight door canopy on carved bracke
and also original ironwork to the street. From here
street is two solid rows of houses. The RED LION on o
side, the NEW MANOR HOUSE on the other mark
beginning. The New Manor House is dated 1839, a
may serve as a warning against that undiscriminati
praise of the Early Victorian which one comes acr
sometimes to-day. The house is bargeboarded and gabl
all right, but of stock bricks and symmetrical, no mo
than a drab suburban villa, picturesque merely in
routine way. After that, overhang cottages on both sic
and such C17 mixtures as WOODHAM HOUSE with t
symmetrical gables, but a doorcase of c. 1700 with carv
brackets. The C16–C17 has also some pargetting to sho
usually, of course, renewed, and occasionally fine expos
timbers, especially the OLD HOUSE on the E side, and
a slightly later date GREEN SHUTTERS on the same si
On the W side GAYTON'S is on a large scale, of bri
with three gables. Then, about halfway down, the mo
palatial mansion in the village is reached: MUCH HA
HAM HALL, seen behind a large Wellingtonia, a five-b
house of 1735 with central Venetian window and hipp
roof, and in line with it farther S the stable range w
arched carriageway and four windows on each side of
Opposite another early C18 house, the same usual ty
and of less unusual size; segmentheaded windows. On t
same side, particularly pretty, CAMDEN COTTAGE, l
with pargetting and an asymmetrical gable, followed
CASTLE HOUSE, a delightful, white, early C19 front
seven bays with a Gothick porch and arched windows w
hood-moulds. Lower down on the same side MORF
COTTAGE, with exposed timbers which may well be C
Close to this is the entrance to MOOR PLACE, a house
1775–9, not bigger originally than the best in the villa,
but placed in large grounds. The social scale operat

effectively, without necessarily much architectural variety. Moor Place was designed by *Robert Mitchell*. It is of brick and has the usual five bays and two storeys. The distinguishing feature on the entrance side is the blank arches on the ground-floor. The interior has a fine central three-flight staircase with iron railings, much discreet stucco-work, and good fireplaces. A wing was added in the s by *Sir Ernest Newton* in 1907, lower, and in his best and most tactful Neo-Georgian.

of Moor Place by the railway station an estate of nearly fifty houses by *P. Mauger & Partners*, begun in 1945.

ound Much Hadham many uncommonly well-kept former farmhouses and cottages, notably at HADHAM CROSS, YEW TREE HOUSE of the early C17 but with a date plate 1697, at GREEN TYE a cottage on the N side of the Green, and GRUDDS FARM with a moat, and at PERRY GREEN, e.g. BUCKLER'S FARM, well modernized in such features as the windows.

NAST HYDE
1¾ m. SW of Hatfield

REAT NAST HYDE. Early C17 brick mansion of two storeys with gables; on the H plan, like North Mimms. The wings project farther to the N than to the S. In the middle of the S front a two-storeyed porch. The space between the wings on the N side is now taken by the C19 addition of a large hall. The original hall is, however, also preserved, as is the staircase with straight-sided balusters and the parlour. The windows are mullioned and transomed, of three to four lights.

of Great Nast Hyde a house built in 1934 by *F. R. S. Yorke*.

NETTLEDEN

T LAURENCE. A brick church of 1811 except for the low embattled W tower which is of flint and dates from the C15. Nave as well as chancel are embattled. The window tracery was originally no doubt simpler than it is now. – BRASS to John Cotton † 1545; the figure *c.* 4 ft long. – MONUMENT. Epitaph to Edmund Bressy † 1612 with wife and children, the usual kneeling figures.

NEW BARNET

ST MARK, Potter's Road, 1898, by *J. L. Pearson*, but not
spectacular example of that excellent architect's wor
Nave only, the E end a temporary structure. Exterior fli
with stone dressings, large Perp aisle windows with fou
centred heads. The aisle arcades with tall piers; r
clerestory.

THE ABBEY, 89 Park Road. The property was before th
Second World War a Folk Museum. For the purpose
TITHE BARN from Birchington in Kent was re-erecte
here. At the time of writing it served as a Nestoria
church. It has recently been converted into a museu
and art centre.

This district, which is included in the East Barnet Urba
District, is entirely part of outer suburban London.

NEWBERRIES PARK *see* RADLETT

NEWNHAM

ST VINCENT. A small church, but with W tower with stai
turret, S aisle and clerestory, and S porch. All this appea
Perp, but the chancel has two small C13 lancet window
and the others of the early C14. And inside both the tow
arch and the short arcade with low octagonal piers an
double-chamfered arches are evidently C14. – FON
Octagonal, Perp, with quatrefoil panels and shields on th
bowl and blank arcading on the stem. – PLATE. Chalic
and Paten, 1568. – TAPESTRY. 1949, by *Percy Sheldri*
in the style of 1500, in memory of Reginald Hine, th
Hitchin historian. – BRASSES. Man, two wives an
children, late C15 (chancel). – Joane Dowman † 16c
and children (chancel).

NEWSELLS PARK *see* BARKWAY

NORTHAW

ST THOMAS THE MARTYR, 1882, by *Kirk & Sons* (
Sleaford (GR). In its rock-facing, its pinnacles on the

tower, and its flowing tracery quite alien in the county. The tracery of the w window is in fact very Sleafordish. – PLATE. Chalice and Paten, 1636; Paten, 1668; Flagon, 1749; Paten, 1785.

of the church the OLD VICARAGE (also known as Manorfields), a pleasing five-bay, two-storeyed, Georgian brick house. S of the church begin the grounds of NORTHAW HOUSE. The house is near their w end. It was built in 1698 and has the proportions of that date. It is seven bays wide with a three-bay pediment and three sets of quoins, at the angles, at the joints between first and second and sixth and seventh bays, and at the angles of the three-bay centre. A semicircular porch of late C18 style on the entrance side. The inside is not original.

of the grounds of Northaw House, in Coopers Lane, FAIRLAWN, another good Georgian five-bay house.

the E–W lane S of the grounds of Northaw House, THE HOOK, an interesting house of its date, 1839. It was largely built from materials of Gobions (*see* p. 96), but has all the characteristics of the progressive villa as illustrated in Loudon's *Encyclopaedia*, the low-pitched, somewhat Italian roofs, the asymmetrical tower of moderate height, the occasional narrow roundheaded windows (a type of house which will no doubt one day be found as pleasing as a Tudor or Georgian house is found now). Inside, an excellent late C17 staircase brought here from Gobions or Gubbins (*q.v.*) when that house was pulled down. It has delicately turned and carved balusters of wide spiral, narrow spiral, and columnar shapes (cf., for example, Cheshunt Great House).

W of The Hook and w of Northaw, NORTHAW PLACE, *c.* 1690 but much altered. Inside, a staircase with wall paintings in the *Thornhill* manner.

NORTHCHURCH

MARY. The w end faces the High Street across the turf of a treeless churchyard. The church has a Totternhoe-stone crossing tower; the rest is flint. The archaeo-logically, if not visually, most interesting fact about

Northchurch is that the S and part of the W wall a
Saxon, and that the thickness of the wall at the W e
proves the existence of a separate square W chamber w
the nave proper. The chancel is a C13 enlargement (see t
large N lancet window now opening into a modern vestr
The masonry of the transepts is partly C13, partly C1
The crossing tower was rebuilt in the C15 and the arch
on which it stands were then strengthened. It has a N
stair-turret. Porch and N aisle are C19. Of the nave wi
dows the first has Dec, the second geometrical tracer
The chancel S windows are Early Perp. – CHEST. Flemis
c. 1500, richly decorated with tracery. – STAINED GLAS
E window of 1883, an early *Kempe*. Several other lat
windows by *Kempe* and his successor *W. E. Tower*.
BRASS TABLET to 'Peter the Wild Boy' who was found
the woods of Herrenhausen near Hanover; S wall, insi
S door.

In the HIGH STREET by the churchyard two uncommon
fine C16 cottages of vertical timbers with brick fillin
More half-timbered cottages on the opposite side of tl
road (Nos 13–25).

GRIMS DYKE (*see* Berkhamsted).

NORTH MIMMS

43a ST MARY. In North Mimms Park, yet not near the hous
The Vicarage of the late C17 close to the church, also
the park. The church has an interesting C14 buildi
history. At the beginning of that century the chanc
seems to have existed; in 1328–29 a N chapel was add
with 2-light simple Dec tracery, and a N aisle with wi
dows of three lights but the same reticulated tracery. Tl
S aisle is nearly contemporary, as proved by the identic
octagonal piers of the (3-bay) arcades with their mould
capitals and double-chamfered arches. A S chapel mu
also have been intended; for a blocked arch appea
at the E of the aisle. But closer examination of the (tripl
chamfered) chancel arch reveals on its E side the begi
nings of a continuation which can only have been mea
for a crossing tower. So the aisles were meant to op

into transepts. This ambitious scheme is by no means
frequent in C14 parish churches. The W tower (with
diagonal buttresses, a C14 W door which has foliage
capitals and fleurons in the voussoirs, 2-light bell-
openings with transomes, and recessed spire) dates from
c. 1440–50. – PULPIT. Elizabethan. One of the panels
has a blank pointed arch instead of the usual squat round
arches of so much Elizabethan furniture. – PLATE.
Chalice c. 1570; covered Cup, c. 1610; German Tankard
1659 (on loan at the British Museum); Flagon, 1707;
Paten, 1717. – MONUMENTS. Brass to a priest, c. 1360
with an excellent broad surround with figures in niches.
God the Father with the soul of the deceased in a cloth
and two angels by his side and in the canopy above the
head of the priest. Obviously a Flemish piece. – Brasses
to Elizabeth Knowles † 1458 and two children; a Knight
late C15; a civilian and his wife (small figures), late C15;
and to Thomas Hewes † 1587 and wife (all in the chancel). Tomb-chest of the C15 with shields in quatrefoils
(Elizabeth Coningsby?). – Tomb-chest of the later C16
with the effigy incised on the lid; flowery pillow, flowery
sleeves. – George Jarvis † 1716, epitaph with gesticulating
demi-figure. – John Lord Somers † 1716, large standing
wall monument in the chancel, with marble door at the
foot, leading into the vestry. A life-size figure of Justice
above against a black obelisk; two lions l. and r.

NORTH MIMMS HOUSE. More famous for its pictures than
for its architecture. Yet the house is one of the best examples of the Late Elizabethan style in the county, inferior perhaps to none but Hatfield. It was originally a
courtyard-house, but appears now on the H-plan. The
N front of great perfection. Two storeys with large four-
to five-light windows with two transomes, slightly projecting gabled wings, and a central porch without gable.
Small cupola behind. The doorway, round-headed and
flanked by remarkably pure Tuscan columns with triglyph frieze, originally led into the Screens Passage of
the Hall. This room is now an Entrance Hall and contains an exquisite French chimneypiece of 1515. On the

s side the arms of the H, in contrast to the N, proje
very far. They are in fact as long as the main rang
Before 1846 a one-storeyed range closed the courtyan
at their s ends. In 1846–7 corridors were added to tl
E and W wings; the courtyard was thus considerab
narrowed. Finally, in 1893–4, *Sir Ernest George & Yat*
built s of the original Great Hall a larger Hall with
central bay window. They also erected a long new s
wing of which only the ground floor loggia with mosa
vaults, lush white marble wall decoration, and an ex
tremely juicy bronze gate remain. The gardens wet
designed by *Sir Ernest George*. The rose garden enjoys
special fame. This is the work of *William Robinson* him
self, the reformer of the English garden towards the en
of the C19.

NORTON

St Nicholas. A small church of no architectural interes
seemingly Perp but with a Norman chancel arch on tl
plainest imposts and an outer doorway of the s porc
which looks like a Late Georgian doorcase. – Font. Earl
C14, octagonal, with tracery and quatrefoil decoration.
Pulpit. C17, with canopy and elementary geometrica
patterns on the panels. – Benches. Simple C15 shape
with little decorative buttresses. – Plate. Early Eliza
bethan Chalice.

OFFLEY

St Mary Magdalene. Nave and aisles are mediava
built of flint and stone, and now cemented. The W towe
is early C19 brick with typical Gothick windows of tha
date (e.g. quatrefoils); the chancel was remodelled
1750. It is the great surprise of the church, externally c
Portland stone with square, pyramid-covered angle pin
nacles, no s or N windows at all and only one lancet at th
E end. Its interior will be viewed after that of the nave
This with its arcades of four bays must be – *c.* 1230; tha
is, the piers are octagonal, on shallow Attic bases, an

ave capitals of individual upright stiff leaves as well as [21a]
he usual stiff-leaf formations. The arches are double-
hamfered. In the s porch a contemporary window or
mall opening (Piscina?) is re-used. – FONT. A most in-
eresting C14 piece, stone, polygonal, with tracery panels
f which some are still entirely flowing, but others equally
learly Perp. So the date must be second half C14, and an
nexpectedly long survival of Dec forms is proved. –
ENCHES. C15, of simple, usual outlines, buttressed. –
ILES. Two in the s aisle wall with C14 or C15 patterns
nd an inscription of 1777 that they were found in that
ear 'which proves that King Offa was buried here'.
The name Offley was supposed to come from Offa, and
he tiles were regarded as Anglo-Saxon work. – PLATE.
A fine set presented in 1730. – MONUMENTS. Brasses to
ohn Sawmel † 1529 with two wives and son and to an
nknown man with three wives and nine sons, also early
16 (both N aisle). – Spectacular monument in the s aisle
o Sir John Spencer † 1699, big standing wall monument
vith reredos background. Semi-reclining figure in wig
nd contemporary clothes and at his feet a Roman
natronly kneeling figure with one hand raised, talking to
Sir John. Two putti with crown and palm branch above.
A piece of the first order, variously attributed by Mrs
Esdaile to *E. Stanton* and *Nost.* – Epitaph to William
Chamber † 1728, by *William Palmer*; no figures but
good ornamentation.

The chancel of Offley church has to be treated
eparately. It was rebuilt or remodelled by Sir Thomas
Salusbury *c.* 1750. It has a broad stuccoed chancel arch, a
oof altered and provided with a skylight later, and an
pse with a draped baldacchino and hanging-down drapes
ound the E window. On the s wall Sir Thomas Salusbury
· 1773 and his wife, uncle and aunt of Mrs Thrale, have
heir own monument, very pretentious and self-confident,
vith the over-life-size standing figure of Sir Thomas and
Lady S. Tradition has it that theirs was a romantic story
f a troth long kept. They were parted but in the end
nited. In the background in relief a rather vulgarly

detailed tree with big drapes hanging off it. Grey ba
ground and a grey sarcophagus. The monument
made by *Nollekens* in 1777, who also did the bust
Samuel Burroughs (father-in-law of a Salusbury) † 1
and of Mrs Maude (friend of Dame Sarah Salusb
† 1796 in the chancel arch, and another (unsigned) b
on the S wall (William Offley † 1789). – Other mo
ments in the chancel chronologically: Sir Henry Pen
† 1752, and his son, excellent allegorical figure again
pink obelisk with a medallion with the profiles of fat
and son. Signed by *Sir Robert Taylor* ('invent et scul
on the drapery. – Sir T. R. Salusbury † 1835, bust
T. Smith. – Two memorials by *Sanders*, 1847 and 18

OFFLEY PLACE. c. 1825, said to be by *Robert Smi*
Five-bay, two-and-a-half-storey mansion with cemen
façade and Tudor porch. C17 work behind in one wi

WESTBURY FARM. At the crossroads, half-timbered
plastered, of c. 1600 or earlier, with additions. In
farmyard a C17 brick and timber dovecote.

LITTLE OFFLEY, 1¼ m. NW. Late Tudor brick ma
house on an H-shaped plan. Symmetrical front with
gables of different size on each end and a centre
modelled and provided with a pediment in 1695. F
Elizabethan wooden fireplace with caryatids in one roo

OLD HALL GREEN

ST EDMUND'S COLLEGE. Better known as the Old H
Green Academy. It was named officially St Edmun
College in 1793 and intended to be on the one hand
successor of the English College at Douai, founded
1568, and the English school at St Omer (run by Eng
Jesuits to the time of the dissolution of their order
France in 1762), and on the other of the small Ror
Catholic school started about 1690 at Tayford and mo
to The Lordship, Standon (q.v.) c. 1749 and to Hall Gr
in 1769. At Hall Green a brick house of 1630 was u
which, with its two curved gables, still exists at the W e
of the present College buildings. It stands together w

livers cottages; and the Roman Catholic Parish Chapel, opened in 1818 (The Hermitage), blends in nicely with them, with its playful Gothick porch and its four arched windows. Its continuation by a light weatherboarded cottage front seems not at all incongruous.

The new college, reinforced by the immigrants from France, decided to build proper premises, an enterprise comparable in scale only with College work at Oxford and Cambridge, but far exceeding what English public schools did at that time. In 1795–9 a school was built, of fifteen bays width and three storeys height. The building which faces E is of stock brick with a three-bay pediment (also one on the W front, where a small cupola rises above it). The three main entrances and bays two and fourteen have surrounds of intermittent vermiculated *Coade* stone rustication. Inside on the ground floor a wide corridor or *ambulacrum* (painted in 1870 to designs said to be by *Führich* of Vienna). The Refectory (altered inside) was an addition of 1805. It is two-storeyed with arched ground floor windows and stands to the SE of the main block. The architect of these early buildings was *James Taylor* of Islington.

In 1845, that is after the Catholic Relief Acts, an important further addition was decided on, a chapel worthy of the traditions and ambitions of the College. *Pugin* was chosen to be the architect. He disliked the existing buildings violently. 'Priest factory' is the term he described them by. His addition in a spectacularly different style is the chapel N of the old building. It was completed in 1853, 59 without the projected tower and spire. It consists of an ante-chapel like those of Oxford colleges and a long, tall, main chapel. The two parts are separated from one another by a big two-bay-deep rood screen, an object of Catholic tradition on whose re-introduction into C19 church architecture *Pugin* was specially keen. The style of the Screen as of the altar and reredos is E.E., but that of the window tracery is of *c.* 1300–30; that is, geometrical to flowing (E window). The furnishings are by *Pugin* too, the red, blue, and yellow floor tiles, and much of the

stained glass. *Pugin*, moreover, built a house for the hea
master (to the SW of the Refectory). It is in truth a sm
stock-brick villa, with a three-bay E front, decorated
two symmetrical bays and two symmetrical gables.

After *Pugin* the Scholfield Chantry was erected as
separate little rather heavy E.E. shrine, S of the Pu
Chapel. Its date is 1862, its architect unrecorded. T
Galilee W of the Pugin Chapel came only in 1922 (arc
tect: *F. A. Walters*).

Further large additions to the College in 1907–38 i
subdued Neo-Georgian style (by *F. A.* and later *E.
Walters*; classrooms block *T. H. B. Scott*, 1922).

EARTHWORK. A rectangular enclosure with moat a
mound 1,400 yds W of the Fox and Hounds Inn, abo
Collier's End on the main road N through Ware to Roy
ton. Between Collier's End and Old Hall Green
Roughground Wood, and the mound is in the NE corn
of the wood. Around the mound is a moat 360 ft long a
86 ft wide. From one end of the moat a ditch runs s
into the wood and turns SE parallel to the moat. The sid
of the enclosure measure 300 ft and 176 ft. The mou
marks the site of a C15 sunk-post windmill, nothing
which is to be seen above ground.

OLD RAMERICK *see* HOLWELL

OXHEY

The pre-C20 appearance of Oxhey is now completely los
The village has grown into an appendix of Bushey,
suburb of Watford and even a suburb of London. T
most interesting area is indeed the new L.C.C. housin
estate in the centre of which wise planners have chosen
preserve a chapel and some old houses with their tree
The main house, OXHEY PLACE, it is true, is not old
than the Victorian age. It is built in a Neo-Jacobean styl
But close to it to the N a farmhouse with a good C16 o
ceiling. Also barns, and to the E a CHAPEL, the best i
dividual building at Oxhey. It was built in 1612 as a pla

rectangle of brick and flint with straightheaded Perp four-light windows. – Original w door. – Fine late C17 Font with Font Cover. – Reredos with twisted columns also late C17. – Altham epitaph of 1616 with kneeling figures, columns, and big semicircular pediment.

around L.C.C. houses (many of the standard two-storeyed steel-frame type designed by *F. Gibberd*), and also several of the new H.C.C. SCHOOLS, both one-storeyed and two-storeyed especially the Hampden Secondary Modern School, Little Oxhey Lane, and the Clarendon Secondary Modern School, Chillwell Gardens, both two-storeyed (*see* Introduction, p. 28). Their variety of composition achieved with identical elements is worth special study.

PANSHANGER

or those who have an eye for the Romantic Gothick this house is of great interest. In 1808 the 5th Earl Cowper had an existing house drastically altered and enlarged by William Atkinson, a pupil of James Wyatt. It is a long low building with battlements and towers and is faced with Atkinson's patent cement. In 1800 G. A. Repton had submitted plans for a new Panshanger but they were not carried out, although the layout of the park is based on suggestions made by G. A. Repton's more famous father, the landscape gardener *Humphry Repton*. The view from the house past the groups of trees down to the lake created by a widening of the river Mimram is superb, It is one of Repton's most perfect schemes. The Red Book recording his plans is at Panshanger. The house itself is a demonstrative reaction against earlier Georgian ideals, not a square and solid symmetrically composed block, keeping proudly in opposition to the surrounding scenery, but a long and low, completely freely grouped front, 350 ft long, with battlements and turrets and occasional bay windows, and cemented to conceal its bricks. The original building is the r. half only, as one looks at the façade standing in the garden, The long and lower l. half was added by *W. Atkinson* in 1819–22 and largely rebuilt

after a fire in 1855. The interior was completely remodelled then. It is now in a grand rather pompous Ne[?]
Italian style with many columns and much thick, heav[?]
and competent wood-carving. The architect responsib[?]
for the conversion does not seem to be recorded.

PATCHETTS GREEN *see* ALDENHAM

PIRTON

A village with a remarkable number of good farm or man[?]
houses around.

ST MARY. Broad crossing tower of stone with diagonal bu[?]
tresses (rebuilt 1883). It is crowned by a Herts spike. It [?]
of the C12 as the arches inside prove. The nave has co[?]
temporary masonry but Dec and Perp windows. T[?]
chancel windows are Perp, but the Piscina inside is C1[?]
The Perp S porch is the only flint-built part of the churc[?]
The S transept is new. – GLASS. C14 and C15 bits in the [?]
and S walls.

In the village several worthwhile houses, notably thre[?]
OLD HALL, SW of the church. Rectangular plastered fli[?]
building with brick quoins and stone dressings. The e[?]
trance with three-light mullioned window above and [?]
gable is dated 1609.

RECTORY FARM. Stone building with a front of two late[?]
gables and a central porch. The doorway is four-centre[?]
of brick. The windows, no doubt originally of three ligh[?]
mullioned, one renewed. Fine big barns by the side. I[?]
side, a fireplace with caryatids and some oak panelli[?]
from Hammond's Farm.

HAMMOND'S FARM. Gabled, of timber and brick, with [?]
four-centred brick doorway.

Away from the village chiefly two houses, one a manor hou[?]
the other a moated farm.

HIGH DOWN. Beautifully placed on the edge of a woo[?]
Stone-built, with a porch with mullioned windows and [?]
gable; the arms allow the porch and probably most of t[?]
house to be dated *c.* 1599 or a little later. The E front h[?]
picturesquely varied projections and gables; the windo[?]

are mullioned and transomed; the gables are bargeboarded. At the back a courtyard, now open to the E and
formed of two lower and presumably older ranges. Four-
centred brick gateway in the N range.

RTON GRANGE, 2 m. NW. A courtyard house inside a
moat, of which three probably low ranges (except for the
Bakehouse and Laundry) were pulled down in the C19.
The remaining range has a centre remodelled *c.* 1700
(hooded doorway and sash windows), symmetrical gables
of *c.* 1600 to the l. and r., and a lower gabled bay at the l.
end of the front. E of it a gatehouse astride the moat.

PISHIOBURY
1 m. s of Sawbridgeworth

emodelling or rebuilding of a Late Tudor mansion by
James Wyatt in 1782. Red brick block of two and a half
storeys with five-bay fronts. Castellated, and on the garden side with three-bay castellated pediment. Ground
floor windows with four-centred arches, upper windows
with hood-moulds. Inside, a fine square central staircase
hall (open courtyard of the preceding house?). The staircase with delicate iron railings rises along three sides of the
wall. Sparsely stuccoed vault and glazed centre dome. In
the Dining Room Jacobean or slightly later panelling,
stone fireplace with tapering pilasters and wooden richly
carved overmantel. – Stables and Barn essentially still *c.*
1600. The lake and planting due to *Capability Brown*.

PORTERS PARK *see* SHENLEY

PUNCHARDON HALL *see* WILLIAN

PUTTENHAM

T MARY. A small church with a low W tower with NW
stair-turret higher than the tower. The masonry is flint
and stone in a chequer pattern. The S aisle is stone with
occasional flint, the clerestory has only two windows each
side. The chancel is lower than the nave. The interior of
the nave has three bays with slim octagonal piers. The S

arcade has double-chamfered arches, the N arcade double
convex chamfering and fine capitals. Both are C14. Th
clerestory and roof are C15. – Below the beams are stand
ing figures of saints. – PULPIT with very rustic C17 carv
ing. – PLATE. Chalice, 1569.

PUTTERIDGE BURY *see* LILLEY

QUEEN HOO
1 m. NW of Bramfield

A delightfully well-preserved Early Elizabethan brick house
very small, and of an uncommon plan. The plan may b
described as a half-E; that is, with two porch-like angl
projections. They have corbelled-out gables on which
even the honeycomb-decorated finials survive. The win
dows are mullioned and also of brick. The nearest paralle
in style is The Lordship, Standon, but Queen Hoo wa
apparently never bigger than it is now (a hunting lodge, i
has been suggested). Two fireplaces with depressed Tudo
arches, and in an upper room remains of Elizabetha
mural figure paintings.

RADLETT

CHRIST CHURCH, 1864, by *Smith & Son*; new nave and
chancel added to the N in 1907 by *Oldrid Scott* (GR). The
older part flint with red brick, yellow brick, and stone
Oldrid Scott's more restrained and more competent.

NEWBERRIES PARK, ½ m. E. This was once a fine mid
Georgian mansion, with well-detailed, trim, Venetian
windows, etc. At the time of writing rather neglected.

THE HOUSE BOAT, road house at the N end of the village
now British Physical Laboratories, 1935, by *W. R
Davidge*. Quite a suitable design for a road house, with
polygonal shingled centre, a brick part with port-holes
and roofs with ship's railings.

KENDAL'S HALL, 1½ m. S. Seven-bay, two-storeyed brick
house. Central door with big segmental pediment on
Ionic pilasters.

RADWELL

. SAINTS. Small church, mostly of the C19. No tower;
ut at the W end of the nave the last bay has an arch as if
·r a tower. – Carved ROYAL ARMS above C14 chancel
·ch. – COMMUNION RAILS. Early C17 square tapering
alusters. – PLATE. Chalice, 1576 (1566?); Paten, 1793;
vo C18 plated Chalices and Patens. – MONUMENTS.
·rass to William Wheteaker, wife, and son who † 1487;
·nall figures (chancel). – Brass to John Bele † 1516 and
vo wives (nave). – Brass to Elizabeth Parker † 1602
·hancel). – Two small epitaphs with kneeling figures,
·595 and 1625. – Monument to Mary Plomer † 1605, the
·ne object in the church describing a visit. Plinth with
·neeling children, pilasters l. and r., achievement on top,
·nd nearly life-size frontally seated effigy with baby by her
·ide. Her foot rests on a skull, her hand holds an hour-
·lass. The carving is thoroughly rustic. The creases in the
·leeve are still done with exactly the same carving con-
·ention as at Chartres about 1150.

RAMERICK see HOLWELL

RAVENSBURGH CASTLE see HEXTON

REDBOURN

MARY. A long, well-documented building history. W
·ower and nave Norman, N aisle arcade slightly later Nor-
·nan, chancel early C14, S aisle mid C14; S chancel chapel
·nd S porch 1444–55, clerestory c. 1478, N aisle c. 1497.
·/isually the best impression is obtained in approaching
·he church from the E. The E end is of stone and flint with
·he E chancel window displaying ogee-reticulated tracery
·nd the big tiled roof coming far down. One small N win-
·low is also Dec. The S view of the church is distinguished
·gainst the N by brick battlements to the aisle, on a hand-
·ome arched and cusped brick corbel-table. The same design
·s used for the S chancel chapel which is a little higher than
·he aisle. The S porch has cusped niches l. and r. of the

entrance. As for the tower it has the shallow buttre
(with bits of Roman brick re-used) and the roundhea
windows of its date. The stair-turret is also shallow. Th
is no crenellation but a tiny spike. Inside, traces of
Norman tower arch can be seen above the smaller l
arch. The nave N arcade of three bays has Norn
circular piers and scalloped capitals of the same shap
at Hemel Hempstead and, as there, with decoration to
scallops. The decoration seems simpler and a little ea
than that of the Hemel Hempstead nave. Arches of
steps with an outer billet label. Exposed remains of
Norman window in the N aisle. The S arcade is la
with octagonal piers, double-chamfered arches. '
chancel arch with its moulded capitals and arch mo
ings does not look later than c. 1300. The Piscina
Sedilia and a recess in the N chancel wall are ogee-hea
– FONT. Handsome, unpretentious early C18 desig
SCREENS. Good and well preserved C15 rood screen. T
broad and tall sections l. and two r. of the doorway. E
section of six lights with the centre mullion going u
the apex of the arch. The three l. and three r. lights ta
each together under separate arches. Elementary F
tracery. The coving of the former rood loft is happily
served. It is now, with the parts above missing, all tra
parent like lacework: seven ribs fanning out from
main springers, and cusped tracery between. – PLA
Chalice and Paten, 1577; Standing Paten and Fla
given in 1728. – MONUMENTS. Brass to Richard Pear
† 1512 and wife. Only the figure of the man and so
children and that of a peacock are preserved (s cha
chapel). – Brass to Sir Richard Rede (?) † 1560, wife
children (chancel). – Epitaph to Eignon Benyon † 1
and his wife † 1732, by *Thomas Bell* of London. The
sign copied from the Halsey monuments at Great G
desden, with the bust under a draped baldacchino
Many minor epitaphs and tablets.

The church lies at the far w end of the triangular COMM
There are several handsome houses and cottages (s
thatched cottages) along it, especially on its E side, ba

ıg on to the houses in the High Street. GREYFRIARS, a abled timber-framed cottage, and CUMBERLAND IOUSE, with a date 1745, seven-bay, two-storey brick ouse with Roman Doric doorcase and arched central indow. In the HIGH STREET more such Georgian mansions, the biggest THE PRIORY, a completely urban early 18 house which might as well stand in Grosvenor quare: five bays, two and a half storeys, with segment-eaded windows and the typical vertical strips and win-ow surrounds of rubbed bricks. To its r. a long low ine-bay house of *c.* 1700, opposite RED HOUSE, late C18, nd farther E REDBOURN HOUSE of seven bays and two toreys with three-bay pediment and added upper half-torey.

E AUBREYS, 1 m. SW. Iron Age hill-fort, oval and comprising 22 acres of ground. The defences on the E and W ides have been damaged by ploughing, but on the NW, where there is a single bank and ditch instead of a double ne, as on the other sides, and an entrance. Another possible entrance in the SE, covered by the house called The Aubreys.

REDHEATH
2½ m. W of Watford

e house, at the time of writing, was on the point of falling lown. Only the W front stands as impressive as formerly: ed brick, nine bays wide, three storeys high, with hipped oof and a broad central cupola. The clock on this is lated 1743. The central door sumptuously decorated with alternatingly rock-face-rusticated pilasters, a key-tone head, and carved brackets supporting a shell-hood. The date 1712 is carved in. The house was built for Charles Finch.

REED

MARY. The sole importance of the church is the sur-ival of Late Anglo-Saxon work in the nave. The angles of the nave have unmistakable long-and-short work, and n addition there is the N doorway, though the shafts with

their volute or spiral capitals and the roll-moulding of
arch might well be later than the Conquest. Unl
tressed C14 W tower; chancel C14 (E end C19). –
aisles; the nave N windows late Perp. – PLATE. Cha
and Paten, 1806.

REED HALL. A Tudor chimney remained when the ho
was rebuilt in the C18. Several more recent alteration

RENSTREET FARM *see* BOVINGDON

RICKMANSWORTH

Rickmansworth was in the early Middle Ages Ryke-me
wearth; that is, a rich moor-meadow; and indeed
characteristic features of the town are its rivers, lakes,
water-meadows, an area as broad as the whole town. I
only to be regretted that the bathing lake, one of the I
near London, has been given the name Aquadrome.

ST MARY. Rebuilt in 1826 and again in 1890. The archi
then was *Sir Arthur Blomfield*. To him belongs eve
thing we see now except the yellow brick aisles with th
typical Early Gothic Revival windows, and the W to
which was kept from an earlier building of 1630. It
thick clasping buttresses, battlements, and a spike in
Herts tradition. Blomfield's interior has the octago
piers and two-centred arches of the county, and a cle
tory. – STAINED GLASS, E window with Crucifixion
Burne-Jones, 1891. – PLATE. Chalice and Paten, 15
Chalice and Paten, *c.* 1600; Chalice and Paten, 16
Salver, 1692; Flagon, 1695. – MONUMENTS. Brass
Thomas Day and wives † 1613 (N aisle). – Plain ton
chest of Henry Cary, Earl of Monmouth † 1661
Epitaph to Sir Thomas Fatherley; later C17, with f
ornamentation.

Around the church lie the most interesting houses of Ri
mansworth: THE BURY (Urban District Council), w
the church, and THE PRIORY. The latter is of brick a
timber-framing and much renewed. The Bury is ea
C17 brick and timber-framing, roughcast, and has ins

wo original staircases and in one room panelling and two
carved overmantels.

CHURCH STREET not far from the church is the
VICARAGE, the nucleus of which is late medieval half-
timber work. The ground floor bay window has brick
tracery at its foot. On the first floor an overhanging
oriel. Picturesque gables. Many C18 and early C19 alterations.

he long HIGH STREET meets the short Church Street at
right angles. It winds its way through the town from E to
w. There are not many specially noteworthy houses in it.
Most of them are by the E end: ST JOAN OF ARC'S
CONVENT SCHOOL, the best Georgian house of Rickmansworth, the usual red brick, with the usual five-bay,
two-and-a-half-storey elevation and a central pedimented
door. Close to it (Messrs Adco) C18 STABLES (with
cupola) of a former brewery. Farther W BASING HOUSE
(No. 46), seven-bay, late C18, then Messrs Swanell & Sly,
timber-framed cottages, and the SWAN HOTEL with
Jacobean staircase, panelling, and fireplaces. The w half
of the street was only built up in the C19, and close to its
w end lies, completely rural, PARSONAGE FARM in Rectory Road.

t farther w in UXBRIDGE ROAD a POST OFFICE of 1950
(by *G. W. Pollard*) showing that the G.P.O. has now
abandoned its Neo-Georgian tradition and is able to do
neat and handsome modern work. Then YORK HOUSE
SCHOOL, Georgian, five bays, two-storeyed red brick,
and farther out LONGLANE FARM, timber-framing and
yellow-washed brick with weatherboarded barns.

ecial buildings: BAPTIST CHURCH, High Street, 1843.
Of modest design, stock brick with lancet windows.

OYAL MASONIC SCHOOL FOR GIRLS, 1928–33, by
Denman & Sons. Large group with the classroom buildings all arranged in a semicircle. The rest is of brick and
Neo-Georgian in style, the more representational buildings with somewhat magniloquent classical detail.

ERCHANT TAYLORS' SCHOOL, 2 m. E, nearer to Moor
Park; 1931–3, by *W. G. Newton*. Not very large, friendly

H.—9

in the grouping. Brick, Neo-Georgian in style, with det
influenced by the Swedish Modern of *c.* 1925.

RIDGE

St Margaret. Nicely placed N of a village Green w:
some weatherboarded barns and a half-timbered cotta;
The church belongs to the C15. It is of flint with sto
dressings and has a low battlemented w tower with b
diagonal buttresses, a tiled nave and lower chancel, anc
very pretty C19 timber porch with bargeboarding a
traceried openings on the sides (*A. Billing*, 1881). Aisl
less interior with two-light straightheaded windows and
good, lively king-post roof. – Large WALL PAINTING
St Christopher, mid C15, very raw. – PLATE. Chalice a:
Salver, 1740; plated Flagon, also C18.

Orchard Mead. Almshouses, designed by *G. G. Swift*
1844.

ROTHAMSTED
1 m. SW of Harpenden

Manor House. Of the medieval house the masonry of th
Hall, the central hall of the present house, facing S, r
mains, and that of the Offices and Kitchen to its E. In th
Jacobean age the house was faced with brick and r
furnished, and about 1630–50 it was enlarged and exte
nally altered. The show-side, the S front, is now of th
period with mullioned and transomed wooden windc
casements, a three-storeyed central porch covered by
Gothick cupola and Dutch gables, two each side, to the
and r., crowned by the typical alternately triangular ar
segmentheaded pediments (a first hint at the coming
the classical style). To the w there are three more suc
gables, and yet two more were added when in the 186
the house was extended to the NW. That Neo C17 wor
was done very competently, but it seems unrecorded b
whom. Many of the fittings were bought at that time b
Sir C. B. Lawes-Wittewronge, and it is impossible now
recognize what belonged to the house originally. Th
Hall has linenfold panelling of *c.* 1550, the room to its r.

big stone fireplace with caryatids and a lintel with four
birds carved in, the room to the r. of that a big Jacobean
wooden fireplace and a strapwork sopraporte. To the l.
of the Hall is a room with a late C16 wall painting of a
battle and opposite a stone fireplace. The Drawing Room
has an elaborate plaster ceiling and a sumptuous fireplace,
both c. 1900 by *Sir T. G. Jackson*. On the first floor is a
stone fireplace with a charming lintel with all sorts of
animals, including unicorn, camel, squirrel, and snake. –
The formal garden dates no doubt from the remodelling
of the 1860s. The fine avenue of elm trees was planted in
1721.

ROYSTON

oyston lies at the crossing of the Roman Ermine Street
with the pre-Roman Icknield Way, and it has been surmised that the strangest monument of Royston, ROY-
STON CAVE, close to the crossing, is in some way connected with this. It is a bottle-shaped cavern c. 28 ft deep
and at the foot c. 17 ft in diameter in which there are very
rudely carved reliefs of the Crucifixion, St Christopher,
etc. Their date is hard to guess. They have been called
Anglo-Saxon, but are more probably of various dates between the C14 and the C17 (the work of unskilled men).
t the important crossroads a monastery of Augustinian
Canons was founded in the C12. The parish church represents the survival of a part of their very large church.

T JOHN AND ST THOMAS. The present church is large
and townish. It lies E of the old road and S of the new
main road of Royston. It looks all of a piece, but is in
fact a post-Reformation adaptation of the monastic
church. Of this the nave and aisles were pulled down. The
wall running W parallel with the N aisle wall of the church
is the N aisle wall of the monastic church. The W tower
stands where the nave must have ended. The rood-stair
has been traced one bay E of the tower. This first bay of
the present nave is different from the others. After that
the nave appears on the s side for two bays as a convincing
piece of mid C13 design, with piers consisting of four big
main shafts and four keeled diagonal shafts, and carrying

octagonal capitals and complexly moulded arches. The
arcade and the rest of the s arcade have mostly octagon
piers. But one on the N side has four main and four sul
sidiary shafts, presumably the result of the re-use of o
materials. This same very understandable device accoun
for the odd blocked archway in the N aisle and for detai
of the W tower, and of the s aisle windows. The E part
the nave is again a part of the monastic church which ca
easily be reconstructed. It represents the originally aisl
less E end of the chancel. On the N side one large lanc
remains complete and the springing of a second can l
recognized. On the s side the tops of all three (with do
tooth ornament) have been exposed in the masonry abov
the arcades. – At what time these arcades were built s
entirely in the spirit of the old work cannot be said. Th
Royal Commission is satisfied with 'in the C17 or C18
and 'at some uncertain period'. Fresh detail research
needed. The present chancel and most of the W tower ir
cluding the W portal are C19. But the Piscina in the char
cel is again a genuine C13 fragment. – PULPIT. Contair
ing tracery from the former SCREEN of which other frag
ments have been used for a DESK. – SCULPTURE. Imag
of the Virgin (headless) and of a bishop (also headless
both of alabaster, C15. – STAINED GLASS. C15 angels i
a N window. – PLATE. Chalice, 1621; fine Paten, 1629
Paten, 1718. – MONUMENTS. Alabaster effigy of a Knigl
two angels at the head, late C14. – Brass to Willia
Tabram, Rector of Therfield, † 1462, demi-figure unde
cusped ogee canopy with thin pinnacles (nave). – Brass t
a man and woman, c. 1500 (nave). – Thin Brass Cross i
stone slab, C15 (chancel). – Against the outer N wall larg
tablets referring to the BELDAM VAULTS close by, th
earlier with scrolly broken pediment records names fror
1725 onwards, the later in a Gothic Revival style (ver
Dec with crocketed ogee canopies) from c. 1830 onwards

PERAMBULATION

The town consists chiefly of the four streets which represen
Ermine Street and Icknield Way. The HIGH STREE

ads down from the S to the main crossroads. It is narrow
d straight. The chief houses are the BULL HOTEL,
arly Victorian yellow brick; Nos 59–65 opposite, C15
astered with overhang, supported on thin brackets; and
os 43–47, a large early C18 house with a four-bay, three-
oreyed centre with giant angle pilasters and four-bay
wer wings. The windows are segmentheaded. More
inor houses in the High Street recognizable by their
assical cornices or by overhangs at the back. Parallel with
.e High Street KING STREET of the same character, but
ith only minor specimens. Off the High Street in JOHN
TREET the stately former CONGREGATIONAL CHURCH
1843 (giant Ionic columns *in antis* and big pediment)
d the modest COURT HOUSE, debased Italianate of
349. From here one arrives at THE PRIORY, apparently
enlarged Georgian house with quoins and pediment,
robably built on part of the site of the domestic quarters
the monastery.

High Street is continued past the crossroads in KNEES-
ORTH STREET. Here are the remains of the Hunting
odge which James I built for himself at Royston. What
:mains is a plastered cottage with overhang and then the
-called PALACE, a two-storey brick house with two big
iimneys towards the street but the rest redone in the C18
ith a shell-hooded door and a Venetian window above. N
f this the street widens and some detached Georgian
ouses appear on the W: the ROOKERY (white brick) and
EW TREE HOUSE (red brick with segmentheaded
indows).

W–E axis has little to offer W of the crossroads (except
e big WORKHOUSE of 1835). E of the crossroads it is
alled MELBOURNE STREET. On the S side of the street
es the church, on the N side chiefly the following houses:
even-bay early C18 (?) red and purple brick house with
oor on carved brackets and rubbed brick trim. Then
ANYERS HOTEL, white brick, at an angle to the street.
he three-bay centre with giant Ionic pilasters. Then a
even-bay stuccoed C18 front hiding a C17 back with
ur-light mullioned windows in two gables. Finally the

TOWN HALL of 1855, yellow brick, like a Non-[c]
formist Chapel.

More Georgian houses to the E of the top of the High St[reet]
towards the Market.

In and near ORCHARD ROAD, just W of Huntingdon R[oad]
an estate of *c.* 90 houses, also a two-storey terrac[e of]
houses for old people; 1945, etc., by *P. Mauger* [&]
Partners.

THERFIELD HEATH, to the W. On the heath five ro[und]
barrows and one long barrow, the only one of its kin[d in]
the county. Of the five Bronze Age barrows the diame[ters]
vary between 27 and 66 ft, and they stand 3–12 ft h[igh.]
The long barrow stands 6–12 ft high and measures 12[0 by]
65 ft.

SANDON MOUNT, Notley Green, in a field between Co[tton]
Lane and the road from Kelshall. The mound is cove[red]
by a clump of trees. Its diameter is *c.* 87 ft and it is [sur]
rounded by a ditch 14 ft across. A gap in the ditch in [the]
NE corner marks a 16-foot-wide entrance. The m[ound]
itself was probably thrown up in the C13 as a look[-out]
place or defensive earthwork, but in the late C14 or e[arly]
C15 the site was used for the erection of a windmill [no]
trace of which is to be seen above the ground.

RUSHDEN

ST MARY. W tower (unbuttressed), nave, and chancel o[f c13.]
The chancel is of white brick and was built in 1849. [The]
rest is essentially C15, including tower arch and cha[ncel]
arch, but with the exception of the S doorway (capital w[ith]
broad leaves) which proves that the nave walls mus[t be]
C14. – FONT. Octagonal, Perp, decorated with s[mall]
panels with quatrefoils or four-lobed leaves in three ti[ers.]

Many very neatly kept cottages in the scattered vill[age.]

JULIANS. Essentially now a house of 1937–9, though m[uch]
of the masonry is Early Georgian and some perhaps e[ven]
Jacobean. The windows of the entrance side and more [of]
the less formal N side are early C18. But doorway [and]
window above, pediment, and lantern are all of the re[cent]

econstruction. Inside, the extremely pretty staircase with
lim twisted balusters is original, and most of the Dining
Room represents a later C18 re-decoration.

RUSSELLS *see* WATFORD

RYE HOUSE *see* HODDESDON

SACOMBE

CATHERINE. Nave and chancel, and sw tower, with
ow stair-turret. The latter was rebuilt in 1865. The whole
church is very much renewed and architecturally of no interest. But it contains two monuments by two of the foremost sculptors of their periods : Thomas Rolt † 1758 by
Rysbrack, an epitaph with flags and other trophies at the
top and lovely cherubs' heads ; and Elizabeth Caswall
† 1815 by *Flaxman*, also an epitaph, rather frigid, with a
standing allegorical figure with raised arm and a kneeling
and weeping one opposite her.

COMBE PARK, built some time between 1802 and 1808.
Yellow brick of two storeys and nine bays with a four-
column, one-storey portico of Greek Doric columns on
the entrance side. On the garden side two bow windows.
In the centre inside, a staircase with restrained iron railing
under an oval dome. The staircase starts as one arm, and
turns at the first landing at right angles into two arms.
They turn again at right angles and so reach an upper
floor gallery (cf. Hyde Hall).

LD RECTORY, Sacombe Green. An exceptionally picturesque timber-framed C15–C17 house. The history can
be followed well. The oldest windows have wooden mullions set diagonally. Slightly later windows on the w side
above the original ones. More alterations in the late C16
and C17 centuries. Carefully restored fairly recently.*

ST ALBANS

troduction, p. 200. Verulamium, p. 201. The Cathedral,
202. Churches and Public Buildings, p. 219. Perambula-
n, p. 223.

* Cf. in detail *East Herts Arch. Soc. Trans.*, 1938.

INTRODUCTION

As one approaches St Albans, one's first sight from m
away is a long ship-like nave and stumpy tower on a hill
is a typically English sight as one knows them from the
proach to Lincoln and Ely, and the impression of the cat
dral city is confirmed on entering the older streets with th
well-to-do Georgian houses. Yet St Albans became the
of a bishop only in 1877. The glorious history of the chu
is that of one of England's greatest abbeys. Its head v
made premier abbot of England in 1154. Its artists and
chroniclers were famous all over England in the C13. Of
domestic buildings of this powerful community hardly a
thing remains, and if it is always difficult to see with ou
mind's eyes what large Benedictine monasteries of
Middle Ages have looked like, it is almost impossible at
Albans. Much might still be recovered by excavation, v
the English have always been readier to raise funds for p
historic or Roman research than for medieval. And so the
Albans before St Alban, that is the Roman city of Ve
lamium is, thanks to the work of the last twenty or twen
five years, much better known than the Abbey. It was one
the biggest and most important Roman towns on Engl
soil. Its site was in the valley of the river Ver, on the s si
where now St Michael's Church stands. The Saxon ab
chose a new place, on the highest eminence, and there
cathedral still stands. To its s the monastic buildings
tended down towards the river, the mill, and fishponds.
the N grew the town. Of its beginnings we know lit
Privileges referring to the buying and selling of cloth w
confirmed by King John in 1202. The growth of the to
was marked (as in so many other places) by more and m
exasperated quarrels with the abbey. By the C15 the to
was however secure, and wealthy enough to raise a belf
The medieval town did not cover much ground. It was co
pact, except for the familiar ribbons of houses along 1
main roads towards S, N, and W, that is towards the outly
village churches of St Stephen, St Peter, and St Michael
nunnery had been founded near St Albans about 1140, 1

site was right outside the town, at Sopwell, by the river.
ter the Dissolution it was converted into a mansion of not
onsiderable size. The other important mansion of St
bans also lay by the river, at the foot of Holywell Hill:
lywell House, where Sarah Jennings, the future Duchess
Marlborough, was born. The Stuart and Georgian
owth of St Albans took place along the three main roads
: Holywell Hill, St Peter's Street, and Fishpool Street;
d this pattern was still virtually unchanged at the end of
e C18. Only then new roads began to be built: the London
ad in 1794, the Hatfield Road in 1824, and Verulam Road
1833. The spaces between the old main roads were filled
only very gradually. There never was a building rush; for
Albans has not undergone any spectacular industrializa-
n. The town had 6,000 inhabitants in 1801, 11,000 in
51, 18,000 in 1911, 29,000 in 1931, and 44,100 in 1951.

VERULAMIUM

rulamium was built near the site of a prehistoric city
excavated some twenty years ago. This lay on the brow
of the hill to the SW of the Roman town, was sacked by
Boudicca in A.D. 61, and rebuilt on a larger scale shortly
after. The early town is below the NW half of the later.
The final Roman city was oval in shape like Wroxeter and
Cirencester. Its walls were built c. A.D. 125–50. They were
of flint with bonding courses of brick. In some places
they still stand to the height of 12 ft. The outer ditch was
80 ft wide and 20 ft deep. There were four gates of which
nothing remains visible, except for the plan of the London
Gate at the end of Watling Street (c. $1\frac{1}{4}$ m. W of St
Michael's). This is laid out in modern flint-work over the
old foundations. The London Gate was 100 ft wide with
semicircular towers. In impressiveness it must have far
exceeded anything Roman surviving in Britain. The main
street from the London Gate was 40 ft wide and 180 ft
long. It led to a TRIUMPHAL ARCH of c. 300 of which
the footings on one side are still visible. By the arch the
street divided, and in the angle was a temple. One fork
led to the FORUM. This was c. 200 by 300 ft in size and

lay where the churchyard of St Michael's Church now
The basilica was in the place of the church. Oppos
were apparently administrative buildings and also (:
corner) a triumphal monument.

To the N of the Forum and a little away is the THEAT
the one building excavated and restored. It is the o
Roman theatre visible in Britain. The size is over 18c
across, the shape is semicircular. There were about 1,6
seats. The stage part consists of the Postscaenium :
stage properties, the Scaena or back colonnade, and t
Pulpitum or stage proper. To the l. is a green-room.

s of the theatre was a TEMPLE of Romano-Celtic type,
in a vast court with internal and external colonnad
Houses have also been found, and one MOSAIC FLO
with hypocaust heating underneath has been preserved
situ. Much more has been assembled in the Verulamiu
Museum and is there exemplarily displayed.

How much of Roman Verulamium still stood in the Midc
Ages can hardly be estimated. Stukeley early in the C
says that people for road-making were carting away 'hu
dreds of cartloads of Roman bricks'.

CATHEDRAL

9 INTRODUCTION. The first impression is one of unbalanc
length: a nave nearly 300 ft long, and no attempt to match
by high towers. The crossing tower is sturdy and see
squatter than it is, because of its uncommon breadth.
towers are completely lacking. That is unfortunate; t
medieval Norman building had planned two w towers, a
in any case the crossing tower would have had a spire, as o
was indeed built in the C13. A spike of Herts type existed
late as 1800 and was taken down only in 1832. In approac
ing the building and getting a closer view of its Norm
parts, the most striking peculiarity is the russet a
blackish-grey colouring of the Roman brick and flint, whi
was originally, of course, all plastered white. As it is t
building has a sombre tone, decidedly joyless. And joyle
also is the interior. We are never made to forget the ove
powering weight of the walls. Piers and arches appear on

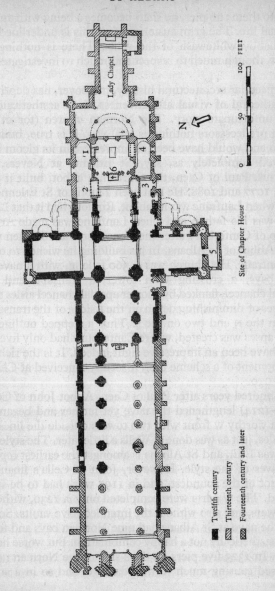

Lady Chapel

Site of Chapter House

N

0   50   100 FEET

Twelfth century

Thirteenth century

Fourteenth century and later

cut into them; no pier, no shaft becomes a being with an in
dividual life. The grim austerity of all this is underlined b
the shabby whitewash of the walls. There is nothing t
attract, though much to respect and much to investigate.

Its peculiar architectural history, moreover, has deprive
the cathedral of visual attractiveness. It is aesthetically
most unfortunate story. The Norman church (for of it
Saxon predecessors nothing is left) was, it is true, built a
one go and would have been as impressive in its gloom if
survived completely as, say, St Étienne at Nevers, c
Tournus. Paul of Caen, the fourteenth abbot, built it be
tween 1077 and 1088. He had been a monk of St Étienne a
Caen when Lanfranc was its abbot. Rumour had it that Lan
franc was his father, and when Lanfranc was made Arch
bishop of Canterbury after the Conquest, Paul of Caen wa
made Abbot of St Albans. In his building he wished to out
do Lanfranc. His church was c. 360 ft long, with a nave o
nine bays, a crossing with tower, a transept, and a
apsidal chancel, flanked by shorter apsidal chancel aisles an
by apses of diminishing depth on the E sides of the transept
two on the N and two on the S. Thus a stepped outline o
seven apses was created, where Canterbury had only five. I
must have been an impressive sight indeed. It is the riches
development of a scheme first, it seems, conceived at Clun
in the C10.

A hundred years after Paul of Caen, Abbot John of Cell
(1195–1214) lengthened the nave yet farther and began t
erect a worthy w front with two towers outside the lines o
the aisles, just as was done at Wells a little later. The style h
used was E.E., and St Albans is amongst the earliest repre
sentatives of the style. However, John of Cella's finance
were not of the soundest, and in 1197 work had to be sus
pended. The w parts were completed only c. 1230, withou
the towers, and also without the intended nave vaults. So ir
1230 the nave at St Albans had nine Norman bays and fou
E.E., aesthetically not a happy combination. But worse hap
pened. In 1323 five piers on the S side of the Norman nave
collapsed causing much further damage, and so in a style

nding with the E.E. w bays but conflicting with the Nor-
n ones opposite, the s side of the Norman nave was re-
lt. There can be no peace for the eye in such conflicting
roundings.

he E parts of the abbey had in the meantime also been
npletely rebuilt. The need for room and also for altars
: so great that even the seven apsed spaces were not suffi-
nt. It is the development we find in most English cathe-
ls. The rebuilding began E of the crossing in 1257 and
nt on till the Lady Chapel was completed about 1320.
is was slow work compared with that under Paul of Caen.
: impetus was evidently lacking. Just as the builders of the
arts of the nave had given up the projected vaults, so the
v chancel, retrochoir, and Lady Chapel had all been
gun with the intention of stone vaulting and all ended
h wooden vaults or ceilings. Had money or enthusiasm
urned after that, the nave might have been entirely re-
lt as at Canterbury later in the C14 or at least entirely
nodelled as at Winchester. The painful conflict between
nd s would then have been avoided.

3ut the separateness of parts of St Albans goes still fur-
r. The monks' choir extends for three bays into the nave.
arge C14 rood screen of solid stone ends it in the w and
is cuts off part of the nave and the view towards the cross-
tower and the E. And another even bigger and heavier
een, the reredos, forms another division farther E.

Finally, to end this tale of unhappy circumstances, St
pans is the only one of the major churches of England
ich has a w front completely, or almost completely, Vic-
ian. It is the work of *Lord Grimthorpe*, done at his own
pense, in 1879. The cathedral was indeed in a sad state
ly in the C19. The Lady Chapel was walled off as a gram-
r school, a public way led through the chancel, and the w
nt was a ruin with the lateral porches walled up. Restora-
n began with a report of 1871 by *Sir G. G. Scott*. But
rk had to be stopped after Scott's death for lack of further
ids. That was when Lord Grimthorpe, a lawyer, amateur
ologian, and architect, aged 63, intervened, and as he is
uted to have spent £130,000 on the abbey it would be

ungracious to speculate what Bodley or Pearson or Old
Scott would have made of so responsible a job.

THE NORMAN ABBEY. All that remains of the Norm
style at St Albans (and it is much and of great pow
belongs, with one exception, to the years immediat
after the Conquest. Paul of Caen began it, probably
1077, that is as soon as he had been made abbot to refo
the lax Saxon monastery. His church was completed a
only eleven years, a miraculous feat. Of its E parts,
scribed above, little survives. We have to go to the tra
sept and the crossing tower to receive the full impact
that mighty and graceless style. The building is of fli
with all strengthening at the angles, round doors a
windows, and in similar places by means of Roman bri
taken freely from old Verulamium. Arches and windo
are completely unadorned (no more than one step b
instead of any mouldings). The walls are articulated
strip-like flat buttresses without set-offs (rather th
lesenes). Paul of Caen might have seen these at St Étien
in Caen, begun in 1064 and consecrated about 1075–
In the N and W walls of the N transepts the ground fl
windows survive, and in both transepts the clerest
windows. Moreover, inside the transept the three eq
openings to the chancel aisles and the apsidal trans
chapels can still be seen. In the S transept two small w
dows remain above them. Of the S front of the S and th
front of the N transept we cannot say much, as Lord
has given the one a spectacular group of E.E. lancets,
other a large rather thin rose-window. In their stead th
had been big Perp windows. The interior system of
transept is of a tall ground floor, a triforium, and a cler
tory with wall passage. The triforium has for each
two pairs of openings. The colonnettes are circular
octagonal or of an odd, decidedly Saxon-looking balus
shape. This has been explained as a re-use of Sax
pieces; it may, however, easily be a survival of a tradit
amongst craftsmen. The tympana of the arches are fil
by a criss-cross of bricks, which was no doubt once whi

15b

washed, as all the rest. On the whitewash originally simple
patterns were painted (an apparent alternation of red and
white blocks of stone, for example, or a sham ashlaring by
red lines to indicate joints or by zigzag lines.*

The crossing tower rests on immensely high arches.
The supporting piers have a double-stepped section for
each side. Above this is a triforium of three twin openings,
and above this two large windows. The rest is hidden by a
wooden ceiling painted early in the C16 with pretty square
panels. The exterior of the crossing tower is entirely of
brick. The builders did not trust flint for construction so
high up in the air. Above the first stage of windows is an
outer gallery of four arches of twin openings on each side,
and above this the bell-stage with two large twin openings and a curious piercing of the tympana by rows of
little triangles. The angles of the tower are strengthened
by buttress-strips which higher up develop into circular
angle supports. The tower is embattled.

Of the E parts, as they were built by Paul of Caen, the
beginning can be traced in the exterior on the N side and
in the interior on both sides. The chancel aisles are groin-
vaulted. On the S side a blocked arch in the first bay
marks the former access from the chancel aisle to the
inner transeptal chapel. In the second bay a pair of quite
tall windows has been found and exposed.

The nave remains complete in the first three bays from
the crossing, at least at arcade and clerestory level. The
flat ceiling is of the C15 but of course replaces an equally
flat Norman ceiling. W of the third bay only the N side is
Norman. The nave has tall arcades with broad rectangular piers, in fact hardly piers at all, but chunks of
solid wall masonry left standing. To appreciate the contrast between this raw treatment of the arcade and the
articulate and elegant arcading of later styles one need
only look at the C13 work farther E. The Early Norman
piers are, as it were, piers only potentially, not yet really.
Their wall character is emphasized by the pilaster-strips or
buttress-strips which rise on their surface and go right up

* Examples must also be looked for in the nave and the chancel aisles.

into the clerestory zone. Towards the arches the piers a:
double-stepped, a small progress against the single-step
ping farther E. But there are not yet any further moul
ings anywhere, nor any capitals, nor any ornaments

Equally unadorned was no doubt the storey above th
arcade. But here some alterations have been made whic
obscure the original state and have in fact until now pr
vented a full appreciation of the design of St Albans. A
things are at present, one sees from inside a deep ur
moulded arch above each arcade bay at the outer end o
which is a three-light C15 looking window. These wir
dows give no light. They lead into the roof of the aisle. A
engraving by Kip and Hawksmoor of 1723 shows, how
ever, that at that time the aisle roof did not reach up s
high and that the windows were of quite a different shape
Evidence inside the present roof shows in fact that th
window wall is a Norman outer wall. So St Albans had n
gallery originally, as all the major Norman churches i
England have, but only a triforium, that is a passage in th
thickness of the wall of the passage itself; all traces hav
now gone, but to the l. and r. of the main upright pilaster
strips shallow piers can still be seen with their bases an
unmoulded capitals on which formerly the arches to
wards the nave must have rested. According to Sir Alfre
Clapham these were large, one arch for each arcade arc
below, like at St Étienne in Caen, but a triforium a
against a gallery can hardly be reconstructed with on
arch of this kind and it seems much more probable tha
the triforium was indeed subdivided towards the nav
more or less as in the transepts. The large brick arche
visible in the outer wall (i.e. the roof-space of the aisle
would then have been mere blank relieving arches. So th
elevation of St Albans was not derived from St Étienn
but from its sister foundation at Caen, Ste Trinité, whic
also possesses (an exception in Normandy as in England
a triforium instead of a gallery. The Trinité also was com
plete by the time Paul of Caen left Normandy. Details o
the C11 triforium at St Albans have no doubt to b
visualized as raw and bare as the arcade.

That St Albans, in the C12, did not shun ornament is proved by the SLYPE, that is the passage between S transept and Chapter House (*see* below) which is decorated with blank arcading with intersected arches. These arches have rings at close intervals so that they look like bent spinal cords. Some of the arcading is still *in situ*, but most of it has been re-erected against the S wall of the S transept. Below it is, also re-set, the highly ornate DOORWAY from the Cloister into the Slype. This has three orders, without any break between jambs and voussoirs, the outer of foliage scrolls, the middle one with two sets of roundheaded crenellations, one on the intrados, the other on the extrados. The inner order is C19 reconstruction. Amongst architectural fragments exhibited in the Slype there are many more pieces of C12 decoration.

THE THIRTEENTH AND FOURTEENTH CENTURIES. What reason can Abbot John de Cella (1195–1214) have had to lengthen yet farther the nave of the church, the nave being the least important part of an abbey church? Or was he only carrying out what had been planned from the beginning? He added three bays and started a proper W façade. The design is wholly in the Gothic style. No compromise with the existing nave is aimed at. Considering the fact that the Gothic chancel at Canterbury had been begun only twenty years before and Lincoln and Wells no more than five, John of Cella was certainly a modern-minded man. However, after only two years, work was stopped for lack of money, and much of what we see now goes back only to William of Trumpington (1214–35). The new bays of the nave have piers of an unusual section. They are basically square, with four attached shafts, but as the angles are broadly chamfered they appear as if they had semi-octagonal shafts in the diagonals. It is a somewhat heavy section, due perhaps to existing square Norman foundations for the lengthening of the nave? The arch mouldings are more complex than can here be described. The arches reach up higher than the Norman ones. Their apexes touch the sill-line of the triforium. For the E.E. extension also has no proper gallery.

The triforium is of two twin-openings per bay, wi
ample dog-tooth decoration along the sill and up t
shafts, and with pierced quatrefoils in the spandrels. T
most interesting thing about the triforium is, however, t
fact that no differentiation is made between the curve
the inner arch of each light and that of the outer ar
above both lights of one twin opening. Thus it looks as
the outer arch started with one broad complex set
mouldings from which some suddenly break off to for
the smaller arch inside—a lack of articulation or logicali
typically English. It exists at Worcester as well, probab
a little earlier (Retrochoir consecrated 1218). Most of th
work on this stage belongs to the second building phas
During the first, that is between 1195 and 1197, vaultir
shafts of Purbeck marble had been attached to the spar
drels of the arcade below. The triforium was prepared
receive their continuation up to the projected vault, b
they were abandoned, as can clearly be seen, and wi
them the plan to vault the nave. The clerestory continu
the wall passage of the Norman nave. On the outside it
handsomely shafted, with a larger arch for each lanc
window and smaller, more pointed, blank arches betwee
The aisle windows were all altered by Lord G. Inside, th
aisles have bare walls (none of the usual English blar
arcading), but the s wall has tripartite vaulting shaf
along the wall, as if for aisle vaults. The existing vault
however, are C19. De Cella's w end was meant to be
grand show-piece, with two w towers standing outside th
nave to widen the façade, and with three deep porche
The idea of towers was given up, the rest was built bu
fell into such dismal decay that it was almost entirely r
built by Lord G. Of the upper parts of the façade nothir
is C13: a nine-light Perp window was demolished b
Lord G. to replace it by his Late Geometrical one. Th
porches are original in their structure, but only in fe
details. The long Purbeck shafts carrying an outer skin
arcading in front of the blank arcading against the bac
walls of the porches, however, can be ascribed to the la
C12. The inside of the front towards nave and aisles

richly adorned with blank lancet arcades. The capitals are
of the crocketed as well as the stiff-leaf type.

The next addition to the church was the replacement of
the Norman E end by one more spacious and more up to
date. The work was started in 1257 close to the crossing.
Here the Norman walls of the chancel and the first bays
of the chancel aisles were left standing and tall blank
arcades applied to the chancel walls. Two entrances into
the chancel from the aisles with odd and very pretty little
tripartite balconies above them (what was their use? they
are inaccessible from outside) were provided. The balconies have three canopies each with three pointed and
cusped arches and three crocketed gables. Farther E, that
is in the Feretory or space for the Shrine, behind the
altar and reredos, the chancel arcades are open, with piers
of four major and four minor shafts. The aisles have
quadripartite rib-vaults. Above the arcade is a small
mostly blank triforium of even little cusped arches, and
above that the clerestory with clusters of nook-shafts and
wall passage. Here also a stone vault was planned, but
only a wooden vault carried out. It is of C13 timber, but
was repainted in the C15 and again recently by *J. C.
Rogers* and *Professor Tristram*. The chancel ends to the E
in an arcade of three bays* and a large and excellent
group of a four-light Geometrical window and two flanking lancets. The large window has two trefoils in circles
and above them a splendid large octofoil, similar to the
contemporary chapter house at Salisbury. E of this the
building is carried on one-storeyed, and on its general
outline, especially from far away, this lowering of the
roof line has an unfortunate effect. In plan the new E
parts seem quite able to balance the long nave; in elevation they don't, except when the building is seen from the
NE or SE. The E exterior consists of the Retrochoir and the
Lady Chapel. Contrary to custom (cf., for example, 18a
Exeter) the Lady Chapel was the last undertaking. The
retrochoir carries on the line of the chancel aisles, but

* Into the springers of the arches odd little blank arcades have been
carved, for no purpose which can now be understood.

uses an octagonal pier to separate the aisles from th
roomy central span. This is not broader than the chance
but appears so because it is so much lower, and also be
cause it has a flat ceiling. All this is not as it was originall
intended. The foundations of columns have been foun
which would have divided the central span into thre
naves as is the case at Salisbury. Against the outer wall
renewed blank arcading, and above it open the window
The window decoration, where it is preserved, is of th
earliest bar-tracery type, two cusped lights with a foile
circle above. Others have the slightly later form of thre
unencircled quatrefoils above the two lights. Yet other
(retrochoir aisle E, Lady Chapel vestibule N and S) go
decisive step farther away from the purity of the E.E
style.

The Lady Chapel itself must be called Dec, although
has none of the fantasies of East Anglia or Yorkshire.
special effort was made here (e.g., the outer walls of thes
E parts were intended to be, and were partly, stone-faced
A vault was also intended, but once more not carried out.
The outer walls have again blank arcading inside, all in it
present form C19. The windows are sumptuously adorned
They have inside bell-flower decoration and in additio
tier above tier of small figures on brackets. Their tracer
is complex. It includes ogee reticulation and small oge
heads to the individual lights of the five-light E window
These are mostly oddly crowned by little crockete
gables, as if they were blank arches, although the glazing
of the window goes on above them in the larger forms c
the arch common to the whole five-light window. Other
wise there are intersections, unencircled trefoils, dagger
arranged cross-wise so as to fill the oblong lozenge-shap
at the top of a four-light window, a wheel of six cuspe
daggers in a circle, with mouchettes in the spandrels, etc
The Royal Commission dates all this as c. 1308. There is
however, no conclusive reason why it should not hav
been completed as late as c. 1320, which is a much mor

---

* The present stone vault is C19. Before it there was a woode
vaulting.

kely date. If one looks at the Sedilia, for example, the harming blank arcading above has much crocketing but o ogees. Thus it appears earlier than, for example, the indow above the Sedilia, which was (an extreme oddity) iven the shape of a spheric triangle. If work was carried n at ground floor level, that is the level of the Sedilia, *c.* 300–10, the more advanced tracery forms may well be a evision of the design made *c.* 1315–20.

In 1323 part of the s side of the Norman nave came own, and instead of a complete rebuilding of the nave, nly this side (six bays long) was redone. The designer ecided to keep to the general scheme of the C13 work arther w. He used piers of the same shape and only djusted his capitals and arch mouldings according to a ifferent taste. He abandoned the C13 vaulting shafts in he arcade spandrels, as he never intended vaults, and ntroduced pretty label stops instead in the form of heads : King, a Queen, a mitred Abbot, and a layman, probably he master mason. His triforium also differs from that of he C13 in such details as the elongated cusping of the rches and the decoration of the spandrels. The earlier log-tooth ornament was replaced by knobbly foliage. The lerestory fenestration is different too, as can be seen out-ide from the s. In the aisles five-partite instead of tri-artite shafts are used and vaults actually carried out.

Some time later in the C14 vestries were built E of the s ransept, where the Norman chapels had been. Their two loorways still exist, as does also the infinitely more laborate late C14 doorway from the s aisle into the Cloister. This is set in a square frame, as pleased the taste f those who believed in the new Perp style. The door rch is very cusped. In the spandrels are those quatrefoils vith shields which appear in the w doors of so many parish churches. To the l. and r. are slim niches with tiny ierne-vaults inside. For the Cloisters, *see* below (Monas-ic Buildings).

The C15, so prominent in most major churches, what-ver their original dates, is almost absent at St Albans except for the nave windows above the Norman arcades).

Lord G. everywhere replaced it by his version of the [

FURNISHINGS. ALTAR AND REREDOS. The rere[
was erected by Abbot Wallingford (1476–92) and [
1,100 marks. It looks repulsively un-genuine now wit[
its *Harry Hems* figures of 1884–90, but its structur[
indeed essentially original, a solid stone wall with t[
tiers of thickly canopied niches. The schematism of [
uprights and horizontals is far stronger than the fanc[
the details (a typical Late Perp feature).* The relief [
inserted in the reredos immediately above the altar i[
Sir Alfred Gilbert. As the reredos cuts awkwardly into[
chancel arcading short STONE SCREENS (with very p[
Perp panelling) were erected in the chancel aisle[
ROOD SCREEN. The rood screen separating not the ch[
cel (i.e. the area E of the crossing) but the monastic c[
from the nave, stands three bays W of the crossing. [
also of stone and was probably built by Abbot de la N[
(1349–96). It has none of the grace and lightness of ea[
C14 *pulpit* such as those of Exeter or Southwell. In[
solid squareness with straight top and only a thin cres[
it is wholly in the new Perp spirit. It has two doors, [
lay-altar between them, and above this seven closely [
niches for images with tall canopies above. More nic[
strangely at a slightly lower sill level to the l. and r. of[
doors. – CHOIR STALLS, 1905, by *Oldrid Scott*. – P[
PIT. In the nave, big and circular, of stone, with [
diaper patterning, designed and given by *Lord Gr*[
thorpe.

ORGAN CASE. By *Oldrid Scott*. – FONT and COV[
1933, by *J. A. R. Blacking*. – SHRINE OF ST ALB[
Erected *c*. 1320, destroyed in 1539, and found in 2,[
pieces in 1872. The base is like a tomb-chest with [
usual quatrefoil decoration. In front of it detached b[
tresses, linked up, it seems, with the main structure o[
higher up. The base itself has four canted niches on e[
of the long sides, decorated inside with blank og[

* Fragments of original stonework from the Reredos removed a[
time of the restoration are preserved in one of the E recesses of t[
transept.

reticulated tracery. Crocketed gables above the niches, the spandrels with excellently carved but badly damaged figures, seated saints, the Martyrdom of St Alban, censing angels, etc. The top of this base formed the platform on which the shrine itself stood. This was always under the watchful eye of a *custos feretri* for whom a special raised box or bridge was constructed late in the C14. – This WATCHING LOFT has only one parallel, the one at Christ Church, Oxford. It is of timber, the ground floor made into cupboards and a narrow staircase, the upper floor coved out like a rood loft. The upper floor is one chamber, open towards the Shrine in eight twin-windows. The detail is all of the simplest Perp, again much like that of rood screens. The designing and carving was probably done by a workshop usually engaged on such jobs. – SHRINE OF ST AMPHIBALUS (N chancel aisle). Here also only the base remains, reconstructed in the C19. It is mid C14 work of clunch, whereas the major shrine of St Alban is partly of Purbeck marble. – DOORS. N wall, N transept, with big Norman iron hinges. – From S aisle to cloister, richly traceried, late C14. – The original W doors, also late C14, of similar design, now in the N transept. – BREAD CUPBOARDS. Late C16, small, in a W recess of the S transept, with balusters instead of doors. – TILES. A few C14–C15 tiles placed in front of an altar in the N transept.

PAINTINGS. St Albans possesses an amount of medieval wall painting unique amongst the major churches of England, even if far inferior to what, for example some French and German churches possess (St Savin, Reichenau). There are first of all traces in many places of the decorative motifs used to enliven the whitewashed wall surfaces, sham ashlaring, alternation of red and white courses, zigzag, foliage scrolls, etc. The whole church must be visualized painted in this fashion. Of the late Middle Ages are the pretty vine scrolls in a N transept N window and the dark green Tudor roses on a strong red background on the piers to the SE of the Shrine of St Alban. There are also traces left of the major figure motifs

which must originally have been everywhere in the mo
important positions, e.g. a mid C13 Christ in Majes
with angels, on the E side of the arch between crossing a
chancel. Similarly there is an earlier C13 figure of
angel on the E wall of the S transept and, on the E wall
the N transept, a C15 scene of Doubting Thomas agair
elaborate canopy work. Then two large C13 figures ha
been uncovered between the clerestory windows at the
end of the N aisle, and finally there is the decoration of t
Norman nave piers themselves. Two of them have lar
C14 figures facing the nave, and five have the precious r
mains of C13 paintings originally no doubt above altar
It is a most interesting fact in itself that altars should ha
stood against all these piers in the nave of an abb
church. Each painting is of two tiers, and in each case t
Crucifixion is on the upper tier. This repetition is aga
interesting, and equally interesting is the variety of trea
ment and sentiment, from the gentleness of the secor
of the painted piers (counting from W) to the majesty
the third, and the terrible distortion of the fifth. In da
they range from *c.* 1215 (first) to *c.* 1275 (fifth).

LATER PAINTINGS. Last Supper; this cannot be t
picture by *Fellows*, painted in 1701. It is obviously la
C18. – The Passing of Queen Eleanor, by *Sir Frank Sal*
bury, 1918, a piece of facile, colourful, historical fiction.

STAINED GLASS. Surprisingly little of interest. E wir
dow 1881, by *Burlison & Grylls*. Lady Chapel S and
windows by *Kempe*, 1896 and 1900. – PLATE. Chalice
1560; two more C16 Chalices; Chalice, 1639; Pate
1697; Spoon, 1709; Flagon, 1721. Spanish Crystal Cros
C16 (on the lay-altar).

MONUMENTS. The most important are the thre
CHANTRY CHAPELS to the N and S of the chancel. The
are Humphrey, Duke of Gloucester's, 1447, Abb
Wheathampstead's † 1465, and Abbot Ramryge's † 151
The most beautiful feature of the Gloucester Tomb do
not belong to it, the late C13 iron grille of rectangul
panels alternatingly built up of vertical and horizont
and of diagonal bars. The chantry itself has a large tr

partite opening to the altar and above stonework of the
design usual in screens, with piers between on which are
three tiers of figures in niches. The vault inside is tra-[25]
ceried. – The Wheathampstead Chantry has a wide four-
centred arch closed by contemporary ironwork and a
heavy straight-topped super-structure with the Abbot's
emblem (wheat ears) and his device, Valles Habundabunt
(of wheat). There is nothing fanciful about the architecture of this tomb. It is deliberately less sumptuous than
that erected by Wheathampstead to his patron the Duke
of Gloucester. The Ramryge Chantry of *c.* 1515–20 is the [26]
most elaborate of the three, a tall ground floor with a close
stone screen, again of the patterns used for stone rood
screens, and above finer and thinner decoration with ogee
arches and polygonal turrets. Amongst the carvings
appear, apart from shields and Ramryge's emblem, the
ram, the Instruments of the Passion and scenes from the
Martyrdom of St Alban. The interior is daintily fan-
vaulted. The door into the chapel is original. – The only
other medieval stone memorial is a RECESS in the S aisle,
arched and cusped, late C13. – On the other hand there is
a large number of BRASSES preserved, and even more indents. Most of the figure brasses have been collected on a
wooden board inside the Wheathampstead Chantry. They
are all of the C15 and early C16 and of no special merit.
Remaining on the floor Ralph Rowlatt † 1543, merchant
of the Staple of Calais (s chancel aisle), and R. Beauner, *c.*
1455, and Sir A Grey † 1480 (chancel). In the chancel
floor a fine tripartite brass canopy with concave sides belonging to the brass of Abbot Stone † 1451. But the finest
brass at St Albans is the large plate of Flemish workmanship to Abbot de la Mare † 1396. It now lies on the tomb-
chest of Abbot Wheathampstead in his chantry. It has
broad buttresses on the sides of the figure with three tiers
of pairs of small figures under canopies and two of single
figures above. In the low top canopy the Lord holding the
Abbot's soul in a cloth, and four angels, the whole done
exceedingly delicately. – Post-medieval monuments are
scanty and not of great interest. Painted epitaph to Ralph

Maynard † 1613 with kneeling figure (s chancel aisle), an
below epitaph without effigy to Charles Maynard † 166
– J. Thrale † 1704, epitaph with two frontal busts again
an altar backplate with weeping putti l. and r. – W. Kir
† 1766, epitaph of variously coloured marbles and wi
charming cherubs' heads at the foot (both s aisle).
Christopher Rawlinson † 1733, large epitaph with lif
size figure of History seated on a sarcophagus against
black obelisk (N transept). – Mrs Mure † 1834, by *Cha
trey*, pure white, with a kneeling female allegory an
Grecian detail. – Bishop T. Legh Claughton, designed l
Oldrid Scott, the figure by *Forsyth*, 1895; alabaster tom
chest with recumbent marble effigy. – A. Blomfield † 189
by *Sir A. Blomfield*, tomb-chest with tracery panels an
poor figures between them (all these N transept).

MONASTIC BUILDINGS. Of these surprisingly litt
can now be seen. It amounts to this : the SLYPE along th
s wall of the s transept.* Then the blank arcading and th
springers of the vault of the CLOISTER. This went alor
the E half of the s side of the nave. The remains are clear
of the early C14. S of the Slype was the Chapter Hou
whose site and size have been ascertained by excavation
s of this probably was the Dormitory, along the s range
the cloister the Refectory, and along the W range th
cellars with probably the Abbot's Lodgings over, or e
tending separately farther W along the nave. The Gue
House, Aula Regia, etc., were farther W still, not far fror
the GATEHOUSE which survives in all its bulk. It stanc
in a line with the s aisle of the church, c. 50 ft away fro
it, with the gateway leading from N to s into the abbe
precincts. The building is due to Abbot de la Mare, th
is belongs to the second half of the C14. It is of flint wi
stone dressings, a big, broad, fortress-like structure. Th
gateway is divided on the N side by a pier into a carriag
way and a pedestrian entrance, but on the s side there
only one very wide and high opening, flanked by re
tangular turrets. The lierne-vault has a central octagon
ribs inscribed into a four-pointed star.

* On its Norman decoration, *see* above.

CHURCHES AND PUBLIC BUILDINGS

t MICHAEL. One of the archaeologically most interesting 15a
churches in the county, which is not at once noticeable,
as the tower and the whole w end are *Lord Grimthorpe's*
work of 1898. On entering, however, an early history of
many stages becomes at once evident and is then borne
out by external features. The nave and chancel walls are
Saxon, probably of the C10. The nave windows with
arches of Roman brick are partly exposed. A similar arch
to a blocked doorway in the s chancel wall. The early C12
added aisles with very heavy low square piers (the Saxon
walls simply left standing). The s aisle was pulled down
later, but the blocked-up arcades remain. Early in the C13
the nave was heightened by a new clerestory. This with its
small lancet windows also remains. So does the slightly
later Lady Chapel, that is the s chancel chapel, much
higher than the aisle so that the clerestory windows here
look into the chapel. The Lady Chapel has very tall roundheaded lancet windows. The e end has a group of two
with one circular window between, the whole framed to
the inside by shafts with moulded capitals and pointed
arches. The doorway from the nave into the chapel and
the s doorway to the church have plain double-chamfered
jambs and arches. Later alterations are the C14 ogee-
headed window and low outer recess in the s chancel wall
(the chancel e window is new), the Dec N aisle e window
of unusual tracery design, several Perp windows, and the
C15 nave roof on carved stone corbels.

FONT. Octagonal, Perp, with quatrefoil decoration. –
PULPIT. Hexagonal, early C17, with tester, decorated
panels, and daintily carved bookrests. – ORGAN, 1950, by
Welch & Lander. – PLATE. Large London-made Chalice,
Paten, Flagon, Almsdish, all of 1736; Almsdish, 1743. –
MONUMENTS. Brass to John Pecock † 1330 and wife (s
chapel). – Brass to a civilian (figure of the wife missing),
within the head of a beautifully ogee-foliated cross, also
c. 1330. – Brass to a Knight, *c.* 1400 (nave, e end). – The
international fame of the church is the monument to Sir

Francis Bacon, the philosopher and Lord Chancello:
† 1626, life-size marble figure seated comfortably an
asleep, an exceptionally 'genre' conception for the date.
ST PETER. As far as the exterior is concerned *Lord Grim*
thorpe's restoration of 1894–5 has made the church
wholly Victorian building. He added a W front (with a big
rather thin rose window and lancets facing the aisles, a v
bay to the nave, rebuilt the N aisle, the crossing tower, an
the chancel, and proudly placed above the rose an inscrip
tion: 'Templum hoc restituit Cathedrae renovator e
auxit.' The transepts had already been pulled down i:
1802. So now the only original feature outside is the
aisle windows, large, of three lights, with simple Per;
tracery. On the N side Lord Grimthorpe corrected thi
mistake and made his Geometrical and Dec, as he ha
made his chancel E.E. So one can read a whole non-exist
ing building history into the stones of the church. Inside
the nave arcades are old, of very tall piers of the usual C1:
four-shaft-four-hollow section. The clerestory was re
built by Lord Grimthorpe. The angel corbels of th
original roof were preserved. The outer wall of the S aisl
has odd wall-shafts, also of C15 style, but possibly earlie
than the nave arcade. They are shorter, too, so that the
neither fit the nave piers nor the aisle windows. – PUL
PIT. With very rich Victorian carving, by *J. A. Goyers* o
Louvain (1863). – SCREEN, 1905, by *Temple Moore*; cor
rect without originality. – ORGAN and CASE. The orga
was made by *Ralph Dallens* for St George's Chapel a
Windsor, went from there to St Martin-in-the-Fields
and finally to St Peter's. Excellent scrolly carving. –
STAINED GLASS. Plenty of fragments of C15 and late
glass in the N windows, but much jumbled up. – The
window by *J. Caprounier* of Brussels, 1867. – The E win
dow by Kempe's successor *Tower*, 1910, entirely in the
Kempe style. – PLATE. Magnificent set of Chalice, Paten
Flagon, and covered Bowl, foreign, given *c.* 1667; Pater
of approximately the same date; Spoon given *c.* 1720–30
Chalice and Paten given in 1785. – MONUMENTS. Bras:
to Roger Pemberton † 1627, wife and children. – Large

ely classical Epitaph to Edward Strong † 1723, with
st at the top in a broken pediment. Strong was chief
aster mason to St Paul's Cathedral. The inscription
ys: 'In Erecting the Edifice of St PAUL, Several years of
s Life were Spent, Even from the Foundation to HIS
ying the Last Stone, And herein (Equally with its In-
nious Architect SR. CHRISTOPHER WREN and its truly
ous Diocesan Bishop COMPTON) He Shared the Felicity
  Seeing both the Beginning and Finishing of that
upendous Fabrick.'

STEPHEN. St Stephen, like St Michael, bears witness to
ose Early Norman decades when the cathedral was
ing rebuilt. The W front of the nave, of rough flint
ickly embedded in mortar, has quoins of Roman brick
d two small roundheaded windows. The front of the
emolished N aisle which was left standing has one more
ch window. The N wall of the nave is a remarkable
limpsest. It contains one large Early Norman window
play only inside; otherwise one might have been
mpted to assign to it a pre-Conquest date). This was
ocked and cut into by a wide Norman arch, probably to
e aisle, which is in style similar to the arcade at St
lichael's. It can hardly be later than c. 1120. This arch is
so blocked. To the W of it an equally blocked pointed
ch. Later, after the aisle had been pulled down, a
ointed doorway was cut into the blocked roundheaded
ay. The chancel masonry must also be Norman, as to it
s chapel was added early in the C13. The two S lancet
indows are original. The S aisle arcade is again not of
e date. The octagonal piers of the W bays have earlier
oulded capitals than those farther E. The difference can
sily be seen. The dates must be late C13 and early C14.
he arches are of uneven width and height too, but all
ouble-chamfered. In the C15 the W door was added and
rther odd additions were made in timber. Instead of a
ancel arch there is a timber frame, and a similar timber
ame at the W end carries a timber bell-turret, original
ven in the two-light timber bell-openings. – FONT. C15
ith much figure carving of indifferent quality, small

figures in cusped niches on the shapely demi-figure
angels with shields on the bowl. – LECTERN. Large F
Lectern of brass with an inscription : 'Georgian Cre
town Episcopus Dunkeldensis.' The inscription date
lectern as between 1524 and 1543. – STAINED GL
Chancel N side by *Hughes*, *c*. 1866, rather pictorial
Raphaelesque; E window 1860, and S aisle window 1
by *Clayton & Bell*. – PLATE. Chalice, Late Elizabet
Salver, plated, 1718; Salver, 1789; Chalice, 183
MONUMENTS. Brass to William Robins † 1482, wife
children (chancel N wall).

CHRIST CHURCH, Verulam Road. Built in 1850
Roman Catholic church but soon taken over by
Church of England. The building is supposed to be a
of the R.C. Church of the Archangel Raphael at Surb
Surrey. This was designed by *Parker* and illustrate
The Builder in 1847. Christ Church is of stone, in
Italian Renaissance style, and of ambitious proport
The W tower is like a campanile, with arched open
and a far projecting roof. The windows are large t
openings, the nave has arcades on columns. Only
chancel is straight-ended (an English custom which
architect evidently had no wish to abandon).

INDEPENDENT CHAPEL, Spicer Street, 1811. Three
with three-bay pediment. Red brick with rubbed b
trim. The bays divided by 'lesenes'. Arched main
dows with Gothic glazing bars.

TOWN HALL, 1829, by *George Smith*. The visual u
charter of St Albans. Until then the town had had the
pearance of a mere country town; now it staked the c
to urban qualities. A giant portico of four fluted I
columns faces St Peter's Street and the N. It is placed
plinth of full ground floor height with the main entra
between robust Tuscan pillars. The portico thus app
to stand too high as if it were on stilts. To the E an
large tripartite windows with straight lintels decorate
wreaths, all in the best Grecian taste. The idea of
whole composition seems to be taken over from Bis
Stortford (*see* p. 64).

AMMAR SCHOOL. The Grammar School was moved to
he Abbey Gatehouse (*see* above) in 1871 and special
uildings were erected. In 1907 new buildings including
he Assembly Hall were started (by *P. C. Blow*). Further
dditions 1910 (School House), 1928, and 1936 (Science
Block). Mostly flint with brick dressings, in a style mixing
ell with the surroundings.
OYNE LODGE INFANTS SCHOOL and GIRLS' GRAM-
IAR SCHOOL, Sandridgebury Lane (*see* Introduction,
. 28).

PERAMBULATION

e centre of medieval St Albans was the CLOCK TOWER,
ne of the rare survivals of an English belfry. It was built
1 1403–12 and is of four stages, unbuttressed, with one-
ght pointed and cusped windows in straightheaded
rames. Near the Clock Tower was the Eleanor Cross to
ommemorate the resting place of Queen Eleanor's dead
ody the night before it was conveyed to Waltham (*q.v.*).
The Cross was pulled down in 1703 and a Market Cross
uilt instead. This in its turn was replaced by the
FOUNTAIN by *Worley* in 1874. From the w and E sides
f the Clock Tower to the N two narrow streets run
arallel: French Row and the Market Place. With their
razy overhangs at all heights and to all depths of pro-
ection they still convey a suggestion of the Middle Ages.
Nos 1–5 FRENCH ROW are indeed pre-Reformation
tructures, even if the exteriors do not tell us much of
hat. But the beams inside the gateways of No. 1 and
Nos 2–4 may well be as old as the C14. In the MARKET
PLACE there is nothing visually so eloquent. The street
as had too many recent alterations. Nos 29–30 indicate
hat in the C17 buildings were taller and more ambitious
1 the Market Place than in less important streets. No. 30
as two symmetrical bay windows, No. 29 three over-
anging gables. No. 29 is dated 1637. – Compare this
vith No. 17 in the HIGH STREET to the E of the Clock
Tower. The High Street also has undergone too much
nodernization to be of value now. But No. 17 is dated
665 and, although it is still gabled, it has now plaster

decoration imitating rustication (the taste for quoins
coming) and plaster panels with wide foliage border
Chequer Street, running parallel with the Market Pl
farther E is again entirely changed. That completes
narrowest medieval nucleus of St Albans. The rest m
now be treated by examining one after another the ribb
thrown out in the main directions.

From the crossing of Chequer Street and High Street,
s runs HOLYWELL HILL straight down to the river V
It is predominantly, but not entirely, a Georgian stre
For the upper half the E side needs more attention, for
lower half the W side. Nos 1–5 are early C18, with
usually tall ground floors owing to the sloping away of
street. No. 1 has giant angle pilasters and an attic sto
above the cornice which they carry. The symmetry of
façade is broken by the big segmentheaded carriagew
The feature repeats in No. 5. Nos 13–21 are more c
tagey, but very attractive in the way in which their lev
climb down. Nos 23–25 is the WHITE HART, a c
timber-framed building, now much restored. Opposit
the first house of interest on the W side: No. 40, built
1783 by *Sir Robert Taylor* for Sir William Domville, la
Lord Mayor of London. It is a big four-square house
white, not red, brick. The façade is of the usual type: f
bays, two and a half storeys, with three-bay pediment a
a doorcase with attached unfluted Ionic columns and
pediment. Originality was not one of Taylor's virtu
Fine wrought-iron lampholders, fine mantelpieces, e
Below No. 40 again no houses of individuality, but
same pretty stepping down of the skylines. Off Holyw
Hill to the W SUMPTER YARD has only one house
note, the OLD RECTORY, five bays, two storeys, late c
with Venetian windows flanking the doorcase.

To the E SOPWELL LANE runs parallel with the riv
flanked by rows of minor two-storeyed houses,* unti
turns towards the river. It was here, close to the riv
that the SOPWELL NUNNERY stood. After the Disso

---

* Including a former Primitive Methodist Chapel of three bays w
pilasters, blank arches, and a one-bay pediment.

:ion the buildings were converted into a private mansion,
nd of this considerable ruins remain, all smothered in
vy. They would look better if their shapes were bared
from the bulky foliage. Sopwell Lane was called the Old
Road when the London Road (*see* below) was the New
Road; that is, the former route to London went by the
Nunnery.

ie direct continuation of Holywell Hill across the river is
St Stephen's Hill, leading up to St Stephen's. The
churchyard has on three sides good buildings: to the w
the KING HARRY, Georgian, of three bays and no par-
ticular merit except that it handsomely closes the vista
where the Watling Street enters the area of St Albans. Its
end is flanked on one side, E of the church, by the
VICARAGE, late C17, with quoins, five bays, two and a
half storeys, and a lower wing on the l. On the other side
of Watling Street, s of the church, Nos 2–8, a Late Georgian group, also of no special character in itself but good
as a foil to the church.

the town of St Albans grew to the s down the hill and
then up again towards St Stephen's, so it grew to the N
until it reached St Peter's and to the w until it reached St
Michael's. The N growth has to be followed from the
point where French Row meets the Market Place. Here
the Market Place widens, after having received this
tributary. Then, as it reaches the Town Hall, it is joined
by Chequer Street and widens again. It is now ST
PETER'S STREET, a tree-planted street of the width and
character of such small-town high streets as one can see in
Herts at Berkhamsted or Stevenage. The visual peculiarity
at St Albans is that the lines of trees are not at equal dis-
tances from the l. and r. frontages. On the w side a good
start with No. 1, late C16 but refaced in the late C17 with
seven bays, two storeys, and three dormers. The centre on
the upper floor is emphasized by a door in a projecting
brick frame which leads to a balcony with iron railings.
After that nothing of importance on this side until St
Peter's Church is reached. But opposite, No. 14, THE
GRANGE, a country house rather than a town house, mid-

Georgian, of purple brick with red brick dressings, with
W front of the usual five bays, with the usual doorca
with attached unfluted Ionic columns, and a S front
two semi-octagonal bays with a Venetian window b
tween. Nos 32–40 is one two-storey group, No. 32 ear
C18, No. 36 early C19 with Gothic glazing bars and fo
mer hood-moulds to the windows, No. 38 late C18. N
40 is bigger and heavier than the others, mid C18, with
ponderous porch. Farther N Nos 58–60, the former
Peter's Workhouse, and then a row of small cottages, N
72–76, distinguished by the odd occasional use of ov
windows. Then the church closes the N view of the stre
which now continues narrower. Opposite the W front
the church an uncommonly good triplet of houses: N
103, built c. 1829 by *George Smith* (of the Town Hall)
the Grecian taste, with a closed porch with Ionizi
pillars. Next to this No. 105, slightly recessed, in th
Tudor taste, an asymmetrical composition, stuccoe
Then IVY HOUSE, No. 107, built for himself by *Stro*
(*see* St Peter's), four bays and three storeys, purple bri
with red dressings, with giant angle pilasters and a doo
case with attached Tuscan columns, a frieze of metop
and triglyphs, and a pediment. Recent additions on bo
sides.

The transition from town to country is (as so often) mark
by Almshouses. N of St Peter's the PEMBERTON ALM
HOUSES of 1627, a simple one-storeyed row of six, with
out gables or any other display features. SE of St Peter's
what is now HATFIELD ROAD the MARLBOROUG
ALMSHOUSES erected in 1736 by Sarah, Duchess
Marlborough. They are an uncommonly large composi
tion, yet modest in height and lacking any representa
tional effects. Open courtyard with a big cedar tre
Buildings on three sides. The wings of nine bays, the r
cessed centre of seventeen with a three-bay pediment wi
carved arms. In this centre the windows have stone su
rounds. The others are of plain mullion and transon
type, rather conservative.

To the W of the Clock Tower a chain of streets, aesthetical

as valuable as Holywell Hill and St Peter's Street but very different in character, because George Street – Romeland Hill – Fishpool Street neither go straight down the hill as Holywell Hill nor possess the spaciousness of St Peter's Street. They skirt the hill and very gradually reach the valley, and they meander in a felicitously accidental way. Starting from the Clock Tower Nos 18–28 GEORGE STREET are mostly medieval with overhanging upper storeys. On the other side only minor houses, except for No. 16 which is Late Georgian, distinguished by the excellent rounded corner (even the door, set in the curve, is rounded). The house leads on into ROMELAND which, with a few low cottages, connects the street with the green in front of the Cathedral. To the S of the Green ABBEY MILL LANE leads down to the river. At its end two remarkable buildings face each other: the FIGHTING COCKS INN, a small octagonal timber-framed house on a brick base, perhaps originally a monastic structure, and the former SILK MILL which dates from the later C18. The building is of brick, nine bays long and three storeys high, the gently arched windows broader than they are tall (as is typical of early factories), and with a small cupola.

Returning to Romeland the continuation of George Street is called ROMELAND·HILL. On its S side is a piece of ground now a graveyard. Originally there had been a square called Roomland with the town pound. The churchyard which has replaced it is of 1812. To the N of the churchyard No. 1 Romeland Hill of only three bays, and then ROMELAND HOUSE, built c. 1710, purple and 58 red brick, seven bays, with three-bay pediment and broad pedimented doorcase on attached Tuscan columns. A Venetian window above it. Good plasterwork inside.

FISHPOOL STREET is a most pleasurable street to walk down, although there is no individual house of the quality of, say, Romeland House or No. 40 Holywell Hill or No. 107 St Peter's Street. Instead of describing consecutively it may therefore be better just to record that there is a variety of overhang houses (No. 13 of three storeys with

plaster panels framed by foliage borders, Nos 38 and 4:
and Nos 166–168 with a door with four-centred arch) an
red brick houses of the usual square proportions (Nos :
56, 122), as well as of the long low type (Nos 59, 137). Th
only bigger house is ST MICHAEL'S MANOR HOUS
late C17 of nine bays, with the entrance on the five-bay v
side (a big porch on coupled Tuscan columns). At th
foot of Fishpool Street the vista is closed by KINGSBUR
MILL, a late C18 brick building with three white weathe
boarded gables of different sizes against tall trees behind
Next to this KINGSBURY MANOR HOUSE, pleasant C1
house with a door taken from the Elizabethan Gorham
bury. Then the street turns, crosses the river, and carrie
on in a southerly direction towards St Michael's. Here
in ST MICHAEL'S STREET, Nos 14–18 show expose
timber-framing. At the far end on the r. is ST GER
MAINS, Late Georgian, stuccoed; on the l. DARROW
FIELD HOUSE or the Dower House (of Gorhambury
early C18, of chequered brick, five bays with a three-ba
wing on the l. The doorcase is later, the Gates, sup
posedly Italian, date from the C17.

Houses such as this were on the outskirts of or outside th
town when they were built. Right in the country was, fo
example, BLEAK HOUSE, in CATHERINE STREET an
Normandy Road, which is now · surrounded by othe
houses. It is also early C18, five bays and two storeys wit
lower three-bay wings. Above the Tuscan doorcase a win
dow with a projecting brick frame with ears. The othe
upper windows have slightly decorated brick lintels. I
NORMANDY ROAD a cottage originally belonging to th
same property. Door with straight hood on richly carve
brackets.

Outside the town still to-day on the W THE PRAE, pretty
long, rambling early C19 house on the road to Dunstable
and on the E OAKLANDS, Hatfield Road, which is
romantic C19 conversion of a Georgian house. Tudo
trim was applied and a castellated tower added which
bears the date 1844. The additions were made for a
F.S.A.

veen 1790 and 1830 three new main roads were created:
ondon Road in 1793, Hatfield Road in 1824, and
erulam Road in 1830. In VERULAM ROAD first nothing
ore remarkable than numbers of plain red brick cottages
hich can thus be dated as *c.* 1830. Then DIOCESAN
OUSE, a large detached red brick house, built as the
erulam Arms and converted by *Caroë*. In LONDON
OAD well-to-do stuccoed villas of about the same date,
anned together by *Smith*, e.g. Nos 25–27 with a veran-
ah on pretty wooden skeleton columns, and Nos 174–
76, a Neo-Norman monstrosity, also by *Smith*. Flint with
d brick dressings, arched windows with Gothic glazing
rs, giant blank roundheaded arches and a zigzag of low-
tched gables on top.

ST PAUL'S WALDEN

, SAINTS. A sizeable, low, all embattled flint church.
he W tower not high, with a higher SE stair-turret and
agle buttresses. The N wall of the nave is so thick as to
uggest an older age than the early C14 windows. The S
sle arcade of five bays has octagonal piers also with early
14 capitals and double-chamfered arches. Of the win-
ows only one (with Kentish tracery) goes with that date.
he others are Perp, as are the upper portions of the
wer and the nave clerestory and also the S chancel
hapel (*see* its blocked arcade to the chancel, with stone
ers consisting of semi-octagonal shafts in the main
es and hollows in the diagonals).

The chancel itself is the great surprise of the church. It[20b]
as remodelled in 1727 by Edward Gilbert of Bury
treet, London, and The Bury, St Paul's Walden. It is
parated from the nave by a gorgeous, if decidedly
orldly, screen with columns, carrying bits of entablature
ad arches, and candelabra on top of the cornice. Inside,
ie chancel is vaulted and stuccoed. On the S wall is a very
screet memorial to the founder, a relief of an urn with
atti and E. G., Obiit 1762. – FONT. Octagonal, Perp,
ith frieze of leaves and embattled top. – SCREEN. Two

sections of one light each, l. and r. of the entrance. E
light has a depressed ogee arch and some tiny I
'panelling' above. – STAINED GLASS. A beautiful Vi
of the early C14 in the tower w window. The figure of
Virgin is mostly brown and olive-green, the chil
clothed in red. – E window (Strathmore Memorial W
dow) by *Hugh Easton*, 1946. – PLATE. Flagon and Sta
ing Paten, 1680. – MONUMENT. H. Stapleford † 1
and wife, small epitaph with the usual kneeling figure
chapel, w wall).

THE BURY. Considerable *Robert Adam* and Neo-El
bethan (1887) additions to Edward Gilbert's house
1740. This is of red brick, two-storeyed, with polyg
bay windows and a central pediment. *Robert Adam*
1767 added a Hall with segmental vault and apses at I
ends, screened off by columns in Adam's favourite m
ner, and Drawing Room and Morning Room beyond
apses. The Drawing Room has bay windows on t
sides. The main entrance to the house in the C18 was
the Hall. In the grounds GARDEN HOUSE, with Goth
pointed, ogee-arched, and quatrefoil windows.

STAGENHOE. Rebuilt after a fire of 1737. Stuccoed elev
bay front. The outer two-bay wings two-storeyed,
rest three-storeyed. Three-bay sculptured pedim
Otherwise balustrades.

SALISBURY HALL *see* SHENLEY

SANDON

ALL SAINTS. Chiefly later C14. w tower originally
buttressed but later propped up by big sloping brick I
tresses without any off-sets. s porch tall with two-li
windows. Nave with four-bay arcades to the ais
Moulded capitals, double-chamfered arches. Chai
arch similar, but with double-hollow-chamfered arcl
The chancel windows are Early Perp, that is also la
C14: still steep, two-centred arches, but panel trace
The tiny Easter Sepulchre inside the chancel (only :
long) has a depressed arch and little crocketed ogee gal

above it, and Sedilia and Piscina are also ogee-crocketed, which would indicate a slightly earlier date. – Indeed a contract exists between the Chapter of St Paul's in London and *Thomas Rykelyng*, stone mason, to pull down the old chancel at Sandon and rebuild it, and that contract is dated 1348. – PULPIT. Jacobean with much incised ornamentation. – SCREEN. C15, of simple design. – BENCHES. C15, complete with seats and backs, not only ends. – STAINED GLASS. Many higgledy-piggledy bits of pre-Reformation glass in the heads of aisle windows. – PLATE. Chalice and Paten, 1688. – MONUMENTS. Brasses to John Fitzjeffery † 1480 and wife; fine, slightly mannered figures; he in the spiky armour of the moment; *c.* 30 in. long. – Nicholas F. Miller † 1747, exceedingly good big epitaph with bust of the fashionable young man in elaborate surround of varied marbles. Who is the sculptor? SANDON BURY. C17 brick house with slightly later s front of five bays and two and a half storeys. Large aisled barn with brick front, and derelict square dovecot. These two buildings seem of late C17 design with brick bands and horizontal and vertical oval windows.

SANDON MOUNT *see* ROYSTON

SANDRIDGE

ST LEONARD. An unpromising church when one approaches it from the w. The w tower and w end in general are all of 1886, and restoration has given the whole building too fresh an appearance. Yet the Roman bricks in the chancel masonry reveal a very great age, and inside a chancel arch of Roman bricks is preserved in the most curious of surroundings. These features may well belong to the church consecrated by Herbert Losinga, Bishop of Norwich (1094–1119). Of the later C12 the nave arcades of three bays with octagonal piers carrying square scalloped capitals with odd angle volutes. The arches have two roll mouldings. The C13 follows with the tower arch left standing when the new tower was built. It has two slight chamfers and rests on renewed shafts with original stiff-

23
30a

leaf capitals. Late in the C14 the renewal of the chan
and at the same time the erection of the stone rood-scr
which (a most remarkable fact) respected the old Ron
brick chancel arch. It was blocked, except for a doorw
with fleurons in jambs and voussoirs and for charm
little figures on sloping ledges to the E of it, and above
two-light straightheaded window opening was ma
To the l. and r. similar three-light openings. The wh
would not look so improbable had not the restorati
of 1886 replaced the upper E wall of the nave above
Screen and the Norman arch by wooden tracery. – FON
Circular, Norman, with intersecting blank arches
colonnades. – PLATE. Chalice and Paten, 1776.

SARRATT

HOLY CROSS. Small church of flint, in its cross-plan a
the masonry of short nave, transepts, and W parts of cha
cel C12 (see particularly the arches between these part
The chancel was lengthened in the C13 (see the doul
Piscina) and again in the C14 (see the design of the
newed E window). The short W tower is of the C17 with
upper storey of the C16, which has pretty brick window
brick quoins, and a brick top with saddleback roof.
PULPIT. C17, hexagonal with ornamented linenfo
panelling and double balusters at the angles; squa
tester. – Plain old BENCHES in the N transept. – WA
PAINTINGS, very faded, on the E wall of the S transept
PLATE. Paten, 1635; tall Chalice and Paten, 1764; Flago
1792. – MONUMENT. William Kingley † 1611 and wi
the usual epitaph with kneeling figures facing each othe
ALMSHOUSES. Opposite the church; plain red brick
1821.

SAWBRIDGEWORTH

One of the best small towns of Herts, built not along a Hig
Street like Berkhamsted or Stevenage, but within a squa
of main streets, all quite small.

ST MARY THE GREAT. A big church, unembattled exce
for the W tower. The tower seems to be C14 (see the tow

rch) but was much repaired in brick in the C16. At that
ime a low stair-turret was added (cf. Hunsdon). The
earliest remaining evidence of the history of the building
s, according to the Royal Commission, a S arch in the
chancel, now hidden. This is supposed to be *c.* 1300. The
N aisle windows must be early C14 (E window replaced
but probably correctly). The date goes well with the
quatrefoil piers and chamfered arches of the N aisle
arcade. The piers are the same in the S arcade but the
arches seem a little later; and the doorway looks indeed
ater too. – FONT, *c.* 1400. Octagonal, with panelled stem
and shields in quatrefoil panels on the bowl. – PULPIT,
1632, but still Jacobean in style. – SCREEN. C15. On each
side of the entrance one very broad four-light division
with panel tracery. – STAINED GLASS. E window, 1864,
by *Hardman*, much less disciplined than at the time when
Pugin designed for him. – MONUMENTS. The church is a
veritable storehouse of monuments. The following fifteen
deserve attention. In the CHANCEL: Reassembled (?) recess for a tomb-chest with three shields in richly cusped
quatrefoils. Shafts to the l. and r. with diagonal honey-
comb decoration. Ogee arches along the top and cresting
above. Indents for brass at the back. Probably early C16. –
Brass to Geoffrey Joslyn † 1470 with two wives, the
figures 2 ft long. – Plain tomb-chest with almost completely defaced figures of John Joscelyn † 1525 and his
wife. – Epitaph to Sir Walter Myldemaye † 1606, wife
and son, with the usual kneeling figures. – Large standing
wall monument to George, Viscount Hewyt, † 1689. Life-
size standing figure *à la Louis le Grand,* one hand on hip,
the other on a helmet. Red marble columns l. and r., and
trophees outside them. Curly broken pediment on top.
On the plinth two putti hold the inscription. – In the S
CHAPEL. Magnificent large Brass to John Leventhorp
† 1425 and wife, the frontal figures life-size. – Standing
wall monument to Sir John Leventhorp † 1625 and wife.
The two effigies, the lady in front, her husband behind
and a little higher, lie under a deep coffered arch with
Victories in the spandrels. Columns on the sides, fourteen

kneeling children in relief on the plinth. – Jerem
Milles † 1797 and his wife † 1835, by *Ternouth*, wit
kneeling mourning woman. – In the NAVE: Late (
fragmentary Brass; twelve sons and six daughters o
Brass to John Chauncy (?) † 1479 and his eight sons
Sir Walter Hewyt † 1637 and wife † 1646, epitaph of bl
and white marble. Very unusual design. The two de
figures in one oval medallion hold hands. White colum
with black capitals l. and r. White gable of two conca
curves *à la chinoise*. – Viscount Jocelyn † 1756, excell
bust before grey obelisk. At foot tondo with mourn
Justice. By *Bacon* (born in 1740; so the recoverment m
be a good deal later than the Viscount's death). – In
S AISLE: Brass of Edward Leventhorp † 1551 and w
He is in armour. – Brass of a woman, 2½ ft long, *c.* 160c
Inside the TOWER: C15 Brass to man and woman
shrouds. – Big Elizabethan Brass to Mrs Mary Lev
thorp † 1566. – Standing wall monument to Sir Thor
Hewit † 1662, signed by *Abraham Story*. Black and wl
marble in a grand Baroque manner. Segmental pedime
Large inscription held by two putti.

In the nice collection of C18 gravestones.

PERAMBULATION

From the church Church Street leads to the crossing of
short main streets: to the s The Square, to the N Knig
Street, to the w Bell Street. In all these there are wor
while houses of the C16–C19, some timber-framed a
plastered, some weatherboarded, and some of George
brick, e.g. No. 1 THE SQUARE, Late Georgian, Fa
GREEN LODGE, at the s end of the The Square, par
Early C18, and some houses and cottages to its s
VANTORTS ROAD. No. 1, The Square forms a pre
group with the end houses of Knight Street and No.
BELL STREET. In Bell Street also a weatherboard
house with far projecting hoist-loft, and farther w No.
(Red House) of *c.* 1720 five bays doorcase with flut
Ionic pilasters, No. 9 of the same type and No. 4 oppos
(The Elms) also similar. Nos 36–46 (including the O

Bell Inn) are timber-framed and plastered and have such features as overhangs and (Bell Inn) small ground-floor bay-windows. In KNIGHT STREET Nos 14–42 a fine uninterrupted row of C17 to C18 houses. Nos 28 and 40 have giant angle pilasters, No. 28 also the rusticated door-pilasters and segmentheaded windows of the early C18. The same type exactly the WHITE LION INN in LONDON ROAD, the W boundary of the old town. The E boundary was the river Stort, and here by the river lies the exceedingly picturesque group of light weatherboarded MILL buildings, now of Messrs T. Burton.

HYDE HALL see p. 143.

PISHIOBURY see p. 187.

SHENLEY

ST BOTOLPH, 1 m. N of the village. The fragment of a larger building for which Maud, Countess of Salisbury, left money in 1424. Chancel and tower arch were pulled down in 1753. The wide nave was originally nave and S aisle. The outer walls are of squared flint with brick dressings. The windows have steep two-centred arches and elementary Perp tracery. – BENCHES. Some with poppyheads. – GALLERY. Remains of a Georgian gallery with Tuscan columns. – STAINED GLASS. Window in N wall, 1907, probably from *Morris & Co.* – PLATE. Chalice and Paten, 1798, Flagon, 1774. – MONUMENTS. Sir Jeremiah Snow † 1704, standing wall monument with two putti and an urn at the top. – In the churchyard plain tomb of Nicholas *Hawksmoor*, the great architect, who lived at Porters Park (*see* below) and died there in 1736.

In the village, LOCK-UP, C18, repaired 1810; brick, plastered, circular, with domed top like a beehive. Pointed door and small barred windows with the inscriptions: Be sober, Do well, Fear not, Be vigilant.

Several houses around the village. By far the most interesting of them:

SALISBURY HALL, 1 m. NE of the church. Brick house surrounded by moat. Built by Sir John Cuttes, Treasurer of Henry VIII, and modernized on the NW side by Sir 42a

Jeremiah Snow late in the C17. The porch and pedimen
and the windows to the r. of it belong to his time; at th
back all is Tudor work. Inside, the most important featur
is six large plaster medallions (*c.* 3 ft diameter) and tw
half-medallions, all with profile heads of Roman Em
perors. They are said to come from Sopwell Nunnery, S
Albans (more probably from the house erected in its stea
in the middle of the C16), and would deserve close
examination.

PORTERS PARK. One of the innumerable buildings of th
Middlesex County Council SHENLEY MENTAL HOS
PITAL. The house which belonged to *Nicholas Hawks
moor* (cf. above) is wholly altered. The stables keep mor
of their C18 appearance. The Hospital is a vast garde
city, remarkably *riant* in its Neo-Georgian architectur
and well-trimmed lawns.

HIGH CANONS, 1 m. SE of the village. Five-bay, two
storey house of 1773, in large grounds.

SHEPHALL

ST MARY. Small; nave and chancel with big tiled roof.
aisle of 1865; no W tower, only a bell-cote. The nav
Roof has arched trusses with broad pointed trefoil tracer
in the spandrels. – SCREEN. Simple, C15. – MONU
MENTS. Several epitaphs to members of the Nodes family
1695, 1697, 1713, 1731.

SHEPHALBURY. Gothic mansion of *c.* 1865 by *T. Roge
Smith*. Red brick and yellow stone, E.E. detail, many
gables, and a stair-turret.

SHEPHALBURY FARM. C17, with big chimney shafts an
much pargetting (especially N gable).

SIX HILLS *see* STEVENAGE

SPELLBROOK
1 m. N of Sawbridgeworth

SPELLBROOK FARM. Early C18 with later C18 porch.
Timber-framed and plastered, 5 bays wide.

REE HORSESHOES INN. With exposed timber-
-aming; picturesque. (MHLG.)

STAGENHOE *see* ST PAUL'S WALDEN

STANDON

MARY. Unique in the county in two features: the large
⊔ porch and the detached tower to the S of the E end of
he aisle. The church stands on rising ground, the E parts
igher than the W end. Hence the chancel is raised by a
umber of steps, the most impressive effect inside. The
hancel is early C13, as proved by two N lancet windows
nd the spectacular chancel arch with three orders of
ig polished shafts (renewed in *G. Godwin's* restoration
f 1865 in pink marble) with shaft-rings and stiff-leaf
apitals, and an arch with dog-tooth ornament (cf. East-
vick). When, in the mid C19, the nave was rebuilt much
vider than before, side openings were cut into the W wall of
he chancel to allow a freer sight of the altar. Of mid C14
vork the following survives: the W doorway, the four-
ight Dec W window with flowing tracery, the aisle win-
lows, especially those to the W and E, and the ogee-headed
ecess in the S aisle. The arcade piers are assigned to the
ame date, but seem later. It is a big church. The arcades
ave five bays. They are tall and have piers with an un-
:ommon section (four attached semi-octagonal shafts and
n the diagonals a keel between two hollows; cf. Tring)
nd two-centred arches. Above a (later) clerestory (with
he windows above the spandrels, not the apexes of the
rches). Of the C15 the tower in its present form and the
ig deep W porch with two windows on each side. – FONT.
Ⅎ very interesting early C13 design; octagonal, with two
iorizontal wavy bands of stylized leaves running around
he bowl. – MONUMENTS. In the chancel Brass to a
neeling Knight, lower part only, 1412. – At the end of
he nave Brasses to a civilian, mid C15; to a Knight of the
Vade family † 1557. – In the N aisle plain tomb-chest,

originally with brass-shields against the sides. On the
the exquisite brasses said to be to John Field † 147
merchant of the 'Stapull of Caleys', and his son J
Field, Squire, represented by the side of his father an
the same size (2 ft 9 in). The son is in armour. Both st
on hillocks with pretty flowers. Below the small figure
some children. The elder John Field had been rich eno
to lend Henry VI £2,000 for the defence of Calais. -
the chancel standing wall monuments to Sir Ralph S
leir † 1587 and Sir Thomas Sadleir † 1606. Both
monuments with recumbent effigies (Sir Ralph alone,
Thomas behind and a little above his wife) under arc
(Sir Ralph's shallow and decorated with fleurons,
Thomas's deeper and coffered) and flanked by colun
In the spandrels of Sir Ralph's are Victories, in thos
Sir Thomas's thin scrolls. The back walls have big b
cartouches, Sir Ralph's also excellent ribbon work. '
tops are achievements; Sir Ralph's has also two obel
at the angles. Both works come obviously from lead
London workshops. By the side of Sir Ralph's monum
his helmets (c16), sword (c14), spurs, and stand
pole.

In the village s of the church the ENDOWED SCHOO
long, even, two-storey house with c16 timber-frame v
brick-nogged infillings, considerably restored. To th
of the church a good early c18 brick house.

Half a mile sw across the river stands THE LORDSH
This includes the remains of an Early Tudor mans
built in 1546 (*see* two date-stones). It had a cen
courtyard. All was pulled down except the w wing
half the s wing. In the w wing was the main entra
in the s wing the Hall. The carriageway with its fo
centred arch remains and the flanking turrets on th
On the w only stumps. The NW angle turret of the ra
has been reconstructed on the old foundations. Th
part of the w wing has several gables and an outer ch
ney. The interior is entirely remodelled, and a new w
to the E of the s end was erected about 1925 after a fire
burnt the Victorian living quarters.

STANSTEAD ABBOTS

ᴛ JAMES. The interest of the church is its open timber s ²²ᵃ
porch, original c15 work, and its N chancel chapel added
in brick in 1577. The windows are still entirely Perp (E
window three four-centred lights under one four-centred
arch, N two-light straightheaded under hood-moulds).
The arcade inside also with its octagonal piers does not
betray any consciousness of the new Italian fashion. –
Inside there are few churches in the county which have so
well preserved an c18 village character. Whitewashed
walls, a c15 kingpost roof plastered, a three-decker PUL-
PIT and high BOX PEWS. – TOWER SCREEN. Tall and
solid; c17. – MONUMENTS. Brass to a Knight, late c15
(chancel). – Brass to W. Saxaye † 1551 (chancel). – Brass
to a man and woman, c. 1550, holding each other's hands
(nave). – Sir Edward Baeshe † 1587, wife and children;
the usual kneeling figures facing each other across a
prayer-desk. The children small below. Lavish strapwork
cartouche behind the main figures. – Robert Jocelyn
† 1806, by the younger *Bacon*, with two urns, anchor,
gun, and Sphinx (he commanded a ship at the taking of
Manila in 1762). – Four epitaphs in the nave; a study in
females mourning over urns: Philip Booth † 1818, by
Manning; H. T. Baucutt Mash † 1825, by *Kendrick* (two
females); Mrs Booth † 1848, no doubt by *Manning*;
Sir Felix Booth 'of 43 Portland Place', † 1850, by *Manning*.

ᴛ ANDREW, 1880, by *Waterhouse*. An unimaginative
routine design, stone outside, nearly all happily covered
by climbers, red brick inside. – PLATE. Chalice and three
Patens, 1714.

ᴛANSTEAD BURY, E of the church. An eminently picturesque front, the result of several centuries' alterations.
The shapes and textures and colours of the approach side
(w) must delight the eye of any painter. The house is the
outcome of the late c17 and early c19 remodelling of a
c15–c16 building of which the half-timbered stair-turret
and a brick wall and gable bear witness. A small addition

to the w front is of darker red brick and dates from
1700. The whole of the garden (E) front of seven ba
with three-bay pediment and dormer windows with alte
nately triangular and segmental pediments is late C17, ,
is also the fine large staircase inside. To the s an early C
façade of three bays and two storeys, as if the whole larg
house were a villa in Hampstead. Originally the Tude
mansion extended much farther to the s. Its building hi
tory is not sufficiently investigated.

BAESHE ALMSHOUSES, ¾ m. NW of the old church, bui
early in the C17. Brick, two-storeyed, with three gable
Altogether six dwellings.

BRIGGENS. The centre block was built c. 1725. Early C
bow window added. Then in 1908 extensions to the N
and NW.

The village street has one remarkable HOUSE. It is date
1752 and appears from the front the usual five-bay, two
and-a-half-storey red brick house of its date, with a hand
some Ionic doorcase. But on its w side it has an apparentl
contemporary circular stair-turret with embattled top, a
if it were a fortified manor house; an early example o
'Strawberry Hill' Gothic. At the E end of the High Stree
in happy opposition to one another the RED LION INN
early C17, with overhang and gables, the OLD CLOC
SCHOOL, also of the C17, with its quoins and tiny cupo
with ogee top, and the Victorian MILL, now a factory,
stock brick block of 1865, three by five bays with gian
blank arcades and a Greek temple roof.

STANSTEAD ST MARGARETS

ST MARGARET. Norman nave (*see* the small window in th
s wall). The chancel is Dec, obviously built for a churc
more important than is the present one. Large E windo
of four lights with early flowing tracery. Contemporary
windows. On the N side the church had an aisle and
chancel chapel which were later pulled down. Sma
Georgian cupola. Inside low BOX PEWS.

STAPLEFORD

MARY. The church stands outside the village. It has a Norman N doorway (one order of colonnettes, the left capital with upright oak leaves, the outer voussoirs zigzag, the inner zigzag on the intrados) and an altered C13 lancet window in the chancel. But its chief characteristic is its N tower which has the porch below, a weatherboarded upper stage, and then an octagonal timber stage and a spire. This changes a medieval church effectively into one mid Victorian. The tower was built in 1874. – PLATE. Chalice and Paten, 1712.

ATERFORD HALL, 1 m. S. Two-storey brick house of c. 1600. Traces of a mullioned brick window with hood-mould on the N side. Fine chimney stack.

STEVENAGE

NICHOLAS. Away from the town to the NE, almost entirely on its own. A flint church with a low W tower with leaded spire. The upper parts and the diagonal brick buttresses are C15, but the tower itself (see its windows and W door) is Norman. The S view of the church is specially rewarding with the various steps in height and in depth. The church is entirely embattled. S porch at the W end of the S aisle, S transept added 1841. Most of the windows point to the C14 (chancel N and S; chancel chapels E straightheaded but with early C14 tracery; N chancel chapel N; odd windows in the aisles). The arcades between chancel and chapels are of the early C14 too. Those in the nave are C15 on C13 bases and shafts. The clerestory and the nave and chancel roofs are also C15. The niche for a statue in the NE corner of the N chapel may be C14 or C15. – FONT. Plain C13, with later ogee-shaped crocketed cover. – SCREENS. Complete set of screens between nave and chancel, aisles and chapels, and also chancel and chapels, the latter as usual more modest, but the principal ones also by no means as lavish as those of East Anglia. – CHOIR SEATS, C15, with MISERICORDS

(mostly leaves; also an angel with spreadout wings, a
a face with leaves growing out of the mouth). – STAIN
GLASS. E window, 1842, S chancel window, 1848, bo
supposed to be by *Wailes* (TK); but can they be by t
same artist? The E window has four saints, with canopi
in traditional colours. The S window is a three-light N
me tangere in gaudy colours (still the painterly approa
of the C18 and by no means yet medievalizing). – PLAT
Chalice and Paten, 1634; Flagon and Paten, 1683.
MONUMENTS. Brass to Stephen Hillard, *c.* 1500, larg
figure of a priest in vestments. – Mutilated effigy of
lady wearing a wimple; an angel and a priest by her p
low; *c.* 1300.

The RECTORY W of the church is by *Sir E. Newton*, 191

HOLY TRINITY, 1861, by *Blomfield*. An early church.
his, before his style became smooth and competent a
stale. Nave and chancel only, with a bellcote. Flint wi
stone, red brick, and white brick adornments. Tiled ro
with bands of fancy tiles. Plate tracery. A new larger na
and chancel were added by *Tate & Popplewell* in 1881–
'and a very good match they made' (GR).

SIX HILLS, ¾ m. S. Barrows. Probably of Roman date an
constructed for burial purposes.

PERAMBULATION

Stevenage is for the time being still chiefly the High Stre
with three short branchings-off on the E. But the Ne
Town, one of the planned satellite towns of after th
Second World War, is growing. It will have its centre s
the present town, industry chiefly W of the railway, an
residential areas mainly to the E on the hills extendin
up to 2 m. in that direction, and as far S as Shephal
The attraction of Stevenage HIGH STREET is the haphaza
tree-planting and the fact that at the N end it widens in
a triangular Green and halfway down to the S it narro
for a while by the placing of an island in it. The narro
street thereby formed on the E is Middle Row. Starti
from the N the BOWLING GREEN has on its own N sid
unfortunately nothing to act as a sufficient back-drop

the approaching High Street. At the E corner is the GRAMMAR SCHOOL, quite extensive now, and incorporating a small one-room building of (redone) brick with open timber roof which is the school, originally founded as Alleyn's Grammar School c. 1562. On the w end Nos 1–7 JULIAN'S ROAD, a group of early C17 cottages. In the HIGH STREET on the E side, still facing the Bowling Green, No. 3, a four-bay C18 front, stuccoed, and No. 5, THE GRANGE, a broad twelve-bay red front with central canted bay window and large carriageway on the l. The house was a coaching inn and dates from the Early Georgian time. A little farther s THE YORKSHIRE GREY, also an inn, lower, with five widely spread windows and door with pediment on Tuscan pilasters. The C18 carries on on the E side, while on the w less happens; it is a pity, however that the architecture of the Woolworth store does not take any notice of the character of the rest of the street. Nos 29–35 on the E again a pleasant Georgian brick group. No. 37, a cross-gabled C16 house, starts the narrower part of the High Street. MIDDLE ROW which splits off here, to join the High Street again lower down, is all red brick cottages, so consistently so that one may well feel reminded of Holland. Opposite on the w side at the junction of the High Street and Middle Row is No. 66, dignified early C19 white brick; No. 68, temp. William and Mary with an eight-bay front and narrow angle pilasters; and Nos 70–72, also c. 1700. The E side is here less interesting and does not produce anything special to its s end. On the w side there are still Nos 94–98, timber-framed with symmetrical gables, and No 106, Late Georgian brick of five bays and three storeys with a doorway with pediment on carved brackets and a charming iron lantern-holder over. Off the s end of the High Street at the beginning of LETCHMORE ROAD immediately behind Holy Trinity the former WORKHOUSE, the best timber-framed building of Stevenage; C16 with symmetrical gables to the l. and r. on an overhanging upper floor.

From here, turning E the NEW TOWN is reached, or from the High Street by Sish Lane. Most of the area so far

built is called Stony Hall. Its visual focus is a long seven-
storeyed block of flats by *Yorke, Rosenberg, & Mardall*
just off Sish Lane. It faces the future centre of the town.
Immediately in front of the flats lies an area for the planting of trees, and then the group is closed a little lower
down by a number of four-storeyed flats. The high block
is built with a reinforced-concrete frame, long open-access
balconies at the back and divers kinds of small motifs as
light relief. In the front view this hankering after variety
has led to a curious, not easily comprehended, rhythm.
The concrete framing shows round one group of window-
balcony-window on the left and round five such groups
on the right. Two similar groups between, however, have
the framework hidden, and on top of that they possess a
different, alternating rhythm of windows and balconies.
The functional justification is a different size of flats behind, but the aesthetic effect remains somewhat restless
for the monumental centre of a neighbourhood. Most of
the smaller housing is two-storeyed in terraces.

The following details may be mentioned. SE of Stony
Hall lies Bedwell North and East, s of Bedwell North
Whomerley Wood, and sw of this Monks Wood. The
architect to the Corporation is *C. Holliday*. The project
called Stony Hall South and the Stony Hall shops,
Whomerley Wood, and the Monks Wood shops were
under the charge of *Stirling Craig*; Sish Lane North and
Monks Wood Hostel of *Cynthia Wood*; Stony Hall East,
Bedwell North and East, and the Monks Wood Public
House of *Oliver Carey*; Monks Wood and the Sish Lane
Hostel of *L. W. Aked*.

In the New Town one uncommonly good public house the
TWIN FOXES by *C. Holliday*, *O. Carey* and *L. G. Vincent*
outstanding in its combination of actively modern forms
with the traditional English pub. Also two notable schools.

BARCLAY SCHOOL, Walkern Road. Co-educational
Secondary Modern School by *Yorke, Rosenberg, &
Mardall*. The size is remarkable and explained by the
planned development of Stevenage New Town. The composition of the school is free and felicitous as well as func-

onally sound. The building has no façade, indeed no
.ce. Yet it is not at all utilitarian in any derogatory sense.
. nice variety of blocks and of materials (light brick,
reeze blocks, random rubble, light weatherboarding).
xcellent details, fixtures, and fabrics inside, e.g. a
/illiam Morris wallpaper on the focal wall of the Dining
[all. A specially interesting detail is the main staircase
arried up on a concrete spine without jointing into the
all or resting on a wall. In front of the entrance against
. curved screen *Henry Moore's* 'Family', man, woman,
.d child.

LKERN ROAD SENIOR MIXED SCHOOL (*see* Intro-
uction, p. 28).

STOCKING PELHAM

MARY. Small church, of chancel and wide nave (the
oyal Commission suggests it might originally have had a
ooden s arcade because the s wall is not in line with the
.ancel). Mid C14 according to the remaining chancel N
indow and the remarkably original nave window. – No
.rnishings of interest.

TORTFORD HALL *see* BISHOPS STORTFORD

TEMPLE DINSLEY

Early Georgian house * of moderate size (seven bays, two
oreys, segmentheaded windows with stone keystones, and
.bbed brick surrounds, central three-bay pediment) so
.uch enlarged by *Lutyens* in 1908 that the whole appears
.tirely a Lutyens house. He added to the main front on
.ch side three-bay extensions with semicircular win-
ows in the top floor, and three further two-bay ranges
ith roofs so steeply pitched that these wings become the
omposition's main feature. Also extensive office ranges.

TEWIN

PETER. A small church on the edge of a scattered village
ut with the RECTORY close by, a five-bay, two-storeyed

* A cottage outside the grounds is dated 1717.

Georgian house with a timber-framed weatherboar
barn, and a stable also timber-framed but with brick
fillings. – The church is partly still of the C11 (*see* a
window on the N side of the nave and the uncovered
mains of inner surrounds of windows on the s side). '
chancel was rebuilt or remodelled in the C13, as is pro
by s lancet windows. Also of the C13 the s aisle with la
windows and an arcade of octagonal piers with sin
moulded capitals. Of the C15 some inserted Perp v
dows, the whole very low w tower with diagonal buttre
and a spike, and the nave roof. A little later still the tim
s porch, badly converted, when the chief monumen
Tewin was removed from its original place outdoors
squeezed into the porch. As this has a high obelisk a
main motif, the effect is painful. The MONUMENT i
General Joseph Sabine, Governor of Gibraltar, † 1
Below the obelisk on the pedestal in the front an
quisitely carved relief of a Roman general (portrait?)
the sides and back trophies and arms. There is a nun
of good epitaphs in the church (1709, 1727, 1733, 17
and also a BRASS: Thomas Pygott † 1610 (s aisle). – FO
Fluted C18 bowl.

MARDEN HILL: *see* p. 165.

TEWIN WATER, 1 m. WNW. Called 'a new and handsc
house' in 1819. Handsome the house certainly is, in
Neo-Greek way, with a w front of seven bays, the ce
recessed and adorned by a pair of coupled Ionic g
columns, the wings by Ionic angle pilasters. The s fr
has two shallow bow windows, attached coupled Io
giant columns between, and a little curved forward I
cony between them. No pediment, just a plain attic.

THEOBALDS

Theobalds was built by William Cecil, Lord Burgh
Queen Elizabeth's leading statesman, about 1564. W
James I visited the palace he was so pleased with it tha
induced Lord Burghley's son, Robert Cecil, his o
prime minister, to exchange it against the old and gloc

brick palace of Hatfield. During the Commonwealth Theobalds was dismantled and all but pulled down. About 1765–70 on a site close to it four small country houses were built instead, known, it seems, as Theobalds Square Of these one remains, OLD PALACE HOUSE, a modest five-bay, two-storey house, apparently with one-bay side wings. It has now an early C19 iron verandah. The second, THE CEDARS, was severely damaged by fire during the C20 and not reconstructed. The other two, Cecil House and Jackson's School, have gone. Of Burghley's palace only one strip of brickwork exists now c. 15 ft high. It forms part of the gardener's cottage of Old Palace House. It seems to have been the SW corner of the Burghley mansion. In addition stretches of the old wall have been identified.

bout ½ m. W is the entrance to what is now known as THEOBALDS PARK. The monumental entrance is nothing less than *Sir Christopher Wren's* TEMPLE BAR, erected in 56 Fleet Street, London, in 1672, and transferred to its present site in 1878. It is a very big gate, much bigger than photographs make one expect. It has two orders of pilasters, the lower rusticated Tuscan, the upper Ionic. The upper storey rises only above the centre part of the lower (on the scheme of the Italian church façade of the Baroque). The main gateway has a wide depressed segmental arch; the entrances for pedestrians are curiously narrow in comparison. The upper storey is flanked by big volutes, again as in Italian church façades. They are decorated with gristly, typical mid C17 forms. In the top pediment a tablet flanked by cornucopias. The quantity and character of the details seems rather French than Italian. The ephemeral architecture of triumphal arches, as publicized in engravings may have influenced Wren. THEOBALDS PARK is a mansion of five bays and two and a half storeys with forward-curving one-storey colonnades and small outer wings. The centre of the garden side is simply a bay window. But to make up for that plainness there are to the l. and r. of the bay window Venetian windows on two floors. The house was built in 1768. Some time later, probably about the middle of the C19, the space behind the colonnades was filled in and structures put up with large Venetian windows towards the garden. Yet later, an Edwardian addition was made of somewhat pretentious character, a broad big tower on the garden side on the l. Its details are reactionary for its day. The clients were not well advised in the choice of their architect. The original part has an Etruscan Entrance Hall and to its l. a staircase with iron railings curving up to the upper floor under a ceiling also decorated in the Etruscan taste. Below the house to the s is an ornamental lake formed out of the New River.

THERFIELD

St Mary, 1878, by *G. E. Pritchett*. He used the chancel and s windows of the old church. Small fragments from other parts of it are kept in the vestry. Also in the vestry COFFIN LID with foliated cross and C14 MONUMENT with tiny recumbent effigy and two female figures. Under the tower wooden epitaph to Ann Turner † 1677, with ornament, figure of Father Time, and a Skeleton.

Many good old houses in the scattered village (Elm House, Tuthill, The Limes, etc.). The best is the RECTORY, no doubt the former manor house. It has a C15 and an early C18 half. The earlier half is a rarity in the county. It has N front of two parts, to the l. a two-light window converted into a door, and above the long windows of the former Chapel. The pointed E window of this can also still be traced. The r. part of the old half on the N side gabled and has a stair-turret. On the ground floor is a four-light window, on the first floor one of two lights. All these windows, also those on the less well preserved s side of the house, are straightheaded, but the individual lights are pointed and cusped. – The r. half of the house to the N and s is clearly early C18: four bays, two storeys, with mansard roof.

Therfield Heath (Barrows): *see* Royston.

THORLEY

JAMES. Norman s doorway. Colonnettes with spiral-fluted shafts and capitals with elementary upright leaves at the angles. Arches with two orders of zigzag. Nave and chancel have C13 lancet windows preserved. No aisles. w tower C15, unbuttressed, with low stair-turret and spike. Tall C15 tower arch; the chancel arch of double-chamfered orders could be C13 still. The chancel Sedilia, however (ogee-headed), must be of the C14. The E and w windows C19 (1846, by *Pritchett*). – FONT. Square, C12, of Purbeck marble, with five shallow blank arches on each side. – REREDOS with side-panels of naturalistically carved flowers and leaves; High Victorian in style (by *J. Day*). The church was restored in 1854 by *Vulliamy*. The PULPIT and COMMUNION RAILS were designed by *Sir G. G. Scott.* – STAINED GLASS. w window, *c.* 1853, still in the painting style of the C18, that is pre-Puginesque. – PLATE. Chalice and Paten, 1562; Patens, 1809 and 1818; Flagon, 1839. – Many minor epitaphs.

THORLEY HALL, close to the church. Good C15 farmhouse with C18 modernizations (s front). Elements of the C15 can still be traced inside.

THROCKING

HOLY TRINITY. The most interesting part is the w tower; of the C13, flint-built and unbuttressed below (*see* the two deeply splayed lancet windows), but completed in brick with roundheaded windows, a corbelled-out stair-turret, and a parapet (originally with pinnacles) in 1660. An ornate brick plate outside records the date. The rest of the church is Perp. – FONT. Octagonal, Perp, with various tracery patterns on the panels of the bowl; the stem is also panelled. – BENCHES. Four in chancel with poppy-heads. – MONUMENTS. Two black floor slabs with unusually fine coats of arms, one to Thomas Soane † 1670, the other to Robert Elwes † 1752. In 1753 *Rysbrack*, one of the two most distinguished sculptors of the period in England,

made the noble epitaph for Elwes: a large, very classi
pedimented inscription tablet and a Rococo cartouc
with coat of arms beneath; no figures. – Hester Elw
† 1770, by *Nollekens*, also an epitaph; with a seated fem
figure by an urn; the decorative detail remarkably N
Grecian for its date.

THUNDRIDGE

Of the old PARISH CHURCH, ½ m. to the E of the new, or
the W tower survives, hidden by trees and covered
creepers. In it is a Norman doorway, not in its origin
position, with zigzag and dog-tooth decoration. To the
of the church even more immersed in the trees is one
brick chimneystack of THUNDRIDGE BURY, the form
manor house.

The new church ST MARY dates from 1853. It is by B
jamin *Ferrey*, rockfaced and with a tower alien to Herts
that it has no battlements but a stair-turret with a spir
let. – PLATE. Flagon, 1775; Chalice and Paten, 1837
MONUMENTS. Caroline Hanbury † 1863, by *The*
Relief of a meticulously carved monument under
weeping willow. – R. C. Hanbury † 1867, also by *The*
with a dull figure of Faith.

YOUNGSBURY, the new manor house, ¾ m. NE. The fr
part is dated 1745, the back early C19. Later alteration
(POLES. By *Sir Ernest George*, late C19. Red brick, in t
Jacobean style, with curved gables. Large curv
scholastic looking additions.)

Small OBELISK erected in 1879 to the memory of Thon
Clarkson, who resolved on this spot in 1785 to devote
life to the abolition of the slave trade. The monume
stands by the side of the main Cambridge road (Erm
Street).

TOTTERIDGE

Totteridge is characteristic of the outermost perimeter
London: a village church still preserved and otherwise sm
Georgian and big wealthy Late Victorian and Edwardi
houses.

t ANDREW, 1790. Aisleless nave of brick with arched window in Gibbs surrounds and heavy w pediment. Pretty weatherboarded bell-turret of 1706. w porch 1845. Chancel and window tracery 1869. – PAINTINGS. Virgin and Saints, demi-figures, by *Lorenzo Lotto*; an early work, presented by Lord Rothermere. St John on Patmos and the Woman of the Apocalypse, both sketches, by *Benjamin West*, uncommonly dramatic, almost in a Tintoretto way. – PULPIT. Jacobean, from Hatfield church. – STAINED GLASS. Chancel by *Clayton & Bell*, nave s and N, one window each, by *Kempe*, 1896 and 1903. – PLATE. Cup, inscribed 1614. – PROCESSIONAL CROSS. Italian, late C13. – MONUMENTS. John Puget † 1805, by *John Bacon, Jnr*, epitaph with urn. – Second World War Memorial, by *T. J. Rushton*.

everal noteworthy houses close to the church. VICARAGE, *Sir Charles Nicholson's* first building, 1892, very simple; BARN, weatherboarded, just NW of the church; GARDEN HILL and SOUTHERNHAY, w of the church, the former Early, the latter Late Georgian.

rom the church TOTTERIDGE LANE runs E towards Barnet and w towards Edgware and Elstree. The following houses in the E half (from E to w) deserve mention: disused CONGREGATIONAL CHAPEL, 1827; OLD HOUSE at the NE corner of TOTTERIDGE GREEN, plain Georgian; THE CROFT at the sw end of the Green, very picturesque Late Victorian with three ranges and a court, roughcast, with Tudor windows, somewhat *à la* Voysey, by *Collcutt*, 1895. – w of the church: THE PRIORY, three-gabled Jacobean but considerably altered and restored. Then a group of pretty Georgian cottages, then GRANGE MANSIONS, a late building by *Nicholson* in the Neo-Georgian style, with Garage originally the stables of The Grange; then the MANOR HOUSE, a good five-bay mid Georgian house; Gothick GATE LODGE to Loxwood; TOTTERIDGE PARK, early C18 and early C19 but enlarged and altered out of recognition; DENHAM FARM HOUSE, with Late Georgian façade to an earlier timber-framed house, and opposite DENHAM, 1877, by *Norman*

Shaw, a picturesque, asymmetrical half-timbered hous
with Stables. On the same side farther w FAIRLAWN
1710, but much altered. THE WARREN up a lane to the
is also by *Nicholson*, and also of no special character.

TRING

There is not much of architectural importance at Trin
except for the church. It lies back from the HIGH
STREET which here widens into a kind of square with
the architecturally deplorable Rose and Crown Hotel on
the other side. The High Street has nice houses; one o
them (No. 23) of three storeys and four bays, late C18. -
In AKEMAN STREET an odd former Nonconformis
chapel with two short projecting wings, and Nos 91–92 o
good C16 half-timber work. In WESTERN ROAD some
pretty Early Victorian houses ending in the BRITANNI.
INN facing w with its porch, that is away from the town
to welcome visitors. On the other side behind the High
Street a fine C16 barn in PARSONAGE PLACE.

SS PETER AND PAUL. The s side appears from the High
Street across the churchyard; flint with random stone, an
oddly mottled effect. It is not specially long and the towe:
is not specially high. It is embattled throughout, with
chequerboard patterning in the s porch and nave battlements. The earliest part of the church is the chancel with
a tall C13 lancet window in the N wall. Otherwise most o:
what is visible is C15 to C16, except for the tower whose
arch to the nave is clearly of early C14 date. The tower
has angle buttresses and a SE stair-turret higher than the
tower battlements. The broad spacious nave has N and s
aisles of six bays with unusual piers which have four attached shafts and in the diagonals thin fillets between
hollows. They were renewed in the restoration of 1880–2
(by *Bodley*), the originals going to Long Marston. The
capitals and arches remained. The shafts are continued in
the clerestory zone by stone shafts on figures of animals,
and these shafts support the old roof. The clerestory windows are of three lights, simple Perp, as are the aisle

ndows, except the larger ones at the E ends of the aisles.
STAINED GLASS by *Kempe*, S chancel windows 1886
d 1890, several others of the 90s. – PLATE. Chalice,
65; two large Flagons and Breadholder, 1713; Bread-
lder, 1723. – MONUMENTS. The monument to Sir
illiam Gore † 1707 and his wife is very sumptuous. It
oudly faces the porch and is the first thing that strikes
e visitor to the church. The sculptor may be *Nost*. Sir
illiam, in the robes of a Lord Mayor of London, and
dy Gore lie comfortably on the concave sides of the
inth of a big urn against an elaborate pedimented back
chitecture. – John Gore † 1763, a dainty epitaph of
ried pale marbles with a small medallion against an
elisk; two putti outside the flanking pilasters. – W.
ay † 1838, by *J. Browne*, with a big seated female figure.
NG PARK, a former Rothschild mansion, brick with
ench pavilion roofs; nothing outside specially splendid
showy.

TYTTENHANGER

e brick house with the ends projecting slightly on the N 48b
entrance side and a little more on the S or garden side.
he brick quoins, the brick window frames, the wooden
ullions and transomes of the windows, the heavy win-
w pediments on the S side, alternatingly triangular and
gmental, the hipped roof and the rather squat cupola,
 is characteristic of a date *c*. 1660. Cussans indeed,
thout quoting any authority, says that Tyttenhanger
as built by Sir Henry Blunt shortly after he had come
to possession in 1654. The magnificent staircase inside 49
ith a balustrade of sumptuous openwork foliage scrolls
so goes well with that date (cf. Ham House, Surrey;
rde Abbey, Dorset). The most characteristic features
 the 1650s, however, are the extremely odd surrounds
 windows on the S and W sides, the undisguised
ymmetry of the W side, the quite crazy doorcases in the
aircase hall, with frames growing angular excrescences
lfway up the sides, and at the top retracted friezes
rrying pediments and similar mannerisms. They are of

wood but remarkably similar in design to the stone d
way at Balls Park, Herts. Only the outer s doorwa
Tyttenhanger with a scrolly open segmental pedimer
delicately carved brackets looks embarrassingly acc
plished for a pre-Wren date. Tyttenhanger, toge
with Balls Park, belongs to a group of mid C17 house
which Mr Colvin has recently suggested *Peter Mil*
the architect. The attribution is based on the fact fc
by Mr Colvin that Mills designed Thorpe Ha
Norfolk.

On the second floor CHAPEL with two-decker pulpit
awkwardly in a window corner, and Ten Commandm
above the fire-place. Hour-glass attached to the pu
In the attic behind the dormer windows a Long Ga
runs along the whole length of the house. – Much li
fold and Elizabethan panelling re-used.

UPP HALL
1¼ m. SE of Braughing

Fine early C17 manor house of brick with straight ga
The main front to the W, originally with a porch.
window openings are very wide and had no doubt b
mullions and transomes (cf. Hadham Hall). Only in th
gables, below small circular openings, do brick mul
and hood-moulds survive. Projecting wings on the E
More spectacular than the house itself its brick B
140 ft long with diapers of vitrified headers. A numb
the original pointed-arched openings remain.

VERULAMIUM *see* ST ALBANS

WALKERN

ST MARY. The exterior does not tell of anything ea
than the C14, until the s doorway is reached whic
clearly Norman (one order of colonnettes). It leads
the s aisle where there is also one fairly large blocked
man window. The arcade of two bays between aisle
nave must be Early Norman. The arches are unmou

nd rest on imposts of the simplest shape. One consists of our little rolls projecting in steps and decorated herring-one-wise (cf. Little Munden). As, moreover, there is no entral pier but simply a piece of thin wall left standing, ne can assume that that wall is pre-Norman. The N rcade of three bays has octagonal piers with simple noulded capitals and double-chamfered arches; clearly :13, though the windows, as those of the S aisle, are Perp. The chancel was, in an extremely ham-fisted way, made E.E. by *Gough* in 1878 and 1882 (arcade to the added N hapel with two Gargantuan arcades each of two lights vith elementary plate tracery). But the Sedilia and Piscina re original C13 work. The W tower is quite tall and has no uttresses. The W window shows that it was built early in he C14 (ogee-reticulated tracery). The tower arch is louble-chamfered. – FONT. Octagonal with coarse cor-elled-out shafts in front of the diagonal panels (C14?). – CREEN. C15. – MONUMENTS. Extremely good effigy of Purbeck marble representing a Knight with flat-topped helm, mid C13 (S aisle). – Brasses to a man and woman, ormerly with scrolls; good quality (N aisle). – Brass to Edward Humbarstone † 1583 and wife (nave W end), with palimpsest of Flemish brass. – Epitaph with two of the usual kneeling figures, 1627 (nave). – Epitaph of David Gorsuch † 1638 and wife, also the composition of the two kneelers facing each other, but, in accordance with the ater date, rather livelier figures, a more classical sur-ound, and some thick fruit hangings. – In the Church-ard a scrolly obelisk (like a candelabrum) on four scrolly eet (Susannah Elwes); Early Georgian no doubt.

NGREGATIONAL CHAPEL, 1810. Just a gabled, lightly pargeboarded front with doorway and one arched window bove.

posite MANOR FARM, one of the usual five-bay, two-torey Georgian façades but perhaps structurally earlier; or the octagonal brick DOVECOTE with blank horizontal val windows is no doubt late C17 (cf. Sandon). – More nteresting houses along the village street to the S: the WHITE LION with a chequered brick five-bay centre and

earlier end-gables, one with an early C19 Gothic doorw[...]
ROOKS NEST FARM with one wing of timber-fram[...]
and brick, the other of brick with projecting porch. [...]
latter wing has large mullioned brick windows.

WALKERN HALL. Early C19 house of five bays and [...]
and a half storeys with two-storey lower wings. Gr[...]
Doric four-column porch, balustraded top.

WALKERN MILL, 1831, of brick, with small roundhead[...]
windows.

WALL HALL see ALDENHAM

WALLINGTON

ST MARY. Perp throughout. Fine S porch with tall entra[...]
and three-light windows. Airy nave with a large S wind[...]
and large N aisle windows. Arcade to the N aisle with pi[...]
with four shafts and four hollows in the diagonals. Th[...]
aisle roof is original. The chancel opens in a four-cent[...]
arch to a N chapel. The rest of the chancel was rebuil[...]
1864. – FONT. Octagonal bowl of Purbeck marble w[...]
two shallow pointed arches in each panel. – SCREEN. C[...]
with very simple tracery. – BENCHES. Completely p[...]
served C15 benches with thin backs. – STAINED GLA[...]
C15 bits in the N chapel. – PLATE. Cup, 1754; Pat[...]
1840. – MONUMENTS. Tomb-chest without effigy; on [...]
sides alternatingly broad panels with shields and narr[...]
niches with small C15 figures under crocketed o[...]
canopies.

WALTHAM CROSS

There is now no break along the Roman Ermine Street [...]
tween London and Middlesex and between Middlesex a[...]
Herts. Some fifty years ago there still was. One can not[...]
between Enfield and Waltham Cross where the pre-V[...]
torian ribbon of houses comes to an end, where the Victor[...]
additions come to an end, and where first the former a[...]
then the latter begin again on the Herts side. Only a quar[...]
mile from the border stands

32a WALTHAM CROSS, one of the Eleanor Crosses, that is [...]
crosses erected by Edward I to commemorate the restin[...]

places of his dead queen, Eleanor of Castile, on the way from Harby in Leicestershire where she had died to Westminster Abbey. There were twelve in all. Most of them have disappeared; only those at Northampton, Geddington, and Waltham remain. Charing Cross was the last of them. The Waltham Cross was begun in 1291. The masons were *Nicholas Dyminge de Reyne* and *Roger Crundale,* and the sculptor or *imaginator* was *Alexander of Abingdon.* The Cross was heavily restored. In fact the second and third stages were rebuilt in 1833 and again in 1883. In 1950 yet another restoration was begun. In the history of Gothic architecture in England, the Eleanor Crosses are of considerable importance. They (and St Stephen's Chapel, Westminster) mark the earliest departure from the purity of the E.E., that is the classic Gothic style, and the dawn of the Dec style with its complexities and sophistication. The Waltham Cross is hexagonal first of all, which is an odd shape, without the axial clarity of the square, circle, or octagon. A glance at the main stage with the figures will explain what is meant by this. There are three figures standing in niches under canopies, the niches framed by the buttress-like supports of the canopies. But on the remaining three sides the rhythm changes and although there are also niches they are not framed by buttresses but have one buttress each right in the middle, in front of the niches, a typical Dec complication. The statues also have no longer the crispness and sharpness of E.E. sculpture (e.g. at Westminster Abbey *c.* 1260–70) but a tendency in the draperies to congeal, as it were, and in the whole figures to become part of a general flowing undulation. Decoration is profuse. The lowest stage has blank two-light arches crowned by crocketed gables and with quatrefoils in the spandrels, still a pure Geometrical kind of tracery. The foliage of the capitals is naturalistic, as far as that can still be seen, and no longer stiff-leaf. The spaces to the l. and r. of the gables are decorated with diapering. All this does hardly go beyond Westminster Abbey. But the upper parts of the second stage have become **a** jungle of crockets

and finials. The self-discipline of the E.E. style is eviden
disappearing.

What there is of interest in Waltham houses is in the HI
STREET, especially S of the Cross on the W side HARO
HOUSE, No. 73, of yellow brick, with an Ionic doorc
and a pediment decorated by a cartouche with the d
1757; and N of the Cross on the E side GREENFIE
HOUSE with a late C18 porch.

HOLY TRINITY, towards the N end of the High Street, w
built in 1832. It is of yellow brick and has the tall, rath
gaunt character of churches of that time. The one-lig
and two-light Perp lancets (an odd combination)
characteristic. No aisles, no galleries. The E parts we
remodelled very well in 1914 by *Ayres*. Tall doul
transeptal openings with piers without any capitals. N
window at all, but N and S windows concealed by
arch across the chancel at the entry to the altar-space.

THEOBALDS: see p. 246.

THEOBALDS: *see* p. 246.

WARE

11b ST MARY. The parish church lies in the centre of the tov
at the very crossing of High Street and Baldock Street.
is a typical Herts town church, of flint, all embattled, a
all too thoroughly restored. Nearly all the windows are r
newed, and it is often not possible to say how accuratel
Those of the show sides of the transepts are an inventi
of *G. Godwin*, who restored the church in 1848. (Furth
restorations 1885 and 1905.) The existence of transepts
the only unusual feature of the church. The W tower
tall, in fact of five stages, has thin angle buttresses and t
characteristic Herts spike. Of the windows the most i
teresting (probably old, because hardly the sort of thi
the Victorians would have invented) are those with flowin
that is *c*. 1330, tracery in the S aisle. The only detail in t
church which goes farther back is one fragment of a
chancel window found and left uncovered. It proves t
chancel to be C13 work. The rest of the window w
destroyed when *c*. 1400 a S chancel chapel was built a
connected with the chancel by an ambitious double ba

ne wide arch subdivided into two by a Purbeck marble
haft (with the well-known four-shafts-and-four-hollows
rofile) and by a spandrel pierced by Perp tracery. The
ave arcades of four bays plus one taller and wider arch
orresponding to the transepts is later still. It has tall slim
iers of a typical complex C15 profile. Only inside the
rches are small capitals employed between shaft and
rch, the main mouldings towards nave and aisle run
hrough uninterrupted. – Pretty C15 recess in the N tran-
ept. – FONT, c. 1400; the most richly decorated medieval 30b
ont in the county; octagonal, of stone, with quatrefoil
anels on the short stem and on the big bowl figures of the
Virgin and the Archangel Gabriel, St Margaret, St Chris-
opher, St George, St Katharine, St James, and St John
he Baptist. Between them demi-figures of angels alter-
ately carrying musical instruments and Instruments of
he Passion. The carving is rather coarse and stocky. –
ULPIT. Mid C17 with raised panels but still tapering
ilasters at the angles. – COMMUNION RAILS. S chapel
nid C17, from Benington, unusual shape, as if panelling
vere made transparent by leaving only the broad frames
nd taking away all the infillings. – PANELLING. S chapel.
Iandsome late C17 work with a top band of openwork
oliage scrolls. – DOOR from chancel to N vestry. C14 or
:15, with three locks. – STAINED GLASS. E and W win-
lows by *Wailes*, 1849–50, strident colours, and the types
f the figures not inspired by the style of c. 1300 but
ather by the Nazarenes or Raphael. – Chapman Allen
vindow, S aisle, c. 1885; a characteristic example of the
gradual influence of the Pre-Raphaelites on the typical
Victorian glass style. By *Shrigley & Hunt*. N transept N
vindow, c. 1910, by *Whall*, inspired by the Pre-Raphael-
tes but refreshingly different from the ordinary run of
arly C20 windows. By the same one N aisle window,
1905. – PLATE. Chalice, 1618; Paten, 1806; small Chalice,
1806. – MONUMENTS. Brasses to Elene Warbulton † 1454
N transept); to a lady, c. 1425 (N transept); to W. Pyrry
† 1470, with wife and children. – Pretty Epitaph to R.
Atkinson † 1756, by *H. Cox*. The usual obelisk but at its

foot to the l. a row of books, to the r. a Rococo cartou
with arms. – W. Murvell † 1826, by *Rouw*, heavy
severely Greek epitaph, white marble. – The church
has nice cast-iron gates and railings.

THE PRIORY (Urban District Council). The remains
of a priory but of the house of the Franciscans at W
The present large house grew out of it after the Diss
tion and exhibits easily recognizable C17 and C18 w
What is earlier and goes back to the Franciscans and
C15 is the S side and part of the W side of the Clois
with openings consisting of three lancet lights und
four-centred arch, and a range projecting to the W f
the W wing. This has straightheaded two-light wind
on two floors with pointed and cusped heads to the
dividual lights, and an open kingpost roof now no lo
accessible. What was the use of the range at the tim
the friars is not known (guest house?).

INFANTS SCHOOL, Park Road (*see* Introduction, p. 28

PERAMBULATION

From the centre Baldock Street leads N, the High St
E to the bridges across the river Lea and the New Ri
Both streets have much to recommend them, mostl
their combination of C16–C17 timber-framed and ga
with C18 red brick houses. In BALDOCK STREET
best building of the earlier type is the BULL INN
overhang, two gables, and two first floor oriel winde
Opposite Nos 43–49 are the usual plastered C17 cotta
The best brick houses are Nos 27 (five bays, three stor
Ionic doorcase) and No. 35, both first half C18. The sa
story *en miniature* Nos 10–12 and No. 8, the for
timber-framed, the latter brick. At the N end of Bald
Street lies on the r. THUNDER HALL, a tall Jacob
brick house with central (former) porch and gable. It
remodelled and cemented over early in the C19,* when
a gatehouse and cloisters were added so that now
whole building seems of that period. Opposite is CANC

---

* It is said by *Wyatt*. Does that mean the elder or the younge.

OTEL, yellow brick with a Greek Doric porch. Then
ae of the most interesting buildings of Ware; CANONS
ALTINGS which incorporates a range of two-storeyed
:d brick malthouses of c. 1600. The W side has a row of
uttresses, the E side one three-light brick window with
ood-mould, still with four-centred heads to the indi-
dual lights.

HIGH STREET runs parallel with the river Lea. The
ouses had originally gardens stretching down to the
ver, and perhaps their most unusual feature is that a
umber of them has gazebos of brick or weatherboarded 7a
y or overhanging the river. Otherwise the street has also
ae alternating rhythm of the gabled and picturesque with
ae straight and regular. Nos 84–88 with three gables and
ome good ceilings inside is the best C16 example. In
omplete contrast to it Nos 74–76, a two-storeyed, urban,
ght-bay, stock brick façade with the shop windows set in
lank arcades. Opposite Nos 61–65 are plastered, two-
oreyed, and gabled houses of the C17; No. 65 has some
15 details remaining inside; No. 67 is mid C18 of purple
rick with rubbed red brick dressings. The same dif-
rence is repeated between Nos 51–53 or 35–37 and the
ood Georgian fronts of Nos 43–47 between them. An
fect worth noting is how WEST STREET runs parallel
ith, and close to, the High Street but opens out into it
a one place about the middle of its course. Here, nobly
:cessed from the High Street, stands the OLD TOWN
ALL, a plain Regency house of seven bays with a heavy
nfluted Ionic. EAST STREET also runs parallel to the
ligh Street. It must be visited because it has in No. 2A
dated example of the usual purple brick front with
abbed brick dressings (1709; with curly lintels to the
:cond, fourth, and sixth upper windows). Next to it an
rchway below a niche opens in a house of about the
ame date. It leads into BLUECOAT YARD. Here on the
. is Bluecoat House, the former manor house of Ware,
C15 timber-framed house (see the front door and some
eams inside) altered in the C16 and C17. It was the
luecoat School from 1674 to 1761. Opposite it a long

terrace of almshouse-like cottages was erected in 1
for nurses and children. They are still entirely
classical in their character, timber-framed with horizo.
windows and dormers. Back to the High Street wh
towards the E end, there is one more good early
house: No. 21 with a carriageway and next to it a d
case with Gibbs surround.

From the E end of the High Street straight on into S
STREET with perhaps the most interesting building
Ware, Messrs Albany's CORN STORES. They incorpo
a large C17 quadrangle of storehouses originally with
open courtyard. The upper floor is reached by or
ladders under lean-to roofs and has open timber roofs
the way round. Such large commercial premises of
early a date are rare indeed.

Across the river and the New River to LONDON RO
Facing the bridges the former AMWELL HOUSE, J
Scott's the Quaker poet's house (Ware Grammar Sch
for Girls), a stately red brick mansion of c. 1730 v
three-storey centre of five bays and far-projecting t
storey wings with Venetian front windows. MILBRC
HOUSE, to the E, now also belongs to the Gram
School. It is of c. 1820, yellow brick, and has at the b
an odd battlemented bow window with Gothick windo
John Scott's gardens were extensive, and their pride,
GROTTO, fortunately still exists (Scott's Road). It
built in the 1770s and is, though on a small scale, far m
complex than Alexander Pope's at Twickenham. Co
pared with the grotto at Stourhead, on the other hand,
minute. But that only enhances the enchantment. It c
sists of quite a number of passages and chambers laid
as intricately as the catacombs of Rome. They are t
varying degree lined with flints, shell, quartz, bits of gl
etc. The daylight is not entirely excluded; in two place
sudden glimpse of the greenery of the garden is caught
a small two-light Gothick and a still smaller circular w
dow. Moreover, the largest room has an indirect skylig
But the second largest room is all in darkness, a room w
a central pillar and originally a number of ribs towa

he walls in the fashion of Gothic chapter houses. The
patterns of the shell decoration vary from chamber to
chamber, sometimes a complete lining, once cemented
walls with a 'polka-dot' pattern of shells, and once a
rellis pattern. The largest rooms are only 12⅓ ft and 6½ ft
n diameter.

NHAMS HALL, 1¼ m. NE. A Queen Anne house of
moderate size with a delightful staircase, converted by *W.
Wood Bethell* in 1900–1 into a vast Neo-Tudor affair (e.g.
with a gallery 107 ft long). The plasterwork by *Lawrence
L. Turner*.

SNEYE, 1½ m. SE, *c.* 1868, by *Waterhouse*. Red brick, with
much diapering, masses of stepped gables, details of
racery, etc., in the E.E. style and much use of red terracotta. Rather harsh and unsympathetic in the general
effect.

WARESIDE

LY TRINITY, 1841, by *Thomas Smith*. Of stock brick in
he Norman style. Nave, wide transepts with galleries in
hem, and apse (polygonal outside). In front of the altar
ails the Puginesque brass to a vicar who died in 1845.
quarter of a mile s of the church a half-timbered house
proudly dated 1843 and indeed happily incorrect in its
arrangement of the timbers.

WATER END FARM *see* WHEATHAMPSTEAD

WATERFORD HALL *see* STAPLEFORD

AYTEMORE CASTLE *see* BISHOPS STORTFORD

WATFORD

tford with *c.* 73,000 inhabitants is by far the largest town
Herts. It is clearly a town of its own, yet with its red
ndon buses, its terminus of a London tube line, and its
ny names and fascia-boards of shops familiar to the Lon-
er, it never allows one to forget that in many ways one is
l in London when one walks through Watford. The urban
a of Watford is wider than its population figure would

make one expect. It extends to the SW through Bushey a
Oxhey and in the SE towards Rickmansworth. New esta
of council houses, both H.C.C. and L.C.C., are growing
rapidly, and Watford's own development is steady too, sir
the town's industries, chiefly brewing (Benskin's) a
printing and its allied trades, are not suffering much und
trade crises.

The old Watford of pre-Victorian days is still eas
discernible. It consists of the church and its closest sy
roundings and the long High Street leading down towar
the river Colne and on to Bushey and London. The riv
skirts on two sides the hill on which the town stands. T
railway crosses the river valley by a fine long and high br
VIADUCT once apparently one of the main sights of W
ford.

ST MARY. Hidden from the High Street by a screen of l
   houses and placed in a large churchyard with an abu
   dance of old trees.* The church itself is of flint, long, bro
   and low, with a big, solid W tower. The tower has diago
   buttresses, battlements, a NE stair-turret, and a spike. T
   chancel dates from the early C13, as can be seen ins
   from the double Piscina and the chancel arch. Its capit
   and double-chamfered arches repeat in the low long
   arcade of the nave. The N arcade is C15, yet at first si
   very similar. Both arcades have octagonal piers and tw
   centred arches. The differences lie in the taller piers,
   more finely moulded capitals, and the slightly tal
   hollow-chamfered arches. The outer walls of the aisl
   the clerestory, the nave roof with beams resting on car
   angels, the S chancel chapel with tall slim octagonal p
   and four-centred arches, and the tower are also C15. T
   N chancel chapel (Morrison Chapel) was added in 1
   (see the Tuscan columns of the arcade to the nave –
   Hatfield church – and the mullioned and transomed
   window). – PULPIT, 1714, by *Richard Bull*, with dain
   carved borders to the panels, etc. – VESTMENT CL
   BOARD, *c.* 1730, Flemish or French, with the four ev.

* The churchyard was altered in 1952.

gelists in medallions. – PLATE. Chalice, 1561; Chalice and
Cover, 1610; two Flagons, 1628; two Breadholders,
1637; Almsdish, 1642. – MONUMENTS. Brasses to Hugh
de Holes † 1415 and his wife † 1416 (?), largish figures, of
good quality; the man, in judge's robes, bigger than the
woman. – Brass to three retainers of the Morrison family;
two of them died in 1610 and 1613. – In the Morrison
Chapel wall monument perhaps to Bridget, widow of
Richard Morrison of Cassiobury and later wife of the
second Earl of Bedford, who built the chapel in 1595 (no
inscription): the usual kneeling figure between two
columns. The monuments to her son and grandson are
the chief glory of Watford church and among the best
sculptural works of their date in the county. Both are by
Nicholas Stone and both of alabaster and touch. Both also
are of the most ambitious type: standing wall monuments
with life-size figures. Sir Charles Morrison † 1590 (made 34
in 1619). He rests semi-reclining between columns supporting two segmental arches and a larger segmental arch
above. To the l. and r. outside the columns two kneeling
figures against baldacchinos of richly crumpled fabric. No
Jacobean mannerisms are left, and the skill of portraiture
is admirable. Opposite the monument to Sir Charles Morrison † 1628 ('splendidissimo et clarissimo viro'). He lies
semi-reclining behind and slightly above his wife's recumbent figure. The monument this time is a tall four-poster
and above the two segmental arches are two gables. Two
kneeling figures outside the columns as in the earlier
monument. – Many minor later monuments, e.g. Anne
Derne † 1790, graceful epitaph of varied marbles, by *J.
Golde* of High Holborn.

ST ANDREW, Church Road, 1857, by *Teulon*. Rather restrained for that architect. s aisle added 1865.

HOLY ROOD (R.C.), Market Street, 1883–90, by *Bentley*,
then about 45 years old. One of the noblest examples of
the refined, knowledgeable, and sensitive Gothic Revival
of that time. The flint exterior combines vestries and
other outer rooms into a square plan. The main accent is
the square NW tower. In addition two turrets with copper

spires. Flint with stone bands in the Herts tradition; th
tracery C14, but other detail clearly influenced by Art
and Crafts innovations. Plain nave, transept of two bay
width with two-storeyed opening to the nave. This an
the elevation of the chancel with square ambulatory an
well-passage above it, in front of the large upper win
dows, are remarkable yet not obtrusively original.

BAPTIST CHURCH, Clarendon Road, 1876–8, by *J. Wall*
Chapman. In a semi-Italian Romanesque style with aps
towards the street and attached campanile with pyrami
roof. Purple brick with red brick dressings.

TOWN HALL, Hemel Hempstead Road and Rickmans
worth Road, 1940, by *C. Cowles-Voysey*. At the mai
traffic junction of Watford and repeating in its plan th
lines of the two streets and the roundabout between them
Above the concave centre a Swedish-modern lantern. Th
building is otherwise in chaste Neo-Georgian forms
With the Hospital next to it, the Library, and the Swim
ming Baths, it forms the nucleus of a civic centre fo
Watford.

MINISTRY OF LABOUR HEADQUARTERS, built close t
Watford Junction railway station as the London Orpha
Asylum by *H. Dawson* in 1869–71. Large group of bric
buildings in an undistinguished Gothic style.

MRS ELIZABETH FULLER FREE SCHOOL (*see* below).

PERAMBULATION

The visual centre of Watford is now by the Town Hall. I
was once by the church. Around the churchyard ther
still are on the N a row of nice low cottages, on the S th
MRS ELIZABETH FULLER FREE SCHOOL, a delightfu
three-bay brick building of 1704 with arched windows
stone quoins, door with segmental pediment and centra
cupola, and on the W the BEDFORD ALMSHOUSES
founded in 1580. They have a five-gabled plastered fron
with the two outer gables a little smaller than the others.
Round the corner in KING STREET: WATFORD PLACE
a white villa of *c.* 1825 with four-column Ionic portico.

and in VICARAGE ROAD the Morrison Almshouses, rebuilt in an uninteresting Neo-Gothic style in 1824.

om the churchyard to the N and E the HIGH STREET can
be reached. In NEW STREET a four-bay, three-storeyed
brick house of early C18 type. At the corner of Church
Street and High Street a C16 half-timbered house with
overhang. To the N the prevalent character of the High
Street is C20 urban. To the S there are still stretches of
small old houses of quite a county town character, especially Nos 129, etc., and on the other side Nos 154, etc. A
little lower down BENSKIN'S BREWERY, the stately C18
dwelling-house towards the street (five bays, two and a
half storeys, with three-bay pediment and lower outer
wings) and behind it the tall Victorian brewing premises
of yellow brick. On the other side of the road some maltings of 1836 still exist. Yet lower down the High Street on
the E side No. 223 with good doorcase (fluted Ionic
pilasters and Venetian window above), on the W side Nos
244–248, an eight-bay, cemented late C17 house. The end
is Frogmore House on the E side, immediately by the
gasometer, a four-bay, three-storeyed house of *c.* 1700
with rusticated doorcase with Roman Doric pilasters,
carved metopes, and a hood on carved brackets.

he High Street N of the church is not entirely without
older houses but they rather tend to be overlooked. Note
HALSEY HOUSE (Conservative Club) on the W side, long
Early Victorian stuccoed façade, and on the E side MON-
MOUTH HOUSE, a completely reconstructed early C17
brick house. The exterior has now four gables; some interior features are preserved in their original state. Past
the Town Hall in the HEMEL HEMPSTEAD ROAD, No.
3 (Education Offices), the best classical house at Watford:
late C17 front of nine bays but not as wide as that number
of windows would make one expect. The bays are very
narrow projections with squeezed-in windows. The central three bays also project, a lively rhythm of forward and
backward movement. – A little to the N in CHURCH
ROAD the SALTER'S COMPANY ALMSHOUSES, 1863,
by *John Collier*, an almost ideal example of charitable mid

Victorian architecture. One long central range and
short projecting wings. Red brick, Tudor style. The cer
motif completely asymmetrical with a tower and a step
gable. Fine cedar trees between the buildings. Ornate i
gates to the street.

Farther out to the NW ($1\frac{1}{2}$ m. from the centre) GRC
MILL HOUSE and HEATH FARM HOUSE, good far
houses, and THE GROVE. The Lodges towards He
Hempstead Road of late C18 stuccoed architecture. T
house was built by *Sir Robert Taylor* in 1756, enlarg
c. 1780 and again *c.* 1850. It is a block of red br
with stone quoins. The centres on the two principal fro
are emphasized by angle pilasters. The E part is ol
than the larger W part. On the other side of Hemel Hen
stead Road is RUSSELL'S, now a H.C.C. Home, a go
red brick house with pediments on two sides. It has
date 1718 on a weathervane. The S entrance is od
placed in the central bow window. Much new H.C
housing of good design to the NE of Russell's and beyo
the North-Western Avenue. Between Kingsway a
Leavesden High Road one of the new H.C.C. SCHOO
(*see* Introduction, p. 28).

Back to Watford by the North-Western Avenue. Just l
yond its E end in COLNE WAY (and off St Albans Roa
ODHAMS PRESS, big brick factory with long low ban
of windows, a symmetrical façade by *Sir Owen Williar*
1937.

LANGLEYBURY *see* p. 152.

REDHEATH *see* p. 191.

WATTON-AT-STONE

ST ANDREW AND ST MARY. An all-embattled flint chur
of the C15 with two porches, a rood stair-turret on the
side, and a tower stair-turret rising higher than the tow
battlements. The N porch is two-storeyed with a bro
stair-turret on the E side. The view from the NE towar
all these various castellated parts is especially enjoyabl
Most of the windows are renewed but represent the Pe

panel' tracery of the originals accurately. The E window is original. The interior has a four-bay arcade with par-icularly characteristic Late Perp piers. They are of a complicated section (the same as at Ware) with a double curve and several hollows and have capitals only to the innermost shafts under the arches. The main mouldings carry on into the voussoirs without any break. A Perp N chapel was added in 1851 and provided with a Neo-Jaco-bean tunnel-vault. – MONUMENTS. Brass to a Knight in armour under ogee canopy with thin buttresses and pinnacles. The figure is said to represent Sir Philip Pele-ot † 1361. It is 4 ft 9 in. long and restored (N chapel). Brass to a civilian, C15 (N chapel). – Brass to a Knight in armour, early C16 (N chapel). – Brass to a civilian, head-less, C15 (N aisle). – Brass to a lady, Early Elizabethan, lower part missing (nave, E end). – Brass to a priest, mid C15, very good large figure (4 ft 9 in.; chancel). – Large incised alabaster slab to John Boteler of Woodhall and his two wives. One of them died in 1471. The inscription runs at the head end, the wrong way up. John Boteler's date of death remained blank (N chapel). – Standing wall monument to Philip Boteler † 1712 and wife. Frontally kneeling figures in a shallow Gothic recess, he in con-temporary costume, she as a Roman matron. They suffer from lack of leg space. – Sir Thomas Rumbold † 1791, by *Bacon*, with a delicate relief of a mourning female in a tondo. Two urns in the shallowest relief to the l. and r. – W. R. Rumbold † 1786, with a big urn wreathed with an oak garland. Probably also by *Bacon* but unsigned.

he best thing in the village is a baluster-shaped early C19 cast-iron PUMP. It stands close to WATTON HALL, a timber-framed plastered house with three parallel over-hang gables to the street. N of them three trefoil brick arches, no doubt Early Tudor, have recently been dis-covered underneath the plaster.

ROOM HALL, ¾ m. w. Late C16 brick house with central porch, central chimney, and on the upper floor partly original windows with brick mullions and four-centred heads to the individual lights.

WATTON WOODHALL see WOODHALL PARK

WELWYN

Nowadays people often forget that Welwyn is not a gard
city but an old little town of much charm and far enou;
away from the garden city not to be entirely swamped]
suburban developments however tasteful.

ST MARY. The exterior is too drastically restored to ha
preserved any of its original character. The SW tow
nave, clerestory, N aisle (with its odd N gable), S aisle wa
and S chancel chapel were newly built in the 1910. Insid
the chancel has a long lancet window in the S wall and tv
blocked ones in the N wall. The E end has a group of thr
stepped-up lancets, with Purbeck marble shafts insid
The Double Piscina has pointed trefoil heads. The chanc
arch is double-chamfered on broadly moulded capital
The forms of these and the arches are repeated in the
arcade of four bays. – SCREEN and COMMUNION RAI
destroyed by fire in 1952. – PLATE. Chalice, 166(
Paten, 1678; Flagon, 1750. – MONUMENT. Edwar
Young, author of *Night Thoughts* and *On Original Con
position*, who was Vicar of Welwyn from 1730 to 1765.

Plenty of enjoyable houses near the church. Immediately]
the SE one of brick and timber; opposite this, acros
CHURCH STREET, a Georgian five-bay house. At the en
of Church Street Wendover Lodge, white Late Georgia
three-bay house with additions. In MILL LANE the for
mer ASSEMBLY ROOMS, just S of the White Horse Inr
red brick, low, of five bays, now divided into cottages. A
the S end of Mill Lane more minor Georgian architectur
Facing the entrance of the road from St Albans the WHIT
HART and its neighbour, both red brick Georgian. Th
White Hart was largely built *c.* 1760–5. A little to the
School Lane leads to NEW PLACE, built in 1880 b
Philip Webb for his brother. It is of brick, L-shapec
with Webb's typical sash-windows with relieving arches
but buttresses and a steep-pitched roof. To the N of th
White Hart High Street runs towards the church. By th

crossing of the river Mimvam BRIDGE on the way towards the church by the bridge BRIDGE COTTAGE with
iron verandah and monkey puzzle, and BRIDGE HOUSE,
and opposite this a house with pretty semicircular porch.
W of the church the WELLINGTON HOTEL with some
old half-timbering but usually *c.* 1725, and then at the
exit to the N more detached Georgian houses. Not one of
all these houses is of the first order; but their grouping
around the church and the streets fanning out from it is
attractive.

OCKLEYS. Nine-bay brick house of 1717 now a school.
Two-storeyed with angle pilasters and attic above the
cornice. Doorway with segmental pediment on Roman
Doric columns. Segmentheaded windows. The dressings
of fine rubbed bricks. – In the grounds an important
ROMAN VILLA has been excavated. This was originally
built of timber and mud in the C1 A.D. It was then a
rectangular house of five rooms with an open colonnade
in front. In the C2 wings were added and the colonnade
was rebuilt. The plan of the villa marked in turf and
brick.

WELWYN GARDEN CITY

Welwyn Garden City was planned and built entirely after
the First World War. It is thus a later creation than Letchworth and the Hampstead Garden Suburb and differs in
characteristic ways from both. It is not pioneer work like
Parker & Unwin's, but the architects of Welwyn, *Louis de
Soissons* and *A. W. Kenyon*, have evidently learnt from the
mistakes of the pioneers.

Welwyn Garden City extends on both sides of the railway 63b
which runs here in a straight line roughly from S to N. To
the E of, and close to the railway is the industrial area;
for a garden city as against a garden suburb must
possess enough industry to ensure it an independent
life. Architecturally best amongst the factories are the
SHREDDED WHEAT COMPANY, 1925, by *L. de Soissons*
and ROCHE PRODUCTS, by *Otto Salvisberg* of Zurich,

1938–40 (addition 1952). Towards w from the railw.
station runs a short boulevard with planted centre. Th
meets at right angles the main N–S artery, also a parkwa
At its N end a semicircular exedra is intended to have in
portant public buildings. At present the main public buil
ings and also the five-storeyed Stores, and the shoppi
area are all by the station and the parkway. This urba
looking area is something that the Hampstead Garde
Suburb lacks and that Letchworth received only slow
and never adequately, owing to its arrested growth.

The residential layout is clearly derived from the *Unw*
ideas and patterns. Old trees are meticulously kep
straight roads are rare, and closes everywhere determi
the pattern. The predominant style of the houses, how
ever, has characteristically changed since Letchworth.
is now a quiet comfortable Neo-Georgian, no longer olde
worldy. The brickwork is mostly exposed.

LUDWICK CORNER, Cole Green Lane. By *Sir Ernest Neu
ton*, 1907.

PENTLEY PARK JUNIOR MIXED AND INFANTS SCHOO
and HOLLYBUSH LANE SECONDARY MODER
SCHOOL (*see* Introduction, p. 28).

The original Welwyn plan provided for a growth to
50,000 inhabitants. In 1948 the Welwyn area was throw
together for planning purposes with Hatfield New Tow
and a revised plan worked out (consulted architect an
planner *Louis de Soissons*). The future populations for th
two are now 36,500 for Welwyn and 25,000 for Hatfiel
Building schemes of the last few years are SOUTH PARK
WAY, LEMSFORD LANE s of this, and, at the other sid
of the railway, about 1½ m. to the E HOMESTEAD COUR
(with several blocks of flats of no special architectura
interest) and, again to the E, COLE GREEN LANE. Her
houses are by *Hening & Chitty*, and *P. Mauger &
Partners*.

WEST HYDE

ST THOMAS, 1844, by *Thomas Smith* (GR). Flint wit
cemented brick dressings. In the Norman style. Nave

transepts, and narrower chancel. A porch and a corresponding excrescence in the angles between transepts and chancel. A roof ridge runs through the transepts and the crossing at right angles to the nave; an odd effect.

WESTBROOK MAY *see* BOXMOOR

WESTMILL

MARY. It is only by looking at the SE angle of the nave that one can recognize the Anglo-Saxon origin of the church. No other feature as early as that exists. The next in order of time is the N arcade (two bays). Two pointed arches, unmoulded, are cut through the Saxon N wall. They look later C12. Then comes the chancel, with one straightheaded C13 window. The others are C19. Altogether the church is too much restored to be very rewarding. The chancel arch is C15, the very tall tower arch and the whole W tower with diagonal buttresses and Herts spike essentially *c.* 1500. – FONT. Octagonal, Perp, with fleurons in quatrefoils, circles, etc.; also blank tracery. – CHANCEL SEATS. Some with poppy-heads and very gaunt long human heads. – BENCHES. Simple C15, buttressed. – COMMUNION RAILS, with twisted balusters, late C17. – PLATE. Chalice, 1563; Paten, 1630; large Paten, 1713.

pretty group of cottages along the S side of the church-yard, started at the E end by the early C18 brick mansion WESTMILL BURY (five bays, two storeys) and its fine brick-fronted barn.

WESTON

OLY TRINITY. The uncommon importance of the church is its Norman crossing with the four crossing arches and 16a the lower part of the tower complete. In addition the N transept with two Norman windows is preserved and the blocked arch which opened no doubt into an apsidal chapel. The S transept also survives though entirely

altered. Presumably the church had two apsidal trans
chapels and an apsidal E end. Of the Norman nave
can say nothing. The Norman parts are of flint with sto
dressings. The upper part of the tower was built in 18
The crossing piers have capitals a little more comp
than most such Norman arches in Herts, and abaci wit
little billet or crescent decoration. The present nave an
aisle (octagonal piers, double-hollow-chamfered arch
with clerestory are Perp. The clerestory windows n
look into the heightened aisle. The nave ceiling is divid
into square panels; the beams rest on grotesque he
corbels. The chancel was rebuilt in 1840 by *Thomas Sm*
in the Norman style. It seems odd to us now to see ho
hundred years ago such a brick chancel with such orn
Norman trim was considered a match for the austerity
the original work. – FONT. Octagonal, Perp, with quat
foil panels. – STAINED GLASS. Chancel N and S wind
still with what may well be glass of *c.* 1840. – PLA
Chalice, 1638; Paten, 1661.

A good village with many pretty houses on the w side av
from the church.

WHEATHAMPSTEAD

ST HELEN. A big flint church with a chancel as long as
nave and a dominating crossing tower with a broach
lead spire starting like a pyramidal roof (an odd outli
due to the C19 restoration). Of a Norman church
foundations of an apse have been discovered. The nave
doubt corresponded to the present nave. The chancel v
added *c.* 1230 (*see* the fine group of three lancet windo
in the E wall, with nook shafts inside, and the N doorw
with dog-tooth decoration). The crossing tower with
heavy treble-stepped piers belongs probably to the la
C13. The early C14 is responsible for the w door (with
ball flower ornament) and the s aisle and s porch. T
two-light windows at the aisle w end and the octago
piers with their moulded capitals and double-hollo
chamfered arches are typical of that date. Of the sai

date are the transepts, and here much money must have
been available and an architect with a good sense of display. The N transept N window is of five lights, the S transept S window of four. Both have ogee-reticulated tracery.
Moreover, the S transept E window has some very original
finely ogee-cusped tracery and big fleurons inside along
jambs and voussoirs. In the N transept the windows have
even two orders of (smaller) fleurons. The E window has
fleurons outside as well, and inside below the sill a delightful blank frieze of crocketed ogee arches with brackets
for statuettes. Nothing else of the Dec style in the county,
with the exception of the E end at St Albans, is quite so
rich. The same designer inserted equally original windows in the chancel N and S walls. The N arcade of the
nave is later than that of the S, although the N aisle has
windows of early C14 date. The clerestory windows were
given their present shape in 1863-6. The only notable
contribution of the later Middle Ages is the charming
canopied Piscina in the chancel tucked in diagonally by
the Sedilia. – FONT. Early C14, octagonal with quatrefoil
circles on finely carved but somewhat decayed leaves. –
PULPIT. Jacobean, from the former chapel at Lamer
House. – BENCHES. In the N transept. From the same
chapel; two benches dated 1631. – SCREEN. Fragments in
the N transept and at the W end, Jacobean, and probably
made up of fragments from a former W gallery. – PAINT-
ING. Mount of Olives by *King*, 1821, large figure. The
frame is in a thin Gothic taste. – STAINED GLASS. *Kempe*,
1893, N aisle, first window from E. – MONUMENTS. A
large number. Brass to Hugh Bostok and wife, *c.* 1436 (N
transept); good large frontal figures; the parents of Abbot
Wheathampstead of St Albans. – Brass to John Heyworth
† 1520 and wife (N transept), small figures slightly in profile. – Man and wife with children, *c.* 1520 (N transept). –
Headless Lady, leg of a Knight and dog at his foot, C15 (S
transept). – Brass Indents chancel N with stone surround.
– John Heyworth † 1558 and wife (N transept), the figures
small, incised in a marble slab, with a modest architectural surround; at the foot simplest strapwork (cf.

Harpenden, Cressye). – Sir John Brocket † 1558 and wif
(s transept): alabaster tomb-chest with recumbent effigie
The decoration with figures and heraldry is just on th
point of leaving the Gothic style and going classical. N
refinements. – Garrard Monument N transept, the larges
in the church, undated and not fully identified. The dat
must be in the 1630s, and the design is conservative fc
that date. Alabaster semi-reclining figures, the husban
behind and slightly above the wife, big architectural sur
round and columns, coffered arch, and allegorical figure
in the spandrels of the arch top achievement. – Man
Garrard tablets in the N transept, one of them, hung u
much too high to be seen, is by *Thorwaldsen* (Charle
Drake G. † 1817: two Grecian figures holding each othe
by the hand; in the style of Athenian stelae).

WATER END FARM, 1¾ m. E, originally a manor house c
the Jennings family. The house lies picturesquely by
ford. It is of brick, has quite an ambitious symmetric
w front with three straight gables, three shallo
two-storeyed bay- windows, and two small straigh
headed doorways. Fine large decorated chimney-stack
The house is said to have been built about 1610.

ROMAN REMAINS, on the N side of the road fron
St Albans to Welwyn. The remains probably repre
sent the capital of Cassivelaunus, the British chieftai
who opposed Julius Caesar in 54 B.C. On the slopes abov
the river Lea are two stretches of earthworks, the v
known as the Devil's Dyke on account of its size. This
1,400 ft long, 130 ft wide, and originally 40 ft deep. On th
E side of this 100-acre enclosure is another ditch, know
as the Slad, 1,200 ft long, 80 ft wide, and 15 ft deep.

WHITWELL

A pretty village with, along the High Street, the Yout
Hostel, red brick, of three bays, *c.* 1700, and three othe
houses of brick and of half-timber work (Bull Inn).

WICKHAM HALL *see* BISHOPS STORTFORD

WIDFORD

ST JOHN THE BAPTIST. Unbuttressed Perp w tower with low rectangular stair-turret, characteristic tower arch, and recessed spire. Nave and chancel under one roof. s porch C19. In the nave above the s doorway a reset C12 zigzag arch. One s window with Dec tracery, the rest Perp and much of the tracery new. – PILLAR PISCINA. A Norman block capital with the front semicircle decorated; early C12, it seems. – DOOR, C14 with C13 ironwork (says the R. Commission). – WALL PAINTINGS. E. and N walls of chancel. On the N wall Christ of the Apocalypse with sword; *c.* 1500. – PLATE. Specially good Chalice of 1562 with Paten.

WIDFORDBURY. C17 farmhouse, but to its E, now used as churchyard wall, the brick wall of a much larger former house with C16 bricks, a four-centred arched doorway, and a larger doorway of the Elizabethan period with pilasters and round arch. Also near the farmhouse an octagonal C16 DOVECOTE.

LAKESWARE, 1 m. w. Rebuilt in 1878 by *George Devey*. The material is red brick, the style Neo-Tudor. The composition and details both as good as the time could make them. The house clearly shows what difference the employment of a sensitive architect makes, even when he works in terms of period imitation.

WIGGINTON

ST BARTHOLOMEW. Small late medieval church, completely renewed in 1881 by *Will. White*. The w end had a separate w chamber. The little C19 turret sits on the joint between it and the nave. – STAINED GLASS. *Kempe* window of 1892 (SS Stephen and Laurence). – PLATE. Chalice and Paten, 1569; the rest 1877.

GRIMS DYKE (*see* Berkhamsted).

WILBURY HILL *see* LETCHWORTH

WILLIAN

ALL SAINTS. In the chancel is a C12 blocked doorway. T.
rest appears C14 and chiefly C15. The chancel E windo
is specially attractive with two orders of shafts insic
Early in the C19 the E end received some blank Dec arca
ing and a reredos to match. – SCREEN. Little of the c
left. – CHANCEL SEATS. With poppy-heads; also o:
with an elephant and castle and one with St John's hea
on the charger. – PLATE. Chalice and Paten, 1718.
MONUMENTS. Brass to Richard Golden † 1446, front
in priest's vestments. – Epitaph with the two usu
kneelers to E. Lacon † 1625 and an even humbler one wi
kneelers to John Chapman † 1624. – Sir Thomas Wils.
† 1656 and wife, with two frontal busts in oval nich
above long inscription.

Near the church the VICARAGE, a small timber-framed co
tage, and PUNCHARDON HALL with a C18 seven-b
brick front.

WOODHALL PARK
1¼ m. SE of Watton-at-Stone

53 The house was built in 1777 by *Thomas Leverton*, t.
architect who probably designed Bedford Square
London. It was an oblong white brick block of seven ba
and two and a half storeys connected by one-storey
links with higher pedimented one-storeyed wings wi
large Venetian windows. The house itself towards t.
garden has rustication to the ground-floor three-b
centre and on it a one-and-a-half-storey attached order
Ionic columns. The outer ground-floor windows ha
pediments on brackets, all very nicely detailed. Abo
1795 the wings were extended on the entrance side and
one-storeyed porch of four pairs of unfluted Ionic colum
was added. *Leverton's* interiors have a style decidedly the
own, different from Adam's or Chamber's or Holland
This comes out most clearly in the central staircase ha
profusely but very delicately decorated with plaster

antique. Oval panels are specially favoured, but the dome lighting the room is circular. The staircase ascends in an elegant sweep without inner supports. It is in one flight without intermediate landings along three walls and leads to a first floor gallery. The Entrance Hall between portico and staircase (originally the Saloon) is decorated in the Etruscan taste. The central room towards the garden has arched windows and blank arches along the other walls. It was originally the entrance. Above it the best room of the upper floor, with a specially pretty ceiling.

WOOLMER GREEN

MICHAEL, 1899–1900, by *R. Weir Schultz*. The exterior in no way remarkable (tower projected but not built). But inside the low panelled room with a big panelled pointed wagon-roof and tie-beams has much character. Rood screen with naturalistic leaf and fruit tracery. The apse arch is lower than the small apse itself.

WOOLMERS or WOOLMER PARK
2 m. SW of Hertingfordbury

The garden front has two canted bay windows at the ends and a long one-storeyed colonnade of severe Tuscan columns between. This seems to date the house as *c.* 1810–20, and the entrance porch, staircase, and passage to the staircase correspond to that date. Yet it seems likely from documents that the brick structure itself was built before 1800.

WORMLEY

LAURENCE. To the N of the house and away from the village. A small church consisting of nave and chancel only, to which in the C19 a S aisle, S porch, and stone bellcote were added. One N window of the nave and the N doorway prove the Norman date of the nave. The chancel has been too much restored to preserve any original features. – FONT. Norman, circular, of very uncommon

design. An upper frieze of broad upright leaves, and be[...]
this panels separated from each other by thick ca[...]
mouldings. In the panels rosettes and groups of upri[...]
leaves. – PULPIT. Jacobean, with termini-caryatids at [...]
angles. – PAINTING. Last Supper, presented by
Abraham Hume of Wormleybury in 1797. Ascribed [...]
Palma Vecchio and purchased from a monastery [...]
Rocchelin Canons near Verona. – PLATE. Flagon, 16[...]
Pewter Almsdish, 1699. – MONUMENTS. Two wh[...]
memorial epitaphs, both with sculpture by *Westmaco*[...]
one to Lord and Lady Farnborough, 1838 and 1837 (w[...]
a large kneeling female figure), the other to Sir Abrah[...]
Hume † 1838 (with portrait bust).

WORMLEYBURY. The house is a square block of yell[...]
brick consisting of basement and two and a half store[...]
To the S is a central canted bay window. There was at f[...]
no other outer decoration. In this form the house [...]
(according to Mr Christopher Gotch's unpublis[...]
thesis) built by *Robert Mylne* in 1767–69. Rainwater he[...]
bear the date 1767, and also one referring to the preced[...]
house: 1734. Mylne was architect to the New River Co[...]
pany (*see* Great Amwell). For the embellishment of [...]
plain house, *Robert Adam* was called in. He adorned o[...]
three rooms, but made an exquisite job of them. T[...]
Entrance Hall has attached columns, an aedicule [...]
Roman Doric columns on each side (a typical early Ad[...]
motif), and most delicate stucco work. Even more p[...]
fuse is the stucco decoration of the Drawing Room, a[...]
here *Angelica Kauffmann* provided her much favou[...]
little painted roundels, etc. – The staircase has an o[...]
dome and classical iron railings. It leads up to a gall[...]
on the first floor. The stucco panels of the staircase w[...]
vary surprisingly by size and shapes. The motif in o[...]
set of them is a large pitcher. All much in the Wedgw[...]
taste. Adam worked at Wormleybury in 1777–9. Sho[...]
after, in 1781–2, Mylne was again paid for work [...]
Wormleybury, and as the sums are considerable, [...]
best work is no doubt the giant portico of stone, ad[...]
on the entrance side. The garden front was left [...]

touched. In front of this lies a made lake, really a widening of the river, and the principal view from the house is
focused towards a big urn on the other side of the lake. –
The stables with a clock turret are close to the house on
the w.

The village stretches along the high road from London, the
same pattern as at Enfield or Broxbourne. It has the usual
remains of gabled and plastered houses (THE LIMES
GARAGE), red brick Georgian houses (WORMLEY
HOUSE), and early C19 yellow brick houses (ARCH
PRODUCTS to the s of Wormley House; with unfluted
Ionic porch and the ground floor windows in blank
arcades).

WYDDIAL

ST GILES. A Perp church, over-restored in the C19. Un- 20a
buttressed w tower, C19 s porch. The special and great
interest of the church is its N aisle and N chancel chapel,
both built of brick and dated by a brass inscription 1532.
The windows are of the usual three-light type under one
arch, all of brick.* The arcade of three bays has brick
piers of the usual type with semi-octagonal shafts and
hollows in the diagonals. The arches are treble-chamfered,
the middle chamfer being hollow. The arch to the N
chapel is also of brick. This triumphant entry of brick
into church building is a significant sign of the Tudor age.
The N chapel has SCREENS to W and S of elaborate early 27
C17 design and BOX PEWS to match in the aisle. –
STAINED GLASS. In two N windows eight smallish panels
with Scenes from the Passion; Flemish mid C16. –
PLATE. Paten, 1734. – MONUMENTS. Brass to John Gille
† 1546, with wife and children (chancel). – Brass to Dame
Margaret Plumbe † 1575, large demi-figure praying
(chancel wall). – Epitaph to Sir William Goulston † 1687,
with twisted columns carrying a scrolly broken pediment
and marble busts in grey niches above the inscription.

WYDDIAL HALL. Built after a fire of 1733. Large white
balustraded house of five by seven bays with canted bay

* A late C16 N doorway is of stone.

windows on the E. But the big outer chimney on the s si
the square two-storeyed porch in the middle of the E si
and other details indicate that enough of the Elizabeth
or Jacobean period remained to be made use of. The a
pearance of the older house is known from Chaun
(1700).

YOUNGSBURY *see* THUNDRIDGE

GLOSSARY

ABACUS: flat slab on the top of a capital (q.v.).

ABUTMENT: solid masonry placed to resist the lateral pressure of a vault.

ACANTHUS: plant with thick fleshy and scalloped leaves used as part of the decoration of a Corinthian capital (q.v.) and in some types of leaf carving.

ACHIEVEMENT OF ARMS: in heraldry, a complete display of armorial bearings.

ACROTERION: foliage-carved block on the end or top of a classical pediment.

ADDOSSED: two human figures, animals, or birds, etc., placed symmetrically so that they turn their backs to each other.

AEDICULE, AEDICULA: framing of a window or door by columns and a pediment (q.v.).

AFFRONTED: two human figures, animals, or birds, etc., placed symmetrically so that they face each other.

AMBULATORY: semicircular or polygonal aisle enclosing an apse (q.v.).

ANNULET: see Shaft-ring.

ANTIS, IN: see Portico.

APSE: vaulted semicircular or polygonal end of a chancel or a chapel.

ARABESQUE: light and fanciful surface decoration using combinations of flowing lines, tendrils, etc., interspersed with vases, animals, etc.

ARCADE: range of arches supported on piers or columns, free-standing; or, BLIND ARCADE, the same attached to a wall.

ARCH: round-headed; i.e. semicircular pointed, i.e. consisting of two curves, each drawn from one centre, and meeting in a point at the top; Segmental, i.e. in the form of a segment; pointed; four-centred, see Fig. 1(a); Tudor, see Fig. 1(b); Ogee, see Fig. 1(c); Stilted, see Fig. 1(d).

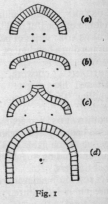

Fig. 1

ARCHITRAVE: lowest of the three main parts of the entablature (q.v.) of an order (q.v.) (see Fig. 11).

ARCHIVOLT: undersurface of an arch (also called Soffit).

ARRIS: sharp edge at the meeting of two surfaces.

ASHLAR: masonry of large blocks wrought to even faces and square edges.

ATRIUM: inner court of a Roman house, also open court in front of a church.

ATTACHED: *see* engaged.

ATTIC: topmost storey of a house, if lower than the others.

AUMBREY: recess or cupboard to hold sacred vessels for Mass and Communion.

BAILEY: open space or court of a fortified castle.

BALDACCHINO: canopy supported on columns.

BALLFLOWER: globular flower of three petals enclosing a small ball. A decoration used in the first quarter of the C14.

BALUSTER: small pillar or column of fanciful outline.

BALUSTRADE: series of balusters supporting a handrail or coping (q.v.).

BARBICAN: outwork, constructed like a gateway, defending the entrance to a castle.

BARGEBOARDS: projecting decorated boards placed against the incline of the gable of a building and hiding the horizontal roof timbers.

BASILICA: in medieval architecture an aisled church with a clerestory.

BASTION: projection at the angle of a fortification.

BATTER: wall with an inclined face.

BATTLEMENT: parapet with a series of indentations or embrasures with raised portions or merlons between (also called Crenellation).

BAYS: internal compartments of a building; each divided from the other not by solid walls but by divisions only marked in the side walls (columns, pilasters etc.) or the ceiling (beams etc.). Also external division of a building by fenestration.

BAY-WINDOW: angular or curved projection of a house front with ample fenestration. If curved also called bow-window; if on an upper floor only also called oriel or oriel window.

BEAKHEAD: Norman ornamental motif consisting of a row of bird or beast heads with beaks pointing downwards and biting usually into a roll moulding.

BELL-COTE: turret usually on the W end of a church to carry the bells.

BILLET: Norman ornamental motif made up of short raised rectangles placed at regular intervals.

BLOCK CAPITAL: Romanesque capital cut from a cube by having the lower angles rounded off to the circular shaft below (also called Cushion Capital) (Fig. 2).

Fig. 2

BOND, ENGLISH or FLEMISH: *see* Brickwork.

BOSS: knob or projection usually placed to cover the intersection of ribs in a vault.

BOW-WINDOW: *see* Bay-Window.

BOX PEW: pew with a high wooden enclosure.

GLOSSARY

ACES: see Roof.

BRACKET: small supporting piece of stone, etc., to carry a projecting horizontal.

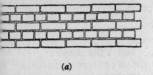

(a)

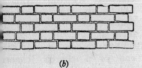

(b)

Fig. 3

BRICKWORK: *Header:* brick laid so that the end only appears on the face of the wall. *Stretcher:*

brick laid so that the side only appears on the face of the wall. *English Bond:* method of laying bricks so that alternate courses or layers on the face of the wall are composed of headers or stretchers only (Fig. 3*a*). *Flemish Bond:* method of laying bricks so that alternate headers and stretchers appear in each course on the face of the wall (Fig. 3*b*).

BROACH: see Spire.

BROKEN PEDIMENT: *see* Pediment.

BUTTRESS: mass of brickwork or masonry projecting from or built against a wall to give additional strength. *Angle Buttresses:* two meeting at an angle of 90° at the angle of a building (Fig. 4*a*). *Clasping Buttress:* one which encases the angle

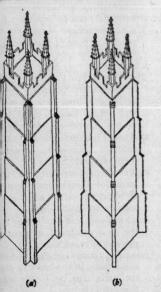
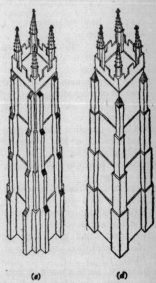

(a)   (b)   (c)   (d)

Fig. 4

(Fig. 4*d*). *Diagonal Buttress:* one placed against the right angle formed by two walls, and more or less equiangular with both (Fig. 4*b*). *Flying Buttress:* arch or half arch transmitting the thrust of a vault or roof from the upper part of a wall to an outer support or buttress. *Setback Buttress:* angle buttress set slightly back from the angle (Fig. 4*c*).

CABLE MOULDING: moulding imitating a twisted cord.

CAMBER: slight rise or upward curve of an otherwise horizontal structure.

CAMPANILE: isolated bell tower.

CANOPY: ornamental covering above an altar, pulpit, niche, etc.

CAP: in a windmill the crowning feature.

CAPITAL: head or top part of a column (q.v.).

CARTOUCHE: tablet with an ornate frame, usually enclosing an inscription.

CARYATID: human figure used instead of a column.

CASTELLATED: decorated with battlements.

CEILURE: panelled and adorned part of a wagon-roof above the rood or the altar.

CENSER: vessel for the burning of incense.

CENTERING: wooden framework used in arch and vault construction and removed when the mortar has set.

CHALICE: small cup used in the Communion service or at Mass.

CHAMFER: surface made by cutting across the square angle of a stone block, piece of woo etc., at an angle of 45° to t two other surfaces.

CHANCEL: that part of the E e of a church in which the alt is placed, usually applied the whole continuation of t nave E of the crossing.

CHANCEL ARCH: arch at the end of the chancel.

CHANTRY CHAPEL: chapel a tached to, or inside, a churc endowed for the saying Masses for the soul of t founder or some other i dividual.

CHEVET: French term for the end of a church (chance ambulatory, and radiatir chapels).

CHEVRON: sculptured mouldir forming a zigzag.

CHOIR: that part of the churc where divine service is sung.

CIBORIUM: box or container fc the consecrated bread. Als used to mean a baldacchin (q.v.).

CINQUEFOIL: *see* Foil.

CLAPPER BRIDGE: bridge mad of large slabs of stone, som built up to make rough pie and other longer ones lai on top to make the roadway.

CLASSIC: here used to mean th moment of highest achieve ment of a style.

CLASSICAL: here used as th term for Greek and Roma architecture and any sub sequent styles copying it.

CLERESTORY: upper storey o the nave walls of a church pierced by windows.

COADE STONE: artificial (cast stone made in the late C18 an the early C19 by Coade an Seely in London.

в: walling material made of
mixed clay and straw.

FFERING: decorating a ceiling
with sunk square or polygonal
ornamental panels.

LLAR-BEAM: see Roof.

LONNADE: range of columns.

LONNETTE: small column.

LUMNA ROSTRATA: column
decorated with carved prows
of ships to celebrate a naval
victory.

MPOSITE: see Orders.

NSOLE: bracket (q.v.) with a
compound curved outline.

PING: capping or covering to
a wall.

RBEL: block of stone pro-
jecting from a wall, supporting
some horizontal feature.

RBEL TABLE: series of corbels,
occurring just below the roof
eaves externally or internally,
often seen in Norman buildings.

RINTHIAN: see Orders.

RNICE: in classical architecture the top section of the
entablature (q.v.). Also for a
projecting decorative feature
along the top of a wall, arch, etc.

VE, COVING: concave undersurface in the nature of a
hollow moulding but on a
larger scale.

VER PATEN: cover to a Communion cup, suitable for use
as a paten or plate for the consecrated bread.

ADLE ROOF: see Wagon-roof.

ENELLATION: see Battlement.

EST, CRESTING: ornamental
finish along the top of a screen,
etc.

OCKET, CROCKETING: deco-
rative features placed on the
sloping sides of spires, pinnacles, gables, etc. in Gothic
architecture, carved in various

leaf shapes and placed at
regular intervals.

CROCKET CAPITAL: see Fig. 5.

Fig. 5

CROSSING: space at the intersection of nave, chancel, and
transepts.

CRUCK: big curved beam supporting both walls and roof of a
cottage.

CRYPT: underground room
usually below the E end of a
church.

CUPOLA: small polygonal or circular domed turret crowning a
roof.

CURTAIN WALL: connecting wall
between the towers of a castle.

CURVILINEAR: see Tracery.

CUSHION CAPITAL: see Block
Capital.

CUSP: in tracery (q.v.) the small
pointed member between two
lobes of a trefoil, quatrefoil, etc.

DADO: decorative covering of
the lower part of a wall.

DAGGER: tracery motif of the
Dec. style. It is a lancet shape
rounded or pointed at the head,
pointed at the foot and cusped
inside (see Fig. 6).

Fig. 6

DAIS: raised platform at one end
of a room.

DEC ('DECORATED'): historical division of English Gothic architecture covering the first half of the C14.

DEMI-COLUMNS: columns half sunk into a wall.

DIAPER WORK: surface decoration composed of square or lozenge shapes.

DOG-TOOTH: typical E.E. ornament consisting of a series of four-cornered stars placed diagonally and raised pyramidally (Fig. 7).

Fig. 7

DOMICAL VAULT: see Vault.

DONJON: see Keep.

DORIC: see Orders.

DORMER (WINDOW): window placed vertically in the sloping plane of a roof.

DRIPSTONE: see Hood-mould.

DRUM: circular or polygonal vertical wall of a dome or cupola.

E.E. ('EARLY ENGLISH'): historical division of English Gothic architecture roughly covering the C13.

EASTER SEPULCHRE: recess with tomb-chest usually in the wall of a chancel, the tomb-chest to receive an effigy of Christ for Easter celebrations.

EAVES: underpart of a sloping roof overhanging a wall.

EAVES CORNICE: cornice below the eaves of a roof.

ECHINUS: quarter round moulding carved with egg and dart pattern, used in classical architecture.

EMBATTLED: see Battlement.

EMBRASURE: small opening the wall or parapet of a for fied building, usually splay on the inside. See Loop.

ENCAUSTIC TILES: earthenwa glazed and decorated tiles us for paving.

ENGAGED COLUMNS: colum attached to, or partly sunk in a wall.

ENGLISH BOND: see Brickwo

ENTABLATURE: in Classi architecture the whole of t horizontal members above column (that is architra frieze, and cornice) (see F 11).

ENTASIS: very slight conv deviation from a straight li used on Greek columns a sometimes on spires to preve an optical illusion of concavi

ENTRESOL: see Mezzanine.

EPITAPH: hanging wall mor ment.

ESCUTCHEON: shield armorial bearings.

EXEDRA: the apsidal end o room. See Apse.

EXTRADOS: outer surface of arch.

FAIENCE: decorated glaz earthenware.

FAN TRACERY: see Tracery.

FAN VAULT: see Vault.

FERETORY: place behind High Altar, where the ch shrine of a church is kept.

FESTOON: carved garland flowers and fruit suspended both ends.

FILLET: narrow flat band r ning down a shaft or alon roll moulding.

FINIAL: in Gothic architect the top of a pinnacle, gable,

bench-end carved into a leaf
or leaf-like form.

AGON: jug for the wine used in
the Communion service.

AMBOYANT: properly the
latest phase of French Gothic
architecture where the window
tracery takes on wavy un-
dulating lines.

ÈCHE: slender wooden spire
on the centre of a roof (also
called Spirelet).

EMISH BOND: see Brickwork.

EURON: decorative carved
flower or leaf.

USH WORK: Decorative use of
flint in conjunction with dressed
stone so as to form pattens:
tracery, initials, etc.

UTING: vertical channelling
in the shaft of a column.

YING BUTTRESS: see Buttress.

IL: lobe formed by the cusping (q.v.) of a circle or an arch.
Trefoil, quatrefoil, cinquefoil,
multifoil, express the number
of leaf shapes to be seen.

LIATED: carved with leaf
shapes.

SSE: ditch.

UR-CENTRED ARCH: see
Arch.

ATER: refectory or dining hall
of a monastery.

ESCO: wall painting on wet
plaster.

IEZE: middle division of a
classical entablature (q.v.) (see
Fig. 11).

ONTAL: covering of the front
of an altar.

ALILEE: chapel or vestibule at
the w end of a church enclosing
the porch. Also called Narthex
(q.v.).

ALLERY: in church architecture upper storey above an

aisle, opened in arches to the
nave. Also called Tribune
(q.v.) and often erroneously
Triforium (q.v.).

GARGOYLE: water spout projecting from the parapet of a
wall or tower; carved into a
human or animal shape.

GAZEBO: lookout tower or
raised summer house in a picturesque garden.

'GEOMETRICAL': see Tracery.

'GIBBS' SURROUND: of a doorway or window. A surround
with alternating larger and
smaller blocks of stone, quoin-
wise, or intermittent large
blocks, sometimes with a
narrow raised band connecting
them up the verticals and along
the extrados of the arch (Fig. 8).

Fig. 8

GROIN: sharp edge at the meeting of two cells of a cross-
vault.

GROINED VAULT: see Vault.

GROTESQUE: fanciful orna-
mental decoration: see also
Arabesque.

HAGIOSCOPE: see Squint.

HALF-TIMBERING: see Timber
Framing.

HALL CHURCH: church in which nave and aisles are of equal height or approximately so.

HAMMER-BEAM: see Roof.

HANAP: large metal cup, generally made for domestic use, standing on an elaborate base and stem; with a very ornate cover frequently crowned with a little steeple.

HEADERS: see Brickwork.

HERRINGBONE WORK: brick, stone, or tile construction where the component blocks are laid diagonally instead of flat. Alternate courses lie in opposing directions to make a zigzag pattern up the face of the wall.

HEXASTYLE: having four detached columns.

HIPPED ROOF: see Roof.

HOOD-MOULD: projecting moulding above an arch or a lintel to throw off water (also called Dripstone or Label).

ICONOGRAPHY: the science of the contents of works of art.

IMPOST: brackets in walls, usually formed of mouldings, on which the ends of an arch rest.

INDENT: shape chiselled out in a stone slab to receive a brass.

INGLENOOK: bench or seat built in beside a fireplace, sometimes covered by the chimney breast, occasionally lit by small windows on each side of the fire.

INTERCOLUMNATION: the space between columns.

IONIC: see Orders (Fig. 11).

JAMB: straight side of an archway, doorway, or window.

KEEL MOULDING: moulding whose outline is in section like that of the keel of a ship.

KEEP: massive tower of a N man castle.

KEYSTONE: middle stone in arch.

KING-POST: see Roof (Fig. 1

LABEL: see Hood-mould.

LABEL STOP: ornamental b at the end of a hood-mo (q.v.).

LANCET WINDOW: slen pointed-arched window.

LANTERN: in architecture, small circular or polygo turret with windows all rou crowning a roof (see Cupola) a dome.

LANTERN CROSS: churchy: cross with lantern-shaped usually with sculptured rep sentations on the sides of top.

LEAN-TO ROOF: roof with c slope only, built against higher wall.

LESENE or PILASTER STRI pilaster without base a capital.

LIERNE: see Vault (Fig. 20).

LINENFOLD: Tudor panelli ornamented with a conve tional representation of a pie of linen laid in vertical fol The piece is repeated in ea panel.

LINTEL: horizontal beam stone bridging an opening.

LOGGIA: recessed colonna (q.v.).

LONG AND SHORT WORK: Saxe quoins (q.v.) consisting stones placed with the lo sides alternately upright a horizontal.

LOUVRE: opening, often wi lantern (q.v.) over, in the ro of a room to let the smol from a central hearth escape.

ENGE: diamond shape.

ETTE: tympanum (q.v.) or
arved opening in a vault.

H GATE: wooden gate struc-
re with a roof and open
des placed at the entrance to
churchyard to provide space
r the reception of a coffin.
he word lych is Saxon and
eans a corpse.

ACHICOLATION: projecting
allery on brackets constructed
n the outside of castle towers
r walls. The gallery has holes
the floor to drop missiles
hrough.

OLICA: ornamented glazed
arthenware.

NSARD: see Roof.

RLON: see Battlement.

TOPE: in classical architecture
of the Doric order (q.v.) the
pace in the frieze between the
riglyphs (Fig. 11).

ZZANINE: low storey placed
etween two higher ones.

SERERE: see Misericord.

SERICORD: bracket placed on
he underside of a hinged choir
tall seat which, when turned
p, provided the occupant of
he seat with a support during
ong periods of standing (also
alled Miserere).

DILLION: small bracket of
which large numbers (modil-
ion frieze) are often placed
elow a cornice (q.v.) in clas-
ical architecture.

TTE: steep mound forming
he main feature of C11 and
12 castles.

UCHETTE: tracery motif in

Fig. 9

curvilinear tracery, a curved
dagger (q.v.) (Fig. 9).

MULLION: vertical post or upright dividing a window into
two or more 'lights'.

NAILHEAD: E.E. ornamental
motif, consisting of small
pyramids regularly repeated
(Fig. 10).

Fig. 10

NARTHEX: enclosed vestibule or
covered porch at the main
entrance to a church (see
Galilee).

NEWEL: central post in a circular or winding staircase;
also the principal post when a
flight of stairs meets a landing.

OBELISK: lofty pillar of square
section tapering at the top and
ending pyramidally.

OGEE: see Arch (Fig. 1c).

ORATORY: small private chapel
in a house.

ORDER: (1) of a doorway or window: series of concentric steps
receding towards the opening;
(2) in classical architecture:
column with base, shaft,
capital, and entablature (q.v.)
according to one of the following styles: Greek Doric,
Roman Doric, Tuscan Doric,
Ionic, Corinthian, Composite.
The established details are
very elaborate, and some
specialist architectural work
should be consulted for further
guidance (see Fig. 11).

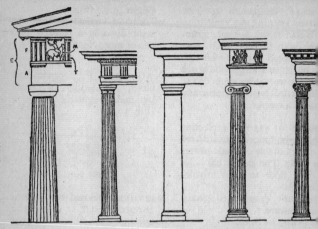

Fig. 11 – Orders of Columns (Greek Doric, Roman Doric, Tuscan, Ionic, Corinth E, Entablature; F, Frieze; A, Architrave; M, Metope; T, Triglyph

ORIEL: *see* Bay Window.

OVERHANG: projection of the upper storey of a house.

OVERSAILING COURSES: series of stone or brick courses, each one projecting beyond the one below it.

PALIMPSEST: (1) *of a brass:* where a metal plate has been re-used by turning over and engraving on the back; (2) *of a wall painting:* where one overlaps and partly obscures an earlier one.

PALLADIAN: architecture following the ideas and principles of Andrea Palladio, 1518–80.

PANTILE: tile of curved S-shaped section.

PARAPET: low wall placed to protect any spot where there is a sudden drop, for example on

a bridge, quay, hillside, hou top, etc.

PARGETTING: plaster work w patterns and ornaments eith in relief or engraved on it.

PARVISE: room over a chur porch. Often used as a scho house or a store room.

PATEN: plate to hold the bre at Communion or Mass.

PATERA: small flat circular oval ornament in classi architecture.

PEDIMENT: low-pitched gal (q.v.) used in classical, Rena sance, and neo-classical arc tecture above a portico a above doors, windows, etc. may be straight-sided or curv segmentally. *Open Pedimen* one where the centre porti of the base is left open. *Brol Pediment:* one where the cen portion of the sloping sides 'broken' out.

DANT: boss (q.v.) elongated
so that it seems to hang down.

DENTIF: concave tri-
angular spandrel used to lead
from the angle of two walls to
the base of a circular dome. It
is constructed as part of the
hemisphere over a diameter the
size of the diagonal of the basic
square (Fig. 12).

Fig 12.

RP (PERPENDICULAR): his-
torical division of English
Gothic architecture roughly
covering the period from 1350
to 1530.

ANO NOBILE: principal storey
of a house with the reception
rooms; usually the first floor.

AZZA: square open space surrounded by buildings, in C17
and C18 English sometimes
used to mean a long colonnade
or loggia.

R: strong, solid support, frequently square in section or of
composite section (compound
pier).

TRA DURA: ornamental or
scenic inlay by means of thin
slabs of stone.

LASTER: shallow pier attached
to a wall.

PILLAR PISCINA: free-standing
piscina on a pillar.

PINNACLE: ornamental form
crowning a spire, tower, buttress, etc., usually of steep
pyramidal, conical, or some
similar shape.

PISCINA: basin for washing the
Communion or Mass vessels,
provided with a drain. Generally set in or against the wall
to the S of an altar.

PLAISANCE: summer-house,
pleasure house near a mansion.

PLATE TRACERY: see Tracery.

PLINTH: projecting base of a
wall or column, generally
chamfered (q.v.) or moulded
at the top.

POPPYHEAD: ornament of leaf
and flower type used to
decorate the tops of bench or
stall-ends.

PORTCULLIS: gate constructed
to rise and fall in vertical
grooves; used in gateways of
castles.

PORTE COCHERE: porch large
enough to admit wheeled
vehicles.

PORTICO: centre-piece of a
house or a church with classical detached or attached
columns and a pediment. A
portico is called *prostyle* or *in
antis* according to whether it
projects from or recedes into
a building. In a portico *in
antis* the columns range with
the side walls.

POSTERN: small gateway at the
back of a building.

PREDELLA: in an altar-piece the
horizontal strip below the
main representation, often
used for a number of sub-
sidiary representations in a
row.

PRESBYTERY: the part of the church lying E of the choir. It is the part where altar is placed.

PRINCIPAL: see Roof (Fig. 13).

PRIORY: monastic house whose head is a prior or prioress, not an abbot or abbess.

PROSTYLE: with free-standing columns in a row.

PULPITUM: stone rood screen in a major church.

PURLIN: see Roof (Figs. 13, 14).

PUTTO: small naked boy.

QUADRANGLE: inner courtyard in a large building complex.

QUARRY: in stained-glass work, a small diamond or square-shaped piece of glass set diagonally.

QUATREFOIL: see Foil.

QUEEN-POSTS: see Roof (Fig. 14).

QUOINS: dressed stones at the angles of a building. Sometimes all the stones are of the same size; more often they are alternately large or small.

RADIATING CHAPELS: chapels projecting radially from an ambulatory or an apse.

RAFTER: see Roof.

RAMPART: stone wall, or wall of earth surrounding a castle, fortress, or fortified city.

RAMPART-WALK: path along the inner face of a rampart.

REBATE: channel or small recess cut into a piece of wood or stone longitudinally to receive the edge of some member that is to be secured in it. The depth of the channel is equal to the thickness of the member to be let into it.

REBUS: pun, a play on wo The literal translation illustration of a name artistic and heraldic purp (Belton=bell, tun).

REEDING: decoration with pa lel convex mouldings touch one another.

REFECTORY: Dining hall; Frater.

RENDERING: plastering of outer wall.

REPOUSSÉ: decoration of m work by relief designs, forn by beating the metal from back.

REREDOS: structure behind above an altar.

RESPOND: half-pier bonded i a wall and carrying one enc an arch.

RETABLE: altar-piece, a pict or piece of carving, stand behind and attached to altar.

RETICULATION: see Trac (Fig. 19).

REVEAL: that part of a ja (q.v.) which lies between glass or door and the outer s face of the wall.

RIB VAULT: see Vault.

ROCOCO: latest phase of Baroque style, current in m Continental countries betwe c. 1720 and c. 1760.

ROMANESQUE: that style architecture which was curre in the C11 and C12 and p ceded the Gothic style England often called Norma

ROOD: cross or crucifix.

ROOD LOFT: singing gallery the top of the rood scree often supported by a coving.

ROOD SCREEN: see Screen.

ROOD STAIRS: stairs to gi access to the rood loft.

: *Hipped:* roof with sloped tead of vertical ends.. *Man-d:* roof with a double slope, e lower slope being larger d steeper than the upper. *ddleback:* tower roof shaped e an ordinary gabled timber f. The following members ve special names: *Rafter:* f-timber sloping up from e wall plate to the ridge. *incipal:* principal rafter, ually corresponding to the in bay divisions of the nave chancel below. *Wall Plate:*

timber laid longitudinally on the top of a wall. *Purlin:* longitudinal member laid parallel with wall plate and ridge beam some way up the slope of the roof. *Tie-beam:* beam connecting the two slopes of a roof across at its foot, usually at the height of the wall plate, to prevent the roof from spreading. *Collar-beam:* tie-beam applied higher up the slope of the roof. *Strut:* upright timber connecting the tie-beam with the rafter above it. *King-post:*

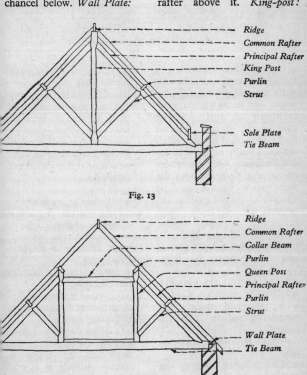

Ridge
Common Rafter
Principal Rafter
King Post
Purlin
Strut

Sole Plate
Tie Beam

Fig. 13

Ridge
Common Rafter
Collar Beam
Purlin
Queen Post
Principal Rafter
Purlin
Strut

Wall Plate
Tie Beam

Fig. 14

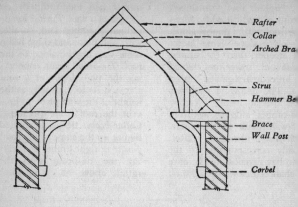

Fig. 15

upright timber connecting a tie-beam and collar-beam with the ridge-beam. *Queen-posts:* two struts placed symmetrically on a tie-beam or collar-beam. *Braces:* inclined timbers inserted to strengthen others. Usually braces connect a collar-beam with the rafters below or a tie-beam with the wall below. Braces can be straight or curved (also called arched). *Hammer-beam:* beam projecting at right angles, usually from the top of a wall, to carry arched braces or struts and arched braces (*see* Figs. 13, 14, 15).

ROSE WINDOW (or WHEEL WINDOW): circular window with patterned tracery arranged to radiate from the centre.

ROTUNDA: building circular in plan.

RUBBLE: building stones, not square or hewn, nor laid in regular courses.

RUSTICATION: Ashlar-work blocks with the margins c wrought and the faces rough specially rock-faced: or ash work of smooth-faced blo with the joints greatly e phasized (smooth rusticatic If only the horizontal joints emphasized it is called band rustication.

SADDLEBACK: *see* Roof.

SALTIRE CROSS: equal-limb cross placed diagonally.

SANCTUARY: area around main altar of a church (Presbytery).

SARCOPHAGUS: elaborat carved coffin.

SCAGLIOLA: material compos of cement and colouring mat to imitate marble.

SCALLOPED CAPITAL: develo ment of the block capital (q. in which the single sem circular surface is elaborat into a series of truncated cor (Fig. 16).

Fig. 16

SCARP: artificial cutting away of the ground to form a steep slope.

SCREEN: *Parclose screen:* screen separating a chapel from the rest of a church. *Rood screen:* screen at the w end of a chancel. Above it on the rood-beam was the rood (q.v.).

SCREENS PASSAGE: passage between the entrances to kitchen, buttery, etc., and the screen behind which lies the hall of a medieval house.

SEDILIA: seats for the priests (usually three) on the s side of the chancel of a church.

SEGMENTAL ARCH: *see* Arch.

SET-OFF: *see* Weathering.

SEXPARTITE: *see* Vaulting.

SGRAFFITO: pattern incised into plaster so as to expose a dark surface underneath.

SHAFT-RING: ring round a circular pier or a shaft attached to a pier.

SILL: lower horizontal part of the frame of a window.

SLATEHANGING: the covering of walls by overlapping rows of slates, on a timber substructure.

SOFFIT: *see* Archivolt.

SOLAR: upper drawing-room of a medieval house.

SOPRAPORTE: painting above the door of a room, usual in the C17 and C18.

SOUNDING BOARD: horizontal board or canopy over a pulpit. Also called Tester.

SPANDREL: triangular surface between one side of an arch, the horizontal drawn from its apex, and the vertical drawn from its springer, also the surface between two arches.

SPIRE: tall pyramidal or conical pointed erection often built on top of a tower, turret, etc. *Broach Spire:* spire which is generally octagonal in plan rising from the top or parapet of a square tower. A small inclined piece of masonry covers the vacant triangular space at each of the four angles of the square and is carried up to a point along the diagonal sides of the octagon. *Needle Spire:* thin spire rising from the centre of a tower roof, well inside the parapet.

SPIRELET: *see* Flèche.

SPLAY: chamfer, usually of the jamb of a window.

SPRINGING: level at which an arch rises from its supports.

SQUINCH: arch or system of concentric arches thrown across the angle between two walls to support a superstructure, for example a dome (Fig. 17).

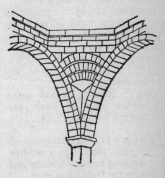

Fig. 17

SQUINT: hole cut in a wall or through a pier to allow a view of the main altar of a church from places whence it could not otherwise be seen (also called Hagioscope).

STALL: carved seat, one in a row, made of wood or stone.

STEEPLE: the tower or spire of a church.

STIFF-LEAF: E.E. type of foliage of many-lobed shapes (Fig. 18).

Fig. 18

STILTED: see Arch.

STOUP: vessel for the reception of holy water, usually placed near a door.

STRAINER ARCH: arch inserted across a room to prevent the walls from leaning.

STRAPWORK: C16 decoration consisting of interlaced bands, and forms similar to fretwork or cut and bent leather.

STRETCHERS: see Brickwork.

STRING COURSE: projecting horizontal band or moulding set in the surface of a wall.

STRUT: see Roof.

STUCCO: plaster work.

STUDS: Upright timbers in timber-framed houses.

SWAG: festoon formed by a carved piece of cloth suspended from both ends.

TABERNACLE: richly ornamented niche (q.v.) or freestanding canopy. Usually contains the Holy Sacrament.

TAZZA: shallow bowl on a foo

TERMINAL FIGURES (TERM TERMINI): upper part of human figure growing out o pier, pilaster, etc., which tap towards the base.

TERRACOTTA: burnt clay, u glazed.

TESSELATED PAVEMENT: dec rative floor or wall coveri made up of tesserae or sm coloured cubes of stone, fitt into a bed of cement.

TESTER: see Sounding Board.

TETRASTYLE: having four tached columns.

THREE-DECKER PULPIT: pul with Clerk's Stall and Readi Desk placed below each oth

TIE-BEAM: see Roof (Figs. 14).

TIERCERON: see Vault (Fig. 2

TILEHANGING: see Slatehan ing.

TIMBER-FRAMING: method construction where walls a built of timber framework wi the spaces filled in by plast or brickwork. Sometimes t timber is covered over wi plaster or boarding laid ho zontally.

TOMB-CHEST: chest-shape stone coffin, the most usu medieval form of funeral mo ument.

TOUCH: soft black marble qua ried near Tournai.

TOURELLE: turret corbelled o from the wall.

TRACERY: intersecting ribwo in the upper part of a windo or used decoratively in blan arches, on vaults, etc. Pla tracery: early form of tracer where decoratively shape openings are cut through th solid stone infilling in the hea

 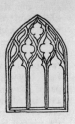 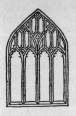 

(a)   (b)   (c)   (d)

Fig. 19

a window. *Bar tracery:* intersecting ribwork made up of slender shafts, continuing the lines of the mullions of windows up to a decorative mesh in the head of the window. *Geometrical tracery:* tracery consisting chiefly of circles or foiled circles. *Intersected tracery:* tracery in which each mullion of a window branches out into two curved bars in such a way that every one of them runs concentrically with the others against the arch of the whole window. The result is that every light of the window is a lancet and every two, three, four, etc., lights together form a pointed arch (Fig. 19a). *Reticulated tracery:* tracery consisting entirely of circles drawn at top and bottom into ogee shapes so that a net-like appearance results (Fig. 19b). *Panel tracery:* tracery forming upright straight-sided panels above lights of a window (Fig. 19, c & d).

TRANSEPT: transverse portion of a cross-shaped church.

TRANSOME: horizontal bar across the opening of a window.

TRANSVERSE ARCH: *see* Vaulting.

TRIBUNE: *see* Gallery.

TRICIPUT, SIGNUM TRICIPUT: sign of the Trinity expressed by three faces belonging to one head.

TRIFORIUM: arcaded wall passage or blank arcading facing the nave at the height of the aisle roof and below the clerestory (q.v.) windows. (*See* Gallery.)

TRIGLYPHS: blocks with vertical grooves separating the metopes (q.v.) in the Doric frieze (Fig. 11).

TROPHY: sculptured group of arms or armour, used as a memorial of victory.

TRUMEAU: stone mullion (q.v.) supporting the tympanum (q.v.) of a wide doorway.

TURRET: very small tower, round or polygonal in plan.

TUSCAN: *see* Order.

TYMPANUM: space between the lintel of a doorway and the arch above it.

UNDERCROFT: vaulted room, sometimes underground, below a church or chapel.

Vault: *Barrel vault:* see Tunnel vault. *Cross-vault:* see Groined vault. *Domical vault:* square or polygonal dome rising direct on a square or polygonal bay, the curved surfaces separated by groins (q.v.). *Fan vault:* vault where all ribs springing from one springer are of the same length, the same distance from the next, and the same curvature. *Groined vault* or *Cross-vault:* vault of two tunnel vaults of identical shape intersecting each other at right angles. *Lierne:* tertiary rib, that is, rib which does not spring either from one of the main springers or the central boss. *Quadripartite vault:* one wherein one bay of vaulting is divided into four parts. *Rib vault:* vault with diagonal ribs projecting along the groins.

Ridge-rib: rib along the lo tudinal or transverse ridge vault. *Sexpartite vault:* wherein one bay of qua partite vaulting is divided two parts transversely so each bay of vaulting has parts. *Tierceron:* secondary that is, rib which issues f one of the main springers the central boss and leads place on a ridge-rib. *Transt arch:* arch separating one of a vault from the n *Tunnel vault* or *Barrel va* vault of semicircular or poi section (Fig. 20).

VAULTING SHAFT: vert member leading to the spri of a vault.

VENETIAN WINDOW: win with three openings, the c tral one arched and wider t the outside ones.

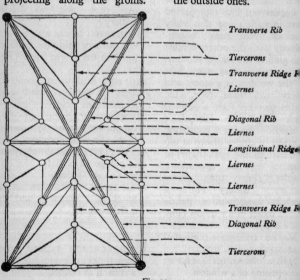

- - - - - - Transverse Rib

- - - - - - Tiercerons

- - - - - - Transverse Ridge F

- - - - - - Liernes

- - - - - - Diagonal Rib

- - - - - - Liernes

- - - - - - Longitudinal Ridge

- - - - - - Liernes

- - - - - - Liernes

- - - - - - Transverse Ridge F

- - - - - - Diagonal Rib

- - - - - - Tiercerons

Fig. 20

VERANDAH: open gallery or balcony with a roof on light, usually metal, supports.

VESICA: Oval with pointed head and foot.

VESTIBULE: ante-room or entrance hall.

VILLA: according to Gwilt (1842) 'a country house for the residence of opulent persons'.

VITRIFIED: made similar to glass.

VOLUTE: spiral scroll, one of the component parts of an Ionic column (see Orders).

VOUSSOIR: wedge-shaped stone used in arch construction.

WAGON-ROOF: roof in which by closely set rafters with arched braces the appearance of the inside of a canvas tilt over a wagon is achieved. Wagon-roofs can be panelled or plastered (ceiled) or left uncovered.

WAINSCOT: timber lining to walls.

WALL PLATE: see Roof.

WATERLEAF: leaf shape used in later C12 capitals. The waterleaf is a broad, unribbed, tapering leaf curving up towards the angle of the abacus and turned in at the top (Fig. 21).

Fig. 21

WEATHER-BOARDING: overlapping horizontal boards, covering a timber-framed wall.

WEATHERING: sloping horizontal surface on sills, buttresses, etc., to throw off water.

WEEPERS: small figures placed in niches along the sides of some medieval tombs (also called Mourners).

WHEEL WINDOW: see Rose Window.

INDEX OF PLATES

303

INDEX OF ARTISTS

INDEX OF PLACES

The references in brackets indicate the square in which the place will be found on the map preceding the title-page